WAUGH DECLARED

The story of Australia's famous cricketing twins

By MARK GATELY

**Foreword by
DOUG WALTERS**

IRONBARK
PRESS

Published in 1992 by Ironbark Press
Level 1, 175 Alison Road, Randwick NSW

© Gately, Mark

National Library of Australia
Cataloguing-In-Publication

Gately, Mark
Waugh Declared: The Story of Australia's Famous Cricketing Twins

ISBN: 1 875471 19 7

1. Waugh, Mark. 2. Waugh, Steve. 3. Cricket Players —
Australia — Biography. I. Title

796.358092

Editor: Norman Tasker
Production: Geoff Armstrong & Ian Heads
Design: Jayem Productions
Finished Art: Kylie Prats
Cover Design: Jayem Productions
Printed by: Globe Press

*Ironbark Press thanks John Fordham, and Northwest
Airlines for their generous support in helping to make
Waugh Declared a reality.*

THANKS

I would like to thank the Waugh family for their generous co-operation during the compilation of this book. All gave freely of their time and memories. In particular Steve and his wife Lynette, Mark and his partner Sue Porter and mother Bev could not have been more helpful, opening their homes and treating me as much more than an intrusive writer. Special thanks also to Essex cricketers Neil Foster and Paul Prichard and their wives Rom and Jo-Anne. Not only did they provide valuable material for the book but generously included me in their social activities while I was in England. It was great fun and much appreciated. Everyone interviewed for this book has my appreciation but a few others that stand out are Brad McNamara, Ian Healy, Tim May and Michael and Julie Bradley. Thanks to all the photographers who contributed, especially Gregg Porteous and Philip Brown, and Trudi Van de Wint of Mane Photo. And to others who assisted in the production, including Geoff Greenwood, Linda Carini and Ginny Harrison. I would like to thank my wife Carol for her support and encouragement and finally my parents Ron and Marie for all they have done for me.

ABOUT THE AUTHOR

Mark Gately has been cricket writer at Sydney's *Daily Telegraph Mirror* since 1990. A graduate of Mitchell CAE, Bathurst, he has been a journalist since 1984. Beginning as a finance writer with *The Sydney Morning Herald* he has also worked as the sporting editor and general writer on *The Northern Herald* and as a sub-editor on *The Sun*, *The Mirror* and *The Telegraph* and *Telegraph Mirror*. In that time he has also travelled extensively in Europe and the USA. He is still an active cricketer, bowling off-spin for Warringah Cricket Club in Sydney's Municipalities and Shires competition and twice playing village cricket in England.

Contents

Foreword by Doug Walters   6

Preface   8

1   Backstreets and Freeways   11

2   Opening Up   15

3   Backyard Battles   20

4   The Guiding Light   36

5   To Be The Best   43

6   For The Love of Sport   54

7   Schooldays   71

8   Working Lives   77

9   The Silly Things Young People Do   81

10   Making The Grade   87

11   Testing Times   101

12   Twin Ambitions   127

13   The Odd Couple   145

14   Fit For Life   152

15   The Other Side of Life   156

16   Playing To Win   170

Statistics   197

Foreword
By Doug Walters

I first laid eyes on Steve and Mark Waugh some ten years ago during my association with indoor cricket. They were both playing representative indoor cricket at the time and they made an immediate impression on me. I thought, "Gee, these boys have some talent; surely they must be able to play as well outdoors." Time has proven that first impression to be correct, but I wonder and hope that we haven't yet seen the best of either of them.

Steve has been likened by many people to my own playing style. Frankly, not having seen too much video of my own play, it's hard for me to judge that view. One thing I do know is that his bat comes through a lot straighter than mine did and his bowling is a lot better. I just wish that I could have bowled the slower ball to the same degree of perfection he has mastered. I will not soon forget that great English summer he had in 1989. As a batsman he tore the English attacks apart and was largely responsible for the drubbing Australia gave England in that series. Steve got his chance to play Test cricket when Kim Hughes and his team opted to tour South Africa in 1985/86. He hadn't played many first class matches at that stage and it was suggested then, as now, that he was rushed in too early. To me that is hogwash. If someone has the ability, (and he obviously did), why hold him back? Age should not be a barrier. I can identify with Steve's highs and lows in cricket, and I think all of us who have played the game can do the same.

Mark, only a couple of minutes the junior twin, had to serve a much longer apprenticeship. I think in fact it was too long. He played 99 first class matches before finally getting the nod and it was unbelievable that when it finally happened this was at the expense of brother Steve. Mark Waugh, the batsman is a complete role model for anyone to follow. He may fairly be compared with Greg Chappell or Colin Cowdrey, or, in technique only, to Geoff Boycott. The more outgoing of the twins, Mark can be forgiven for getting out on many occasions. To the onlooker, the game for such a talented player, often appears very easy. I've heard it said regularly of Mark Waugh that seeing him make even a half dozen runs is worth the admission price. The timing and composure that Mark shows makes him without doubt one of the most feared batsmen in any team in world cricket today — and he will be that for a long time to come. His bowling is steady, and, like Steve's possesses genuine variety. Although we will read more about his batting than his bowling, this side of his cricket cannot be taken lightly as Mark is more than capable of taking anyone's wicket at any level of cricket.

Genuine all-rounder Steve and Mark share another quality — they are both great fielders. Perhaps those early days in indoor cricket when I first glimpsed them, primed their reflexes. As fieldsmen they are equal to the best I have seen or expect to ever see — in all parts of the field. They were born "naturals" but the reality is that many people who have natural ability do not use this gift to its fullest extent. The Waugh's early backyard "Test Matches" and hours of practice since then have brought them just rewards; that alone is an ideal lesson for any inspiring youngster to learn. To watch the ease with which a catch is taken, or see the ability shown in throwing accurately and fast in any fashion, makes one realise that this is not something which just comes naturally, but something that has required the great deal of time and effort which they have both put into their fielding. I have been fortunate to have played with Mark and Steve in promotional matches throughout the country areas of NSW and it has been a revelation to have seen first hand just how competitive the two brothers are. The respect shown to them by bowlers and batsmen alike must have helped anyone who has played against them or even come and watched them.

The success that the twins have had hasn't altered either one of them. They are both personable, modest young men — only too happy to pass on any tips which may help ambitious young admirers. The "future captain" tag has been bandied around by some experts particularly in relation to Steve. I have no doubt that either would make a good captain, but there is plenty of time down the track for that. For now I'd prefer to see them just concentrate on their own performances and continue to delight crowds around the world the way they have done these recent years. Cricket is lucky to have them.

Doug Walters

Preface

Twins are celebrated in myth and legend, and have gradually assumed a special, if smallish, place in the folklore of the modern sporting world too. The mythology of the Greeks and Romans is laced with twin images — Apollo and Diana, Hercules and Iphicles, Castor and Pollux, Romulus and Remus. Twins in primitive cultures often were linked to the gods, or to supernatural beliefs. North American Mohave Indians believed that twins controlled thunder, rain and lightning. In mythology Castor and Pollux, the heroic sons of Zeus and Leda had power over the wind and waves and were known as the seafarers' guardians.

In many cultures twins are considered lucky. And so it was for the game of cricket in Australia when Bev Waugh then of Earlwood, Sydney gave birth to her two sons, Stephen and Mark on June 2, 1965. Steve appeared first and subsequent events in the cricket world gave some support to the belief of the African Yoruba tribe — that the first-born is supposedly sent into daylight by the other twin to check things out. In topline cricket, at least, Mark was to again be the follower ... the later bloomer.

High-achieving twins in sport are fairly rare birds, and the accomplishments of the Waugh brothers rank with the very best of them. English cricket had the Bedser twins — Alec, a champion at Test level, and Eric who played county cricket for Surrey for many years. From Sydney rugby union ranks came the identical Dawson twins, Chris and Paul, who gained much publicity during excellent careers in both union and then, rugby league. The brilliant Ella brothers Glen and Mark (plus younger brother Gary) were dazzling performers on the rugby union stage throughout their careers. In rugby ranks too were the Boyce brothers, Stuart and Jim, both swift and athletic, both reaching international status, playing on the wings for Australia in Test matches.

The distinguished Sydney sports historian George Crawford has records of seven pairs of twins playing Australian Rules football at a high level between the 1940s and 1960s. American tennis twins Tim and Tom Gullikson reached a Wimbledon doubles final. And one of Australia's most loved sportspeople, the great sprinter Betty Cuthbert was a twin — — her sister Marie a talented field athlete.

In rugby league in Australia more recently much attention has been paid to Queensland's richly talented Walters brothers — Kevin and Kerrod, the twins, and older brother Steve, all of them Australian representatives.

Australian cricket though in all its long years has nothing to match the story of the Waugh twins, of Steve — and Mark, four minutes his junior. The closest parallel is with Victoria's Nagel twins of more than half a century ago — Lisle, who played a Test in 1932, and Vernon, a Sheffield Shield cricketer.

In Waugh Declared author Mark Gately set out to track the fascinating story of how it came to pass that two brothers, so alike and yet so different, could arrive at the same milestone in their chosen game — the winning of places in the Australian cricket team.

To tell the story Gately interviewed a vast range of friends and family who spin like satellites around the focal point of Steve and Mark Waugh. At the height of the English summer, 1992, he joined Mark Waugh in Colchester England, where Mark was staying during his commission with county side Essex. In interviews snatched between matches and conversations in the long English twilights Gately gleaned the Waugh story from Mark's side of the fence. English cricketers Neil Foster and Graham Gooch gave generously of their time, and of their opinions in talking of the two gifted brothers. Steve, interviewed in Sydney, had already given his version of the story.

The result of it all was this book — Waugh Declared, a slice of cricket literature with a captivating difference. The book tells thoroughly, entertainly and very often revealingly of the deeds and adventures of the brothers. The later cricket chapters, with the boys in the full flush of their careers as Mark chases Steve into the baggy green cap of Australia, capture the essence of a great Aussie sporting story.

But, much more than that, in Waugh Declared author Gately carefully constructs the framework of their growing years, building a fascinating portrait of the factors that led to two rather shy boys from Sydney's western suburbs becoming champions and record breakers of the cricket field. The book, at its various levels, is much more than just another sporting story. At one dimension it gives a valuable picture of working class family life in the Sydney of the 1960s and 70s. At another it is about the perennial quest of the sportswriter — the searching for the "why" ... the reasons why certain people become champions.

Finally, it is about success and excellence, about talent fulfilled — a happy and inspiring book for young sportsmen and one which bears the universal message: if you have the talent, and you have the dream and you have the determination — and especially if you are prepared to pay the price of hard work, then you will make it. Steve and Mark Waugh, Bankstown boys, paid that price ... and this is their story.

— Ian Heads

Steve (top) and Mark ...
Bulldog boys and
proud of it.

(Gregg Porteous)

ONE

Backstreets and Freeways

THE MARVELLOUS physical talents of Stephen and Mark Waugh are there for all to see. Arguably Australian cricket's most skilful players, there is beauty in their power and grace. Whether batting, bowling or fielding, their athleticism and class stand out even in the exalted circles in which they move and compete. Excitement is never too far away when the Waughs are on the field. They demand to be at the heart of the action. It is that exuberant competitiveness which completes two of the most promotable packages in professional sports.

Very little imagination is required to glory in the deeds of the Waugh brothers. But cricket, like the movies, is entertainment, and fans, like moviegoers, want more for their money than just the action they pay to see. They want flesh on their heroes. While larger-than-life characters like fast bowler Merv Hughes are happy to oblige the Waughs have been a little less forthcoming. They are simply shy young men who have always felt more comfortable doing rather than saying. As a result the cricketing public has been forced to form its opinions second hand, through the media or from the stands. Not surprisingly, many untruths and half-truths have been born and gained currency. True, what you see is pretty much what you get with the Waugh twins, but there are many more aspects of their character that don't surface on the cricket field — the sense of humour that is never too far beneath the surface, the loyalty, the practical jokes, the sense of adventure, the faults and foibles. The end result of their upbringing is not just two of world cricket's most talented players — Mark and Steve are two complex individuals shaped by a variety of fascinating people.

Despite their aristocratic bearing on the field and the imperious way in which they can assault opposition bowlers, these are not young men who have been given a rails run in life. Mark and Steve Waugh come from the Australian heartland. Not the mythical red dust and hard yakka of the bush, but the modern reality. The Waugh twins are the proud product of suburbia and their hard-working parents. Born to a teenage mother and father in Sydney's western suburbs, their childhood was short on luxuries but rich in life's necessities — love, companionship, good food and plenty of good clean fun. Theirs is a fairytale that almost everyone can relate to — playing in the backyard from dawn until dusk, imitating heroes and keeping score. There are the broken windows and lost balls, scrapes, scraps and tears, ingenious invention and sheer joy of childhood play that everyone can empathise with.

There is no doubt Steve and Mark were born with the physical tools necessary for success but it is just as certain that no-one ever worked harder to succeed. As children and teenagers they shouldered a breath-taking burden, turning out for as many as three teams in a week — all year round. They took the field for their district club, school and a variety of representative teams stretching from the local Bankstown area right to the pinnacle of

Australian honours. And all demanded their piece of flesh — demanded that either or both of the Waugh twins win them the game. Doing their bit meant scoring the key goal, hammering a big hundred or taking crucial wickets, not just turning up and playing their position. Thousands of gifted young athletes have been tested and found wanting by similar demands but the Waughs thrived. The joy of competition kept them fresh as a daisy and hungry for more. So strong was Steve and Mark's competitive instinct that when their teenage growing pains became anything but normal under the stresses of their many commitments they shrugged it off and kept on playing. Sport was always their relaxation and their obsession.

Their progress through the junior ranks was a tit-for-tat race for glory. Although "public" opinion attempted to categorise them and pit them against one another from the time they were 13 or 14 they remained focused on their goal, driving each other to greater heights. The twins have been able to strike an extraordinary balance their whole lives, indulging in the fiercest competition but refusing to entertain the accompanying anger and jealousy. It is one of the less obvious aspects of their character and the one most often misunderstood by those who don't know them. Their relationship often defies explanation and rationalisation, but be sure that a fierce bond lurks beneath those reserved exteriors.

After sharing a life for 17 years, sharing a room and clothes, a career and friends, Mark and Steve's paths diverged after they had made first grade at Bankstown. Steve took the freeway to the top while Mark had to struggle through the backstreets and countless frustrating stop lights. But just because things were happening quickly for Steve it did not mean they were always fun. Elevated to the Test team at one of its lowest ebbs, he fought not only Australia's tormentors but himself, his youth and his own inexperience. Success was rare and it was during these grim battles that he was burdened with the inaccurate tag of a dour, even sour, competitor. Few realised just how wrong that character assessment was. A brilliant stroke-maker of undoubted promise, Steve fought tenaciously to regain the run-scoring touch that had deserted him after so many loyal years. Slowly things started to turn around and flashes of his true talent began to shine through. A 70 against England, a couple of brave 90s against the West Indies. But rather than ease the pressure on Steve it only changed the nature of the monkey on his back. Now people wanted to know why he wasn't scoring hundreds.

It was more than 40 Test innings before Steve was hit once more with the new Bradman tag, an unwanted mantle forced upon him in 1989. Such a rating was stretching matters, but through his magnificent Ashes tour of England a little media hysteria was certainly in order. Steve set many records and joined some pretty illustrious company with his statistical onslaught, which included bettering Sir Donald Bradman's lofty 1930 strike rate of 3.70 runs per over. Plundering runs at a better rate than the voracious Don is an achievement anyone would be happy to put on their resume.

Mark, meanwhile, was making his mistakes and growing up in the relative obscurity of Shield cricket. While it may have been easier on the face of it he still had his burdens to carry. Scoring hundreds and taking wickets was no longer enough. He had to rid himself of unflattering tags like "soft" and "lazy", and then had to prove himself over and over again. Thousands of runs and prestigious awards such as his two Sheffield Shield Player of the Year awards, and being named one of Wisden's five cricketers of the year for 1990, hammered home the quality of his credentials. Crucial in his development was a stint with Essex in the English county cricket championship.

There is nowhere to hide when you are playing cricket six days a week and shouldering

Above: Schoolboy terrors ... Steve (Fifth from the left, back row) and Mark (far right, front row) with fellow members of the 1976 NSW Primary Schools representative side.

Left: The spoils of success. Steve (left) and Mark were worried that they would have to share the bat awarded to weekly winners of the NSWCA-Sunday Telegraph Encouragement award but sports editor Bob Cooper (pictured) ensured there would be no arguments.

Below: Allround aces ... Mark (left) was the better tennis player while Steve held the edge at soccer. The multi-talented brothers represented State primary schools at both sports.

the added burden of being the side's overseas player. Many years of experience and maturing were telescoped into two-and-a-bit seasons of county cricket. Mark was able to hone his game against the best fast bowlers in the world on wickets that varied wildly in quality and character. Also looming large was the example of England and Essex captain Graham Gooch.

Not since Greg Chappell had an Australian batsman had to prove his case so emphatically — Mark scoring more than 7000 first class runs before he got his shot at the big time. The parallels between the two do not end there either. In his Test debut Waugh, like Chappell, came to the wicket with his country in trouble against England and peeled off a hundred to save his side. It was an innings that justifiably attracted lavish praise and predictions of success for many years to come. He then went on the 1991 tour of the West Indies and topped the averages for Australia, who went down 2-1 on one of the tougher tours of recent years. But just to prove that no-one was safe, Mark was dropped for the final Test of the 1991-92 series against India, just 12 months after making his debut. He quickly won a recall to the side for the tour of Sri Lanka — a tour Steve was most unlucky to miss after his fine season with NSW.

Mark's debut was a difficult time for the Waugh family because it came at Steve's expense. Despite the jumble of conflicting emotions both men handled the situation with class and restraint, as they had throughout the whole "Mark-for-Steve" build-up. Only a month before the axe fell the pair had combined for a world record fifth wicket partnership against Western Australia in Perth, and they went on to combine for hundreds against WA twice the following season. Sadly the pair have played Test cricket together just twice, in the West Indies, so the majority of the international cricketing public has been denied the pleasure of seeing them strut their stuff in tandem on the Test stage — a pleasure Australia's opponents will be more than happy to forego for many years to come.

TWO

Opening Up

MARK and Steve Waugh set the tone for their extraordinary life right from the very start. Many of those blessed with prodigious talents indulge in a taste for the grand entrance and a fascination with the limelight, but the Waugh twins have never liked to make a fuss. Certainly they announced their impending arrival emphatically enough, but having raised expectations they gave the event their own special twist.

"I went into labour every night for two weeks at about one o'clock in the morning," recalled their mother Bev. "I'd wake up in the middle of the night. I'd have the bags packed and Rodger panicking because I was down to five minutes. But by the time we got packed and got everything ready the pains would subside. That would last for about an hour and happened every night for a week. In the end we got too tense so the doctor put me into hospital. They were only a week off being due then. Then every night at one o'clock the same thing would happen. Every night. So in the end they didn't take any notice of me, they just let me go.

The start of something special. Young Panania parents Rodger and Bev Waugh hold the future of Australian cricket in their hands.

Left: Stunned prankster ... Steve (left) found to his surprise that pinching Mark's dummy wasn't a good idea after all.

Below: Easy to please. Steve (left) and Mark loved nothing better than hopping into a box and playing for hours.

Bottom left: Brotherly love ... Mark (left) and Steve provide positive proof that any rumours of fraternal friction are wrong.

Bottom right: Off to school ... the twins ready for their first day at primary school.

"Then on the second of June, the day they were due, I couldn't eat lunch. I had pains in the middle of the day and I said this is it. It was."

The doctor responsible for the delivery had never handled twins before and, in a most generous gesture, decided to involve his students. Yet to make their first appearance, and the twins were already drawing a crowd. Whether or not they were daunted by the large audience awaiting them or, as is more likely, they desired a little peace and quiet, the stars of the show slipped quietly in at a time most inconvenient to the doctor and his students. The distinction of delivering the Waughs went to a humble nurse who handled the honour with aplomb and then ran around the hospital gleefully announcing the news to anyone who would listen. Not only had she never delivered twins before, she had never delivered a baby. Not a bad debut. The birth had caught everyone out except for mother Bev, and so on one of the rare occasions in their life Mark and Steve disappointed the large prospective crowd but, not for the last time, touched the lives of those lucky enough to share in the moment.

Physically they scrubbed up pretty well although Steve won't thank his mother for her description of their initial appearance. "Steve had a big crop of black hair and he was really pretty. Whenever anyone looked at them they would say 'oh lovely, twins — a boy and a girl'. Stephen was always referred to as the girl with his pretty face. Mark didn't have much hair at all. Stephen had a lot of black hair, very long."

The first hint that something special was in the offing had come from Bev's doctor who told her during the pregnancy that she was either a month out or she was going to have twins. For a 19-year-old sports star this was not exactly thrilling news at first. It wasn't something Bev was expecting — like so many things in life it was something that happened to other people. But it wasn't too long before reality hit and she had to deal with the situation.

The young couple were living with Rodger's parents at the time in Earlwood and they were ecstatic at the news. Rodger had been an only child, as had his mother, and if he had been unable to produce male off-spring that would have been the end of the Waugh name — and all those terrific headlines.

In the less-enlightened times of the mid-sixties there was no rest for the workers. Bev was forced by circumstances and society to go straight back to work. A teacher, she was under a bond to the Education Department and had to return to school a mere six weeks after the twins were born. This would have been a massive blow to a 19-year-old trying to cope with twin boys but her mother and mother-in-law pitched in and shouldered much of the burden. The Bournes put Bev and Rodger up before the happy day and the Waughs took over after the birth. Each cared for a baby while Bev was at work, but they had to swap early on because Rodger's mother, Ella, had suffered from polio as a teen and struggled to cope physically with Mark. While she was remarkably active Mark was a bit too heavy for her to manage.

"I never felt guilty about leaving them to go to work because I knew I was leaving them with my parents," said Bev. "I never could have left them with someone else."

Mark and Steve exhibited their quiet, unflappable demeanour at an early age. Bev took them in a stroller to the local markets at Earlwood not too long after they were born. She thinks it may, in fact, have been their very first outing. Having completed her shopping Bev balanced her groceries on the roof of the stroller for the trip home but got in a bit of trouble negotiating the kerb after crossing busy William Street. The pram couldn't cope with the weight and physical manoeuvre and called it a day, folding up and spilling the groceries all over the road. Bev said there were oranges and things rolling everywhere. Passers-by helped her recover her food and then opened up the collapsed pram. There were the twins, as quiet as can be. Bev said they did not make a sound through the entire episode.

Bev said that Mark walked a little earlier than normal at nine and a half months while Steve followed suit about six weeks later. And they began talking at around 18 months. Bev claims they had their own special language to begin with and called each other Moonie and Goolie, she can't remember which was which. Right from the beginning they favoured an economic approach to speech. And the words they did use were well-chosen.

"They weren't mad, mad talkers," said Bev. "Girls are good talkers. And they followed that pattern all the way through. They have been fairly quiet. Steve was always the noisier one, more mischievous.

"I know one of Stephen's first words wasn't a real good word. He picked up a swear word. One of his first sentences was 'a little bloody fool kid'."

Mrs Waugh's pet name for Steve was "My Little Rabbit". When asked why she explained: "He was a little bloke. You could cuddle him up and squeeze him." It was also an appropriate description of his energy levels. "He used to tear around," said Mrs Bourne. "He used to go that fast."

"Steve was always running around like a mad chook," added Rodger. "He was a real goer."

By all accounts Steve and Mark were cheerful little chaps when they were young. Rarely whingeing and happy to amuse themselves, they undoubtedly eased the burden on their mother and various minders. One baby-management aid which proved very popular with both mother and children was the good old pacifier. Though both probably regret ever having admitted it they were both very fond of their dummies when they were toddlers. They hung onto them for a long time, Mark almost until the moment he first went to school.

The whole family remarks upon how quiet and independent the two boys were as toddlers. Right from the beginning they were confident and secure enough to amuse themselves. While it seems silly to describe toddlers as mature, Bev and the two grandmothers swear that there was none of the self-centred demand for constant attention that drives so many young parents to distraction.

"They always kept themselves really well occupied," said Bev. "Playing with cardboard boxes or anything that looked remotely like a ball or a bat or anything like that. The only toys they really enjoyed were train sets and lego blocks. There wasn't any point in buying them anything else because they would just improvise. Improvise with cardboard boxes and saucepans and just generally occupy each other. They entertained themselves."

Bev probably helped her own cause by involving the boys in nearly everything she did. Instead of viewing household chores as grim tasks she had to rush through before the kids threw a spanner into the works she often treated them as activities where everyone could play. She even included them in the things she regarded as fun herself and could have used as outlets for relaxation away from the boys. "They used to love to help in the garden. I'm a mad gardener too. I grow vegetables and things. They used to get into the dirt and in a terrible mess but they'd help me plant seeds and watch them grow."

Given his immaculate grooming that must have been one of the few times that Mark got down in the dirt. Or maybe time has blurred Bev's memory. Even she admitted later: "Mark never liked to get very dirty, but Stephen didn't mind if he got grubby."

Mark backed that up. "I still don't like getting dirty. When I was playing soccer I would get stuck into it I suppose but I didn't like playing in the mud. Even now I'll only dive if I have to. I prefer not to."

There are those who give currency to the mischievous and misguided rumour that the twins don't like each other. But anyone hoping for confirmation of such malicious thoughts is doomed to disappointment. There was very little strife when the two amused themselves and plenty of photographs to prove it. "They always played well together. They didn't cry very much," said Mrs Bourne. "They didn't really fight. They were so busy and interested in what was going on. I never heard them say they were bored. They weren't any trouble. Not like we thought twins would be, not like the twins I knew.

Mark was always more cautious than his twin. Steve was the adventurous one, the one looking to get into a little mischief according to Bev. And he didn't waste any time waiting to see what the world was like. Once, when still a toddler, he went missing when in the care of Mrs Bourne. "Steve had a little toy dog, a little plastic dog. He was only about 18 months old and mum couldn't find him," said Bev. "He'd gone walking and someone brought him back from a couple of streets up. He said he was taking the dog for a walk. But Mark wouldn't do anything like that, something he knew he would get in trouble for.

"They might be playing with the hose in the little pool up the back and Stephen would grab hold of it and chase Mark with it. He just had the devil in him.. Stand them still to try and take a photo and Steve would be doing something sneaky to make Mark move. He wasn't that naughty, he never caused any great hassles. He just had that streak of mischief in him."

They also managed some mischief as a team. On one occasion they decided to help their mother find the freshest fruit in the local green grocers. "They were in a stroller, or maybe just toddlers, and there was a great big pyramid of tomatoes. Tomatoes just went everywhere. Rolled down the street. Went everywhere.

"The other time they embarrassed me was in David Jones. I was trying on underwear and had them both with me. They were told to stand just outside my cubicle and I kept peeking under to see if they were there. Then I looked and they weren't there. I only had underwear on at this stage so I couldn't chase them. They were having a great time. They were running along peeking under every cubicle, seeing all these ladies trying on their underwear."

Rodger, like most fathers, was in charge of the discipline. "Rodger never told those kids two or three times," said Mrs Bourne. "It had to be once and they jolly well knew he meant it."

"Their father was very strict," confirmed Bev. "They wouldn't dare stand on a lounge or anything. They were well-behaved. You could put anything out that you wanted to and they knew not to touch.

"I think they just knew. I don't think all that much was said, they just seemed to know how far they could go. They respected his discipline. I would say they were fairly easy to discipline. You told them they couldn't do something once or twice, they knew they couldn't do it. If they were told they couldn't touch something it meant forever, not just today. They sometimes tried a few little things with me because, being with me most of the time, like most children they wanted to see if they can break a few rules now and then. If we went for a long trip they knew they had to sit still, that was it. They never questioned it, they just did it. It was pretty unreasonable to expect an 18-month-old to sit still for a period of three or four hours at a time but they did it. They were good travellers. They would just sit up in the back of the car, for up to 10 hours, and you wouldn't here a peep out of them. They would just look out the window. We didn't realise how good they were.

THREE

Backyard Battles

THE DOMINANT theme in Mark and Steve's lives has been the fact that they are twins — at times it has even overshadowed their extraordinary sporting talents. Whatever the topic of discussion the fact of their twin-ness will invariably pop up at some stage. But it is a fascination more to outsiders than themselves. Both say they first realised they were twins because of the identical outfits they wore when they were young, many of them created by their mother. But both added that it wasn't something they thought about a lot. It just was.

"I never had a problem with being a twin," said Mark. "It was just like having a normal brother."

Looking back Steve believes it was an advantage. "We were both pretty shy so I think when you are going to new places, and especially in sporting teams when you are going away, it is always handy to have someone there you know and you can pull back on or rely on. I suppose you felt a bit safer going away."

He said their first trip away to Canberra when they were just seven was "a bit scary". "We had never been out of home before by ourselves and we got billeted with this nice lady. She didn't have any kids so she treated us like we were her own. So it felt a lot easier but it was still a pretty frightening experience looking back on it. Being away for a week and not knowing anyone and being in a different part of the world."

Unlike future trips the twins got up to the minimum of mischief. "We were too scared to do anything," said Steve.

Their good relations as toddlers didn't sour as they got older. In fact they chose to spend the vast majority of their time together. Neither seemed to have any desire to go it alone, each naturally including the other in whatever they were doing. Even after they started school, when a mate came over to their house it was a case of him joining them, not the odd twin having to tag along. Whether they would have grown up laconic and dry-witted whatever the circumstances is open to debate, but maybe their non-stop playing as youngsters gave them a taste for deed rather than word. Their mother certainly believes their apparent lack of verbal communication had its roots there. "They spent heaps of time in each others' company. They didn't really need to talk. Anything they had to say they sort of said with an action. They said with a ball or a bat or chasing one another.

"I can't remember them fighting much over toys. Not when I look at other children and see the way they grab each others' things and get really possessive." Bev and Rodger could reasonably claim responsibility for the twins' lack of selfishness. They consciously removed many of the potential sources of friction between the two young children. But, just as importantly, they gave them gifts that made them share. "They used to get similar things

Above: And baby makes three ... Steve (left) and Mark have always been very close to brother Dean (centre).

Above: Tiny dynamo ... Even in the backyard Steve was keen to hit the ball, any ball, as far and as hard as he could.

Right: Aren't they sweet? Steve (left) and Mark after rummaging through Mum's closet.

Above: Easy rider ... right from the very start Mark
was hell on wheels.

Right: Western suburbs Wimbledon ... Steve is all
set to serve it up but Mark doesn't seem so sure.

which I suppose helped solve the problem when they opened their presents at Christmas. I don't think one would have liked to see the other get something he didn't get so they always got similar things. Maybe a different colour or part of a set of something so they learned to share. Part of a lego set or part of a shuttlecock set. One would get a shuttlecock set and one might get a little baseball set. Usually things that they could share anyway."

Mark and Steve's play was not just energy-expending sporting games or simple curiosity, their industrious use of pots and pans and boxes as toddlers also exhibited an active imagination. As they grew older they also indulged in play-acting that they would probably prefer remained a skeleton in the closet. Their mother's closet. You see they were regular raiders of Bev's wardrobe. Incriminating photos showed a taste and fashion sense that would have been cause for concern had it persisted into puberty and adolescence. "They loved to dress up," said Mrs Waugh. "Steve always liked a tie and Mark always had a handbag." Bev said that as little fellows they both loved hats. Apparently it was often a battle to get them off their heads at bedtime. One of their favourite pranks when visiting the Waugh's Earlwood home was to steal great-grandma's walking stick and great-grandpa's pipe and run off and play with them. Bev said Steve continued to be the ring-leader whether there was a game to be played, new territory to be explored or mischief afoot .

"Stephen was more curious and adventurous than Mark," said Bev. "Mark used to follow along behind. Stephen would investigate and want to stick his finger under a log or something and Mark would stand and watch him do it and then join in when he knew it was safe. When we were on holidays Stephen would always be the first to go in the water and then Mark would follow. He was always much, much more wary.

"I remember once Steve went inside to get an iceblock when we were playing out in the backyard. It was a hot day and I was out there playing with them too, being just as silly as they were. Steve had been gone a bit too long so I went inside. We had a fridge with the little freezer on top and all I could see was Stephen up there on a chair and his whole head, I thought it was stuck in the freezer box. But what happened was he decided it was pretty hot and he thought he would have a lick of the ice on the side of the icebox and his tongue stuck to the ice. He lost half his tongue that day. But if either of them was clumsy it was Mark. Mark seemed to be the one who would always trip over. Mark and Dean were the two clumsy ones for some reason."

Mark's timidness may have kept him out of strife more often than not but that's not to say there was never any trouble. One day Bev took Mark, Steve and Dean to an adventure playground. After playing for a while Mark became frozen by fright at the top of the large slippery dip. Seeing he would go neither backwards or forwards Bev decided to go up after him. When she got to the top she discovered he had found some courage and was already at the bottom of the slippery dip. Having climbed all that way Bev, despite wearing leather boots and a long leather coat which she described as probably her most expensive item of clothing at the time, decided to take the quick way down. Unfortunately the coat caught at the top of the slide and by the time she reached the bottom it had ripped all the way around at hip height. That, needless to say, was the end of their day at the park.

Clumsy and timid he may have been but Mark, by his own admission and with supporting testimony from close friends and family, also hated to get into trouble. Still, sometimes you just can't help bad luck. He was found out despite his best efforts once when he was in hospital to have some allergy tests done. "They served corn flakes with tinned peaches, which he didn't like, and rather than get in trouble for not eating them he tipped the lot behind his bedhead and said he'd eaten them," recalled Bev, who added that it did not take the nurses long to uncover his little fib.

Another more embarrassing episode occurred when Mark was in first grade. "Girls are a bit more precocious at that age, probably get up to a few more things," said Bev. "The boys are sort of shy, scared little things. The teacher had gone out of the room and the little girl behind Mark, I think she fancied him, she stuck a pin in his bottom. It hurt him pretty badly so Mark stood up and pulled his pants down to check out where he was hurt and the teacher came back into the room and caught Mark with his pants down in front of the girl behind him. So he was in pretty bad trouble for that.

"He said 'but mum it was her fault. I was only taking my pants down because she stuck a pin in me and I wanted to see what happened'. I explained it to the teacher a year or two later and she laughed. But he had to wear that one himself. They've got to learn that life's tough."

Such an event would have been pretty traumatic but Mark claims he can't remember anything like it ever having happened to him. "I think mum's making that up. I can't remember that." That's not to say he claimed to be a perfect angel. "Actually I remember in primary school there was me and Stephen and someone else and we had to push a TV, it was on a trolley, down some steps. Well, one step. And it fell off and smashed. We got into a bit of trouble over that." He will admit that he wasn't quite as boisterous as his brother. "I suppose I was a bit more quiet. Not shy, quiet I would say. I used to stick up for myself. Steve was probably a bit more mischievous. "

When asked if he was still a cautious person Mark had a couple of bob each way: "I've probably grown out of that, I think. I'm still pretty much an average type, just run of the mill, normal. I don't think I'm too adventurous or risque."

Their play soon began to gain more and more purpose until they were irrevocably on the path that would lead to the great cricket arenas of the world. The boys discovered that play is twice as much fun if there is a reason to it, so they started to play games where they could keep score and which had a winner and a loser at the end. Before too long playtime was one long, fierce contest of skill and strength. That, in turn, meant Bev never had any trouble getting them to eat their dinner or get eight hours sleep a night. In fact their enthusiasm soon became excessive in both areas. "I think it had to do with the amount of sport we played," recalled Mark. "I can't remember any afternoon from seven until we were 18 when we didn't play any sport. Very rarely. It would be a couple of days at most that we never actually played any sport. Keeping fit and always active I suppose you needed your sleep for the next day."

It was a natural progression for two kids who were constantly searching for something to keep each other amused. But it marked the end of doing anything for its own sake. Everything from now on had a purpose.

Bev said they got much of their inspiration from televised sport. "Depending on what sport was on television at the time, whether it was the Olympic Games or it might have been badminton, golf or cricket, they'd sit there and watch intently for three or four hours then they would go out into the backyard and turn it into virtually whatever sport they had been watching. It was golf they would get cans and turn them upside down and hammer them into the ground to make the holes. It wasn't a real big backyard but they'd improvise and turn it into that sort of arena. I'd have to call them in for tea and then as soon as they'd had tea they would be back out with the light on playing again."

Two such active and imaginative boys trying to recreate the environs of Royal St Andrews or the Sydney Cricket Ground in the confined space of a suburban backyard would normally endanger not only life and limb but the surrounding homes as well — particularly the windows. But Bev swears there were very few mishaps. "There could have been only one broken window in all the hours they've spent around this house. A few sore heads. I think that speaks for their reflexes. There would always be someone there to catch it. Even if they had their back to the ball they seemed to be able to catch it or stop it going into a window." That is not to say the boys were perfect. However special their physical talents there was no magic preventing the glass from shattering. Although rare, breakages did occur but, ever protective, Bev managed to cover for the boys and limit the fall-out.

In fact the events detailed in this book promise to be a revelation to Rodger. But Bev's first attempt at damage control involved a third party which made it a little difficult to keep things quiet.

"They had a little practice golf set they were given for Christmas and with a little practice golf set the ball is not a proper golf ball, it is just a very light little ball. And they were playing out in the backyard. You could do a great big swing and it wouldn't matter how hard you hit the ball, it wouldn't travel any distance in the air because it was so light, it was like a shuttlecock. Anyway, somehow or other, a real golf ball was put down by mistake, because they had real golf balls as well.

"Stephen took this terrific swing, connected with the real golf ball and it went straight through the toilet window of a house behind ours. The guy was in there on the toilet and Stephen had to explain how he had this practice ball but the one he hit wasn't the practice one. Insurance paid for that one."

That was the breakage everyone knew about. Bev may have had a foot in each camp but she was still prepared to engineer a cover-up that worked so well the family disciplinarian remains unaware of one of the rare occasions when his well-behaved off-spring went off the rails. Let's just hope he's got a good sense of humour. Bev lifts the lid on the long-kept secret.

Eyes on the prize ... excelling at cricket did not stop the Waughs from dazzling on the soccer field.

"Stephen was throwing oranges from the top of the stairs to Danny, who was only fairly small, only three or four. Huge big oranges. Danny was standing right near the back door, in front of our back window. Danny is a pretty good catcher and Stephen is a pretty good thrower. Stephen started throwing harder and the oranges got bigger. He must have had a bag of them up there. He was just hurling one after another and Danny stepped aside from one. He just couldn't cope with it and it went through the back window. We got that repaired before their father got home, before I went to squash, that was all repaired within an hour."

"That was a good cover-up story," said Steve. "It was as good as gold. When the old man came home he didn't know the difference. He still hasn't found out about that. The first time will be when he sees the book. I'm a bit worried about that. We were always throwing stuff about the house. Even now when we go around there. It is a miracle we haven't smashed more windows."

Sometimes the damage done was physical. When the twins were 12 Bev and Rodger gave the three eldest boys a golf set each for Christmas. They were practising that morning out in the yard when Steve became disgusted with his mother's efforts and offered to show her the correct technique. "I stood behind him but being used to tennis I was too close. Steve took a terrific swing and hit me fair in the nose," said Bev. There wasn't much sympathy for her though. "I got in trouble for spoiling Christmas day," she said.

After flirting with a variety of sports cricket had caught their eye and the boys were becoming serious suitors. It was a romance made in heaven. The twins played their fair share of cricket at school and at the park with mates but they preferred the one-on-one contests in the less-than-ideal venue of their own home. Conditions were a little cramped but where there's a will there's a way and, as history shows, it certainly didn't do them any harm. The field of combat was either the sloping driveway or the front yard, each boasting its own peculiarities and advantages. Because of the end-to-end slope the driveway gave the bowler an extra yard or two of pace while the sharp left-to-right tilt of the front yard wicket meant that the off-cutter was a very profitable delivery. The driveway demanded strict strokemaking because virtually anything in the air was out. Those rules relaxed in the front yard where the batsman earned six runs for anything hit over the fence.

Relaxed was not a word that was really appropriate for their backyard contests. The competitive genes they had inherited from Rodger and Bev were starting to kick in now. Brotherly love ran a poor second to winning. On the field anyway. "It was always pretty fierce. A lot of arguments," said Steve. "We had to get the bat out of each other's hands. Used to pin each other a bit, too, with bouncers. That probably comes through in our bowling now. The tendency to bowl a few short ones, that stems from our backyard cricket. We were always trying to knock each other's head off.

"There were times when a couple of us would go crying to mum saying we had been whacked with a bat. Stuff like that. She had to come out and calm things down a few times when it got out of control. Half the games used to turn into brandings. Someone would bowl and hit the other and they would throw it back and we would play brandings for about half an hour until someone got hit badly and they would go inside crying. One of us would wet the ball so it would sting a bit more. There were always a lot of balls lying around in the garden and on the roofs. So we were never short of balls to throw at each other."

The twins were never satisfied with simply matching their own considerable talents against one another. They had to introduce new quirks to make the games even more difficult. Curiously, whether by accident or design, any rule or equipment change always seemed to handicap the batsman. They would tape the ball up or shave fur off one side to make it swing more and they would use a stump or a cheap kid's bat to make things even tougher. "We were always trying to improvise and make it a bit harder than it was before," said Steve. "You would get a tennis ball and tape half of it so it would swing, anything you could find you'd use. Table tennis balls or tennis balls or cricket balls. There always used to be some sort of ball in the backyard and you could improvise whether you had a bat or a fence paling. There was always something you could play with. It's probably half the reason kids found it difficult when they came to play in our backyard. They were playing on our turf and didn't know the rules. And they weren't batting with a proper bat and different balls so we had a bit of a field day going through them.

"A lot of times we would bat left-handed or bowl left-handed or play French cricket but most of the time it was pretty full-on. There wasn't too much charity stuff. I used to bowl a bit of spin but it used to get carted pretty easily so we were back on the quick stuff. I wasn't real accurate but it was always bowl as quick as you can down the hill and try and fudge over the line. Try and knock him out, or get him out."

And if there were no balls at all that was no problem either. After the boys had exhausted their own supply and their father's Saturday coaching stock they just made their own said Bev. "They used to get little bits of foam and tape them up. Things like that. If they lost all their balls, if they had all disappeared, they would make some up somehow or other. A foam one wasn't firm enough to be hit so they would find some method of wrapping miles of tape around it. I can remember insulating tape was a pretty heavily used item."

It wasn't just batting and bowling that had them entranced. Their enthusiasm for cricket became complete and made the kitchen a dangerous place to be. For guys that loved food so much they didn't have much respect for it. Please pass the butter took on a whole new meaning. And the wise would never, ever, ask for an egg. Bev said cutting a piece of fruit became a new adventure for her. "Oranges that started off with just being gently thrown would end up inedible or maybe a nice avocado was suddenly inedible. Not because they dropped it, they didn't drop things much, but you'd cut it open and it would be all soft and you'd suddenly realise what had happened to it. It had been used as a ball."

A feature of many Australians' childhood backyard battles was the championing of favourite players. Often the struggle to earn the right of representing the hero of the day was as fierce as the cricket. The Waughs, though, had little time for personalities. The game was the thing. Mark can remember the odd attempt at imitation but Steve drew a blank. "I can't remember actually imitating a particular player but we took sides. We would toss to see who was Australia and who was England. Hills or valleys. You'd never take the Poms, you would always want to be the Australians. But that was as far as that sort of thing went. We would just basically keep a running score and try to beat each other.

"Sometimes we used to try to imitate some of the players," said Mark. "Jeff Thomson, sometimes we used to try and bowl like him. And Dougie Walters. I always liked Dougie Walters. I just liked the way he played. His attitude. His casual attitude, nothing seemed to worry him. But it's a bit hard to model yourself on Dougie. His smoking and drinking and whatever."

They may have not got much directly from Kevin Douglas Walters but they turned out to be his spiritual heirs in their natural approach to the game. He did it his way and the Waughs would do it theirs. "We had a bit of coaching but nothing that changed anything," said Mark. "We just watched cricket on TV and just developed our own game. We never copied anyone. It's just a natural thing."

The pair would also play soccer and rugby league in the yard. Just one-on-one, barging away. Funnily enough this was where they imitated players and ironically, for two such flamboyant cricketers, props were more often than not the stars of the show. Steve followed Western Suburbs so he would be Tommy Raudonikis or John Donnelly or Les Boyd or John Ribot. Mark, on the other hand, was a Sharks man by virtue of the football jumper Bev gave him one year. So they went their separate ways to Lidcombe Oval and Endeavour Field but in later years both switched to the Canterbury Bulldogs. Still the hero's name Mark can recall choosing to honour in front-yard combat came from neither Cronulla nor Canterbury and is not exactly a stellar figure in rugby league mythology — St George prop Barry Beath. "I don't know why," said Mark. "He wasn't that much of a legend." They never experienced any strong desire to play, turning out once or twice for the school.

"We did actually play a couple of games of proper league at school. I was five-eighth and Mark was on the wing. He was a bit of a cat," laughed Steve. "Doesn't like the rough stuff too much. I remember scoring a try from a line drop out. It was the highlight of my Rugby League career. Weren't real keen on the tackles. I was penalised first tackle for going in with a clenched fist, but I never even knew I did it. So I thought I'd better get out of this game."

Mark resented that little dig at his courage but was forced to admit there might have been something to it. "I was pretty tough at soccer. I just didn't fancy playing league. I don't know, it might have been the head contact. I was probably scared of being belted. The heavy contact. I've never had a fight in my life. We fought against each other but when we fought we didn't punch each other in the head, just in the stomach or whatever. Besides that I've never had a fight outside, school or anywhere else. But for some reason whenever we were in the front yard we used to play pretty hard at rugby league."

Not every game was played with all-consuming intensity. Steve's best mate in primary school, Doug Nurka, recalled the boys adopted a game from the popular television show *Almost Anything Goes*. They would get a sheet of plastic out on the lawn, cover it with soap and water and try and play football on that.

Because the Waughs lived on a busy street the young twins were not allowed to have a bike. Instead Beverley and Roger bought them scooters. As with all their other toys a way was found to compete with them in the confines of the house. They set up a racing course down the sloping driveway which took a sharp S past the back corner of the house on the left and the garage on the right. Many were the spills according to Stephen, particularly when Dean graduated to the circuit. "We used to have plenty of scooter races down the driveway," said Steve. "And we used to have a hell of a lot of crashes. If you didn't negotiate the last bend you went straight into the garage. There wasn't much room up there. You'd fight for an early possie down that hill and if your brakes didn't work you were gone."

It appears there wasn't a competition-free zone in either the Waugh lives or the Waugh household. If the weather was bad they would just take the ongoing battle indoors for card games, home-made pinball machines, carpet bowls, board games or unique little games of their own creation. And while no-one would question their sportsmanship on the cricket field Bev said that cheating was part and parcel of getting the upper hand at home.

"Stephen probably had a bit more cunning and because he had such a good memory you had to be a really good cheat to get away with it. But as far as winning and losing I think they would both agree it was about 50-50. Or 25-25-25-25 when the other two came along. It didn't really matter what they did, schoolwork, athletics. I can remember them going in an orange race just as a novelty event and they dead-heated for first, Stephen and Mark. They were in completely different lanes and kept having sneaky little looks across at each other and they took the oranges in completely different order but they ended up in a dead heat.

Not content with starring on the sports field and earning trips interstate Steve and Mark were terrors at schoolyard games as well. Whether it was flicking football cards or playing marbles that Waugh competitive streak ensured that they went home, pockets bulging with trophies. Recalled Bev: "I'd say to Mark and Stephen ' do you want me to buy some cards?' and they would say 'no, we don't need to buy any. Just one will do'. They'd come home with pockets full, and the same with marbles. They would start off with one marble and in the end they must have had every other kid's marbles in the school."

The twins also did their fair share of spectating. They were regulars at the cricket Tests each season and attended one or two Shield matches with their cricket coaches when younger. They were also there when the big soccer matches came to town. "I remember sitting in all the old stands at the Cricket Ground watching Test matches," said Steve. "Sitting there the whole day and watching it. It was packed in those days. I used to enjoy Test cricket a lot. A lot of young people don't like watching it but I used to always listen to it on the radio or watch it on TV or go out there. I could listen to the Test cricket all day on the radio."

Childhood hobbies and pastimes that didn't involve scoring flickered very briefly. "At one stage I built a few model airplanes and I collected stamps," said Mark. "Only for a little while, I got bored with that."

Lest anyone think that Steve and Marks' world was one confined to food, sleep and a variety of bouncing balls then let it be known that sport is not all they watched on TV. As kids they developed a taste for programmes that now are the height of kitsche. Their favourite four shows were, in no particular order, *Gilligan's Island*, *The Brady Bunch*, *Lost In Space* and *The Munsters*. Then there were the cartoons like the Wacky Races which featured arch-villain Dick Dastardly and his sidekick Muttley. Steve can still name all the cars and the competitors they were driven by. Their affection for *The Brady Bunch* is interesting because the Waughs represent a much more realistic suburban Australian version of Hollywood's saccharine-sweet "perfect" family.

Childhood friend Mark Grant was a keen observer of the Waugh household. They began as opponents on the field as young children but eventually went to the same high school and became firm friends. Not only were they playmates but the Grant and Waugh houses became interchangeable. "My brother and I used to stay over at their place and they used to stay at ours," said Mark Grant.

Now a teacher, Grant was sensitive to the atmosphere at the Waughs'. Not that you had to be incredibly perceptive to recognise the fierce competitive environment. "At home competition was always encouraged, especially by Mrs Waugh," he said. "She was especially keen to see her kids get the just rewards for their talents. She was very supportive of her kids. The kids grew up in an environment where it was accepted that competition was good and everyone thrived on competition and I don't think it's had any adverse effect on their characters."

"It was a game of wits and a game of words," recalled his brother Scott. "Who was going to do the dishes or what television show they were going to watch. There was always one playing off against the other."

The local rules, intense competition and the sheer physical talents of the Waugh twins would have been a pretty daunting combination on their own but when you threw in two ultra-competitive young parents and a couple of brothers as well it becomes quite an intimidating package. But far from being overwhelmed Mark Grant said the atmosphere was quite heady. "It was intimidating in terms of the success it brought. You wished it was you.

But I don't think you were ever made to feel in awe of anyone, weren't made to feel second class. Mr and Mrs Waugh never made me feel like that and Mark and Steve certainly didn't. I enjoyed going over there.

"Homework was always done when it was too dark to play outside. It was just a good fun place to be, everyone was always laughing."

It seems that Mark Grant was more than a match for the livewire Waughs. He said Steve and he were mad table tennis players, indulging in mammoth tests of skill on the weekends and during holidays towards the end of high school which would require the victor to win 25 games or more. He also testified to the enthusiasm with which Bev became involved. And the wicked delight with which it was welcomed.

"The boys really enjoyed beating mum," he said. "It was really good to see them giving mum a hard time. They were able to beat everyone and mum was no exception."

Scott Grant said the teenage Waughs and Grants spent the majority of their school holidays at a gymnasium at Condell Park. "We used to go there and spend the whole day playing sport. For $5 you could play tennis, cricket, squash or pool. Just having a game of squash for an hour was a big deal." He never saw any spite in the fierce battles though. "Mark and Steve get on a lot better than most people think. They were definitely very friendly but also very competitive. They competed ferociously."

Mark Grant said the normal household chores often suffered because of the family's hectic lifestyle. With Rodger either working, coaching or playing tennis and Bev spreading herself between four active boys and their teams it is not surprising that it wasn't a model home. Well, as far as tidiness went anyway. No-one could criticise the way Bev and Rodger handled the kids. "They were always a family on the go," said Grant. "Tea was a quick snack, the house was constantly changing and always a mess. It wasn't a pig sty, it just wasn't as important as where they were coming from and where they were going to."

Another reason for any untidiness in and around the house was the lack of elbow grease expended in this particular area by the boys. Bev is such a workaholic that, consciously or unconsciously, she let the boys get away with murder. There was the odd attempt to teach them various chores but general ineptitude meant they didn't last long. "They certainly weren't handy around the place. I suppose it was because time didn't allow but we tried to teach them to mow lawns and things like that. They certainly weren't very gifted in that area."

Rodger and Bev's participation in tennis satellite tournaments gave the family a regular circuit of holiday venues. The Waughs would pack up and travel to places like Gloucester, Bathurst and Taree for three or four days at a time each year. That gave the boys a steady circle of out-of-town friends. It was also a big adventure they always looked forward to.

"We would get excited every year about going away in the car," said Steve. "That went on for about 10 years and was the extent of our holidays and probably the most time we spent with each other. Those trips were great fun, getting up at three in the morning and packing into the car. I used to stand on the left side of the car and Mark would be on the rightside, up the back of the car hanging onto the roof straps. We used to stand up there for three and fours hours at a time, just looking out the windows. Later on when there was three or four of us we used to pile into the back of the Holden with all the pillows and sheets and everything.

"We used to have good friends at those times as well because the same group of people used to go and they used to have kids as well so we looked forward to seeing them each year. They were always keen on sport so we would get up there and play cricket for about three hours, then tennis, then soccer. We'd play sport about 10 hours a day. Or you could go off

A hero's hero. The Waughs have both always admired Australian Test great Doug Walters. Ern McQuillan

by yourself and do what ever you wanted — go exploring or whatever, get up to a bit of mischief. Actually we played in a few of the tournaments after that."

As has been previously mentioned the Waughs' hectic lifestyle has given them a fondness for sleep. "We were always pretty poor wakers-up," said Steve. "The bell would ring for school at 8.45am and we'd lob in there about 8.44 every morning. We always used to sleep in wherever we'd go. We used to rely on mum to get us up, get us going."

"Our whole family's pretty keen on sleep," said Mark. "Mum, she likes her sleep, and the other blokes, Dean and Daniel, they're probably worse than me and Stephen. I don't know why, it's just a family trait. I suppose it's good in one way, you can get to sleep and relax and take your mind off things.

"The family had a reputation for not so much being late all the time but cutting it fine. We used to be late four out of five days. There was three of us — me, Dean and Stephen – – in high school. I always used to be ready on time, of course, but we had to wait for the other two because mum used to drive us to school. It was always Dean or Steve that was late. Every day. I used to have to suffer the consequences as well even though I was ready. I used to be a bit frustrated, I used to get bloody annoyed."

Both Bev and Rodger admit they rarely saw the twins physically fight but that news brought a chuckle from both Mark and Steve. "Jeez, she must have had her eyes closed half the time," said Steve. "No, we had plenty of fights. I think there were a couple of years when we got a bit ugly towards each other. I suppose we were growing up and I suppose you go through a few changes. Thirteen, fourteen, fifteen and we were probably getting a bit serious about our sports then.

"I'd say it was the only time we probably got jealous of each other. Those couple of years there. I suppose there was a bit of competition to see who was the best of the two at that stage and occasionally we'd have your typical brotherly fight. But I don't think we actually hit each other in the head too many times. It was more of a nasty one in the kidneys or the headlock and a Chinese burn, stuff like that. There weren't too many serious injuries but we hopped into it a few times if mum wasn't around. We were always scared of mum and dad. Dad used to chase us around with a belt if we got stuck into each other too much so we would try to do it fairly sneakily."

While agreeing on the subject of fraternal violence Mark did not think jealousy was ever a big problem. "There might have been the odd occasion we were jealous but it was never something that happened a lot between us," said Mark. "All brothers probably get jealous of each other at some stage about something but it was never a major issue with us. We used to do everything pretty much the same so there was nothing really to be jealous of. I used to get jealous if he got more food on his plate."

Mrs Bourne said the twins adored their brother Dean from the start. Maybe having to share with each other put an early stop to any jealousy or sibling rivalry because all three had similar feelings when Danny came along. Dean wanted to be just like his older brothers and made an earlier start at just about everything. He began playing competitive soccer at three and adored his first pair of boots and socks so much that Mrs Bourne recalls arriving while he was having an afternoon nap — in his socks and soccer boots. "He wouldn't take them off. He had to be the same as the others," she recalled.

"They both got great enjoyment out of their younger brothers when they came along," said Bev. "They were fantastic with them. They weren't very old when Dean was born but they were 10 when Danny was born so they were both old enough to take responsibility for him. They never treated him roughly. Lots of people said: 'you've got all boys and now

Clockwise from top left: Father Rodger and younger brother Dean, unconcerned at the threat of twin sharpshooters Steve (with hat tilted back) and Mark; Steve, Dean and Mark ready to charge for the front gate; Mark, Dean, Steve and Danny in 1975; Two future Test cricketers — Steve (left) and Mark, aged 10; Mark, Dean and Steve, about to start filling the trophy cabinet.

Top: The Waugh brothers, September 1992 — (clockwise from bottom left) Steve, Danny, Dean and Mark. *(Trudi Van de Wint)*

Below: The groom and company. Steve (second from right), on the morning of his wedding, with his best man, Brad McNamara (far left) and groomsmen, Tony Fort and Mark Taylor (right). *(Trudi Van de Wint)*

Right : Mark, pictured in something slightly less conventional than usual cricket gear, during a benefit match for Essex teammate Derek Pringle in 1992.

you've got another one. He's going to have a tough time'. But they were unbelievably gentle. Like little mother hens. I don't think he was ever roughly treated or hurt at all."

Well, maybe once. Steve and Mark had been left in charge of Danny and it soon became obvious he required a change of nappy. As neither was willing to get to the root of the problem they formulated a strategy that removed the need for any dirty work. Each took a leg and directed Dean, who was in charge of the hose, to wash poor Danny down. Reports are that there was no stinting on the water pressure.

"I can't remember whose idea it was," said Mark. "We thought it was a good idea though. None of us was going to wipe his bum for him so we had to do something."

Nevertheless Bev believes Danny was very fortunate. "They never gave him a hard time at all. They've always been very protective of him, especially now that they've done well. When Danny was born they came over and checked him out, they weren't worried about me, they knew I was all right. The first thing they said was: 'It looks like he's got good arms, good legs. He'll be able to play good cricket, good tennis. He'll be a good sportsman'."

Both remain close to Danny but it is Stephen who has developed a special bond with the youngest Waugh. Bankstown-Canterbury Cricket Club president Brian Freedman, who has known the Waugh family since the twins were eight years old, recalled one incident which he feels typified the relationship. Bankstown were playing St George in a 1987 first grade semi-final and the Bulldogs had been asked to bat on a wet Hurstville Oval wicket. Steve batted brilliantly to score 93 out of 160. "As he left the field Steve quietly said 'that's 80 too many'," said Freedman. "He took three quick wickets before bad light stopped play, had a few drinks with the boys and then he and Lynette took Danny (who would have been about 12 at the time) to the pictures. Then he came back next day and polished them off." It was not the first or the last time that Steve would take Danny along when he was going out with Lynette. He still does.

It is interesting to read the comments on Mark and Steve's primary school reports. In third grade it was written that "Mark (who was class captain) works well. He is quite mature, very reliable and popular. A pleasant personality. Works conscientiously. Almost tradesmanlike, reliable". While in fifth grade "Mark is a great student. Everything is done to perfection with great attention to detail". And a year later "polite and well-mannered at all times".

Steve, on the other hand, was described as "sensitive and emotional". In November 1973 it was said he was "too energetic sometimes. A keen sense of humour. A sensitive type whose behaviour lapses are an over-reaction to embarrassment".

While later in their school years Mark and Steve came more to fit the mould of knuckle-headed athletes, that was more because of environment and their almost complete obsession with sport rather than because they were genuinely stupid. Indeed a lot of intelligent and diligent students would like Steve's score of just over 300.

So much of what they have become is undoubtedly a result of where they were raised but it might have been so different. Keith and Dorothy Bourne came to Sydney after Keith was transferred from his teaching job in Greenthorpe. He had taught at six successive one-teacher country schools and had decided with his wife to move to the coast to allow Bev to live near her high school. In Greenthorpe she was leaving home at 7am and not getting home until 5pm because of the huge distances she had to travel. They also wanted to live near the sea. If they had been granted their preference the Bournes would have ended up on the northern beaches. Keith had looked at a school in Brookvale and the Bournes actually had a house picked out at Collaroy Plateau when the call came from East Hills. Who can say what might have happened if the boys had lived cheek-by-jowl with the lure of the sea.

FOUR

The Guiding Light

BEVERLY Waugh is such an extraordinary woman that she deserves a whole chapter, if not a book, to herself. With respect to Rodger she has been the centre of the Waugh universe. Her energy is awesome. Even now she drives herself constantly, although these days it is a little more for herself. That she has raised four boys so well and seen two of them succeed as Test cricketers and another make the NSW squad is a tremendous tribute to the woman. What is more of a tribute is the way she would scoff dismissively at anyone who attempted to offer even faint praise — she believes it is simply her job.

For 20 years she has driven boys to sport, prepared teas, scored, stood on sidelines and sat in stands too numerous to mention but she is still there to support each of her sons when they step out on to the field. Of course she can't be there when the twins are touring with Australia or Mark is playing for Essex in England, but when the game is in Sydney she is there. Likewise she refuses to miss Dean and Danny's grade games — even though they are playing in separate teams.

"I don't know how many people have said to me 'how do you cope?'," said Bev. "'How awful', they say, 'fancy having to go and watch cricket'. But I enjoyed it. A lot of people find it difficult but I liked it and still do. I wanted to be with them. I enjoyed watching them and mixing with other people. Some of the enjoyment has gone out of it, though, as it's got more serious."

The rushing around did take its toll physically and mentally on Bev. One Saturday when the twins were six or seven Bev had the barest amount of time to get the twins to their game at Padstow from Dean's at Milperra. Complicating the matter was the fact that someone had backed into the car. She rang her mother and asked to borrow Dorothea's little vehicle and was allowed to on the condition that she took care of it because it wasn't insured. The boys were getting nervous and Bev was going as fast as she could when a great big sheepdog ran out in front of the car. "I didn't have time to do anything," said Bev. "I hit it and it sailed over the car. We were so concerned about the dog. I was upset and the kids were upset but the old man who owned it said 'don't worry ,it's not your fault.' Steve and Mark had to run straight on to the field. Then I walked around the front of the car and saw that there had been about $400 worth of damage done."

On another occasion they were travelling to a game at Toongabbie but seemed to be taking an awful long time to get there. Mark was panicking and eventually Bev realised she had completely lost her sense of direction and they were heading towards Katoomba. She was often caught speeding in her haste to get from one game to another. "I got out of it once when I cried," said Bev. "The boys never forgave me for embarrassing them."

The Waugh family. Clockwise from bottom left: Steve, Danny, Bev, Rodger, Dean, and Mark.

Her reasons for taking up squash also speak volumes about her character. Bev, a former junior tennis champion, was having trouble keeping up with the demands of her clan 10 years ago. But instead of reducing her punishing workload she decided to get fit enough to cope. She took up squash rather than return to tennis because it was something she could do at night that didn't take up much time. "It was the only thing I could fit in," she said. "I wanted to get as fit as I could in the shortest time."

Having decided to tackle squash it is typical that she did not just try to become competent, she immediately immersed herself in a quest to get better. The result was that eight years later, at the age of 44, she was playing in both the open and senior divisions of the women's world squash championship.

"I really like it, I like the competition," she said at the time. "It gives you an incentive to improve, to see how far you can go. And the boys have been very encouraging. I think they realise how much time I put into their cricket." Bev said she appreciates the chance to prove to herself and others what she is capable of achieving after having her tennis career cut short by motherhood. But she admitted that squash had another advantage. "With squash I can get right away from cricket, let all the tensions out on court." Of course, being a Waugh, she did not just go for the joy of participation. She won two rounds of the open championship and was runner-up in her division of the senior titles.

Being a teen mother seems to have been a plus rather than a minus for Bev. Rather than allowing the obvious difficulties to overwhelm her she has taken advantage of her youth and enthusiasm to get into each part of the boys' lives, not just those traditionally occupied by the mother. "I probably should have been in cooking tea or doing the washing up but if there was a game on I'd get involved," she said. While it was difficult for Rodger to escape his "father" role because he spent so much time providing for the family. Bev blurred her "mother" role because her constant contact with the boys allowed her to play and share their jokes full rein.

Bev was out playing with them during the day, being silly in the kitchen or the backyard, making a mess and having fun.

"I suppose we saw more of mum and she took us to more of the games, but that was probably only because Dad was always coaching tennis on the weekends and playing a lot of tennis himself, so Mum sort of had to take a back seat with her tennis career," said Steve. "She probably took us to more sporting events but I'd say they were both equally keen and both gave us a lot of encouragement."

"Mum never had a favourite," said Mark. "Or I don't think she did. She spent as much time with each of us as the other one. Gave us as much attention. She's a very determined sort of person. You knew if she started something she would always finish it. Even with her squash over the last couple of years. The determination she has shown to go from a seventh grader to a player in the world squash open. Once she puts her mind to something she does it. Discipline and determination. Quite often she trains harder than us. Running around the block and going to the gym. She's got plenty of guts."

Given her massive involvement in the twins' sporting career it is amazing that she has alienated very few people. And those more for her enthusiasm and the simple fact of her sons' success than anything negative that she may have done. The coaches of junior teams cop more than their share of flak from sporting parents but they had some very nice things to say about Bev.

"Bev was always the force behind them," said soccer coach Ron Mannell. "I'm sure Rodger was supportive but he was nowhere near the force Bev was. She was behind them 150 per cent. I can remember her sitting out in the cold at Bankstown Oval watching them play. If you had a team full of Bev Waughs you'd never have to worry."

The Panania East Hills cricket club had an annual awards picnic and one of the yearly events was an egg tossing competition for the adults. Bev was a repeated winner partnering coach Alan Dougherty's son Neil.

Despite her highly competitive background Bev did not involve her sons in sport just for the simple competitive and physical aspects, she also saw it as a valuable tool in shaping their characters. And she was not just interested in winners. "She used to worry more about one of them going bad than one of them going good," agreed Alan Dougherty.

Either by word or deed Bev has passed on a clearly defined, simple and strong set of values to her sons. Again, Rodger deserves no small credit for the way the boys have turned out but it is hard to ignore the link between the boys and their mother. Their competitiveness, bluntness, sportsmanship, loyalty, sense of fun, level-headedness, concern for others — the list goes on and on. She is a strong-willed woman and fortunately this has brought nothing but good.

"Probably my biggest belief is that actions speak louder than words," said Bev. "People can hurt you with the things they say to you, and as the boys got older and became good at sport, of course they had to take a lot of sarcasm, especially as I was a teacher. A lot of kids thought they were picked because I was a teacher and knew all the other teachers. Sometimes they would get dropped from a side and be really upset about it. Just generally in everyday life they might get upset about something. They'd find someone had cheated them or a teacher thought they did something they didn't do. I always taught them that ultimately your actions will speak for you. You don't need to go and carry on and make a big fuss. Ultimately that's the biggest thing I've tried to teach them. And to be kind to people, especially people who are less fortunate than yourself. I've got a lot to do with disabled and handicapped children and I think in dealing with them you learn a lot about life. I tried to make the boys aware of how fortunate they are being healthy, able, quite bright. They've got just about everything going for them.

"Don't ever forget that not everyone is like that. You have got to really give thought to other people, just don't think about yourself all the time. Be considerate, compassionate, kind. But you've also got to be tough too. Don't cry much. I don't think that's anything I've actually taught them but I don't think they've seen me crack up very much. I think a lot of children cry just to get attention. They knew that unless it was really worth crying for not very much notice would be taken of them."

There in a nutshell is the genesis of their stoic demeanour. "I can never remember crying much or being a real sook or having a bad temper," said Mark. "I think dad was pretty strong on discipline and if he thought we were putting on an act or something he would get stuck into us."

"I think most of it, a lot of it, is not said. I think they follow a lot by example," said Bev. "I mean they've seen my husband and I play a lot of sport and I think they would go a lot by the way they saw us react."

And by the way they saw others react. "Outside the family you can teach your children to learn from people who don't have very desirable traits in their character," said Bev. "For example, if I saw a kid cry or a parent go crook on their kid at sport we would sort of discuss that on the way home and I'd say 'look, if I ever upset you with something I say to you, you let me know because I don't want you to be unhappy'."

They also tried to ensure that the boys didn't get over-excited about their achievements. "I can't see the point in being highly elated because where's the other end of the scale?" said Bev.

Bev and Rodger did not lose sight of the fact that the most important goal in childrens' sport is having fun. "That's probably the biggest thing," she said, "Once something loses its enjoyment there is something wrong. Once you get to the top level in sport then it is serious and some of the enjoyment does go out of it but basically everything they did they enjoyed doing. They played baseball, they played competition golf, they probably could have chosen any sport and gone right to the top but they enjoyed all those sports."

Part of ensuring that the boys enjoyed themselves was making sure they didn't build up unrealistic expectations of themselves, giving them a wider perspective on the game. Making them look out as well as in. "If you do lose or get beaten or something knocks you back, rather than be too hard on yourself sometimes look to see if someone was better than you, which is quite often the case, and if they were appreciate that and tell them 'you know, you were too good today' because a lot of people can't do that. And a lot of parents can't say that about someone else's child. So I taught them to appreciate that sometimes someone is better than them physically or mentally. I mean they know just about everyone is a better mechanic than them. It's important to appreciate the fact that other people are good at some things and you're good at some things."

If it is easy to see what Bev has passed on to Steve and Mark it is just as easy to see where she got it from. Her parents also appear to have been superb role models. "My father never talked about anyone else," said Bev. "That's probably where I got actions speak louder than words, from him, because during my tennis career and my brother's cricket career Dad was always a strong influence. You always knew he was there yet he was never critical of our performances, only in a helpful way. I can remember so many times that I was cheated at tennis and I'd think 'why can't my dad stick up for me like other children's parents do? They complain to the umpire and the officials. Why doesn't dad do that for me?' He used to say to me 'you know, you eventually come through. You prove it through your actions'. I think that trait has come through to me and, hopefully, passed on."

Although their grandfather's influence has, sadly, been almost totally second-hand through Bev they have had 27 years of first-class first-hand experience of their grandmother's example. The similarities between Bev and her mother Dorothea are striking and it is not just physical. She is also a remarkably energetic woman with a bright and breezy outlook on life. "I'm one of those fitness grannies," said Mrs Bourne. "I don't want to get sick but I'm not a crank about it. I'm the oldest one at tennis but that doesn't worry me. I'm going to play as long as I can. I play tennis three times a week, I go to bingo, I go for a walk. There's plenty to do and I'm very happy. The life you have in your body, not money, is the most important thing in my book. Life and good health. Every hour is a bonus. If ever I get depressed I go out and do something about it. Peace of mind is the greatest thing in the world to have. (But) you've got to have fun in life. You can't be too stiff and regimented."

There was very little physical discipline in the Waugh household. Bev said Rodger would have given them a few smacks, but she said she could count on one hand the number of times she struck them. "It usually ended up a huge joke," she said. "As they got older and they did something I thought deserved the strap it was probably me playing part of the game, too. They'd start running and I'd start running."

"Mum could never catch us with the belt so we used to get away with that," said Steve. "We used to torment her something shocking, I think, looking back on it. She'd chase us around the house. We'd dive in somewhere and wait half an hour and that would be it. We'd be safe."

Well not always. Bev said she did connect on the odd occasion. "I'll never forget once, I haven't really hit Stephen since this time, he must have been about 12 I think. He did something I thought deserved punishment. He started running through the house and he said: 'you can't catch me' and I said 'yes I can'. He took a flying leap over a chair at the back of the table and on the way through he hit his head on one of his father's tennis trophies — it's

However many sports they try and triumph in, cricket will always be number one for the four Waugh boys, here pictured in December 1988.

a clock. That's what started it, that's why I had to hit him, because he'd knocked the clock off the wall and it would no longer go. He kept running and I kept chasing. Eventually I got him. His father used to say when we were sitting there at tea and the clock was still up on the wall, 'gee that clock's stopped again, we must get some new batteries for it'. And we would look at each other and try to keep a straight face. We knew the clock would never work again."

That's not to say Bev completely sheltered them. Both Bev and Rodger, but Bev in particular, seemed to have been able to walk that fine line between giving every assistance possible without becoming interfering — constructive rather than destructive. Bev has always sought to ensure the boys are aware of their responsibilities and learn to take responsibility for their lives. She refused to order them to do things like their homework. She said people need to be aware of what they have to do and the consequences they will suffer if they don't.

"If they don't do it that's their problem. You can't really make someone do something. I reminded them sometimes. If it was getting late and they were outside I might say to them 'oh, you better come in now or you won't have time to do your homework'. In a way that's the same thing isn't it? You are just reminding them to do it. There would have been times, I'd say, when they didn't get it done."

She gives a lot of credit for their relatively trouble-free passage through life to sport and their own decision to pursue it so enthusiastically. "I've always had a lot to do with children, teaching them and coaching them, and the ones who don't seem to have sport seem to be the ones who get together, go into town at night, go to pubs and clubs, get into drugs. I'm not saying that as a general rule but if you are involved in a sport you use up all that physical energy and if you can use it up doing something you like it's got to be healthier for you.

"I never forced them to do anything. If anything I'd probably have to try to say 'come inside' or 'maybe you shouldn't play on the weekend' or 'maybe you shouldn't try out for this team or that team'. It was the opposite if anything. And you would meet some terrific people. They had lots of great teachers and coaches who have spent time with them. I think they appreciated other people giving their time freely.

"But there was a side where I did worry about them over-using their bodies. Danny is much more low-profiled. He could be in just about every team going at the top level at the moment but he is playing a bit of golf, playing soccer once on the weekend and not for the school, and at school he plays baseball. Just a little bit of everything. He could be a top golfer. He could be lots of things but it was too hard on Steve's and Mark's bodies.

"At the time I was bashing my head up against a brick wall trying to explain to coaches that they were being too hard on young children because being in different teams you are training for three or four different coaches. You are training for a school side. You are training for a club side. You are training for a rep side. You are training for a NSW side. They all wanted the best, sometimes for their own egos, too. I felt like saying sometimes 'look, my two don't need to train, they're training somewhere else'. But then that would single them out if they didn't train with the others. They expected 100 per cent and they always gave 100 per cent but it was just too much wear and tear on their bodies. I don't want that to end up happening to Danny."

FIVE

To Be The Best

ATTITUDE is only half the battle. The tens of thousands of enthusiastic hackers who hit the sporting fields of Australia each weekend bear testimony to that fact. Even starker is the example of the teenagers and adults who don't play ANYTHING because of the intense pressure they were put under by their parents when young. Encouragement and a competitive example and all the backyard Tests in the world aren't going to get a person to the real thing unless they have the physical tools. Much is made of so-called "self-made players" but that is a relative term. Generally speaking, anybody who makes it to the top in cricket or any other sport is still physically gifted — there are some things you just can't train for.

And when it comes to being blessed with talent there have been few more blessed than Mark and Steve Waugh. They have everything — speed, power, elegance. But it comes as no surprise that the boys possess such wonderful physical gifts. While many an avid punter will tell you that breeding doesn't necessarily guarantee stardom it is hard to imagine a better bloodline than that possessed by Mark and Steve.

On Rodger's side his grandfather Arthur was a fine lawn bowler, his father Ned a footballer who represented country and later played bowls and mother Ella an excellent young tennis player before polio struck. Not only did she walk again, she then took up lawn bowls and still defiantly refuses to succumb to a wheelchair despite being in her mid seventies. Bev's father was also a good cricketer and tennis. Her mother Dorothea is a keen tennis player, turning out three times a week despite being in her 73rd year.

"Sport's been our whole life," said Rodger.

Both Beverley and Rodger were outstanding junior tennis players, which is how they met and fell in love. A love match on the tennis courts. Had they been older and a little more well known they might have had to suffer through much the same corny headline puns their sons have endured. Rodger is still a fine player in the masters group while Beverley, who represented NSW just before she became a mother, has made a success of squash in recent years, playing in the World Open that was held in Sydney in October 1990. As a teen Rodger was in the same group as Tony Roche and Allan Stone. He was ranked seven or eight in Australia as a 19-year-old but his young family and the lack of money in tennis forced him to choose a career in the bank. He boasted a win over Roche in the Australian under-17 doubles final but his successes did not often translate into places in representative teams and it is those disappointments and a lingering sense of injustice that fuels his fierce desire to see his family do well.

Given his history Rodger would seem the perfect candidate for the role of interfering parent, who uses their talented child to fulfil their own thwarted sporting dreams. At the very least one would expect him to indulge in a little simple jealousy. But he says as he watches the boys becoming rich and famous, he doesn't resent his own lack of opportunity.

"I'm not disappointed," said Rodger. "There wasn't all that much money in tennis and

I was happy doing what I was doing. That never worried me, I never resented having to give up tennis."

Neither is he hurt that they chose cricket ahead of his own sport. "They could have been anything in any sport," he said. "It didn't worry me in the least. I'm actually quite pleased they didn't take up tennis because from my point of view a lot of back-biting and politics went on there. Little did I know there was going to be so much politics in bloody cricket."

They were never barred from tennis, and actually represented NSW Primary Schools at interstate level, but when they were forced by their punishing schedule to choose between sports the family had a conference and it was decided that tennis would be the sport to go.

"Nothing against people involved in tennis, but they do tend to become pretty selfish," said Bev. "It's the same with any sport which is you playing for yourself. Parents get really niggardly and I suppose it is a selfish sport. You tend not to be able to play for anyone other than yourself, you're always thinking of yourself. I always knew they were going to be involved in something and consciously, yes, we put them into a team sport, which we thought had better character-building qualities. They were too young for tennis anyway."

There was no particular reason for cricket being the sport of choice. In fact the first sport they dabbled in was baseball. They played tee-ball for just one year and, apart from endlessly playing the same team, Mark and Steve's only real memory was their purple uniforms. Rodger and Bev planned to give them a taste of a broad range of sports and it was just happy chance that saw them latch on to cricket. So many people are fond of saying that the boys could have been a success at anything they turned their hand to and there were other sports, soccer in particular, that competed fiercely for their favour.

"Dad was always pretty tough without being over the top," said Steve. "Because mum and dad got married at 18 and had us at 19 it stopped both their careers, so I think in a way they were a little bit frustrated that they didn't go on with their own careers and probably hoped a couple of us would go on and do something that they couldn't. So I suppose there was a fair bit of pressure in that regard. But they were never over the top and they were always fair about things. They didn't push us too far and if we didn't do well they weren't too critical. But they always taught us to play the game pretty tough and always try and give it 100 per cent. They gave us values."

You certainly don't have to be Albert Einstein to work out where the twins got their competitive streak from if you know anything about the family at all. "We're not very good social players," admitted Roger. "We're out to beat each other all the time. Bev and I were both very competitive and I guess watching us in country tournaments and doing well rubbed off on them."

Steve's wife Lynette can vouch that the trait is still alive and well right the way through the Waugh family. "When I play tennis with the family they always argue about who I'm going to play with. Even Danny doesn't want to play with me. I can sit there for an hour before anyone asks me to play," said Lynette. To which Steve mischievously replied: "Can't spoil a good game."

While they are human and have over-stepped the boundary on occasion Beverley and Rodger, who has never been backward in coming forward if he feels his sons have copped the rough end of the deal, appear to have done a remarkable job as sporting parents. Not for them the emotional and physical abuse of their own children, the manipulation of other people, the cheating or the whole sordid mess of being a "sporting parent". They have provided a positive example and all the support — financial, logistical and moral — that the

Danny, Steve, Mark and Dean are a chip off the old block when it comes to sport. Each has inherited the athleticism and competitiveness that made Rodger a top-class tennis player. Both Steve and Mark emphasise how much they owe their father. *(Trudi Van de Wint)*

boys needed. They resisted the temptation to use their childrens' talents to live out their own fantasies or as a status weapon to wield against the people around them.

When asked if he had influenced the twins' level-headed on-field conduct by word or example Rodger admitted that his wife was probably more influential in that respect. "Beverley would have told them she didn't want to see them do anything stupid. She was always well-behaved. I was a bit temperamental on the tennis court. Not that much but I used to get cheesed off sometimes. Some of the decisions they get now upset me more than anyone else I think. Because I've been through it all. I've been to the stage where I've played reasonably top tennis and I've had a few disappointments. I feel I don't want them to have the same disappointments."

It is a debt the twins are happy to acknowledge. "They were very important," said Mark. "We watched them play sport and they were competitive but always good sports. They always shook hands. They never abused umpires. I suppose when we started playing it was just a natural thing to us not to abuse people. If we did something wrong I'm sure mum and dad would have said that to us. They stressed being competitive but that winning isn't everything, or it wasn't in those days. They taught us to go and shake our opponent's hand and say 'well played'."

Bev and Rodger were also keen to point out the negative examples. "A lot of kids we played against in juniors, they'd lose a game and they'd bawl their eyes out," said Steve. "I could never imagine myself doing that. Mum and dad pointed to them and said 'you never want to do that sort of thing. Keep your head up high if you go down'. I can never imagine crying over a game of soccer or cricket. I can't see it. I think mainly it's parents putting pressure on their kids, really forcing them to win, forcing them to do well. I can't really imagine a kid crying just because he lost a game of soccer. It has to be the parents."

"Our coaches too," said Mark. "Our coaches in our younger days have got to take a bit of the credit. Quite often you see coaches these days for whom winning is everything. They go around and get all the good players in the district, get them to play for the one team, and they win every year. If they don't win they get upset with the kids — the parents and the coaches. The coaches we had were good all the way through. I would say it is a combination of mum and dad and the coaches we had."

The boys got there first taste of sport on the tennis court. Dorothea Bourne recalled the twins' first attempts: "Rodger coached tennis Saturday mornings for 20 years. The twins were hitting up with him one day, they were about five, and they'd throw the ball up trying to serve and fall flat on their backs trying to hit it. But they soon mastered the art."

Rodger said he first had an inkling of what was to come when he started hitting the boys catches on the tennis court. Again they were only around five at the time but already they had good hands.

"I couldn't believe it," said Rodger. "At that stage I thought 'they're not dropping too many, we've got some talent here'."

One of Rodger's tennis acquaintances had insured his young daughter with Lloyds of London so that if she played Wimbledon in 20 years time he would collect a big payout. He suggested that Rodger do the same thing with the twins: "I should have done it," said Rodger. "I don't know how much it would have cost, probably next to nothing. I've regretted it ever since."

Being so young and close to the boys in age Bev and Rodger were as much siblings as parents, Bev in particular. It was common for either or both of them to take part in the boys' backyard contests. And there was no patronising, if Bev or Rodger played they played to win. Steve and Mark got no easy points, no matter how old they were.

"They were non-stop at sport when I think about it but I was like that," said Rodger. "I used to like playing everything myself so I'd be involved. And wherever we went I'd give them a hit with the racquets. We'd have a bit of a bash after the game or whenever we had some spare time. They loved sport so they'd jump at the chance, they'd have a ball. If they weren't playing tennis they'd be kicking a soccer ball around. I didn't make them do anything, they just liked doing it. We were young people so we were probably more energetic than the run-of-the-mill parent would have been. Golf they'd always beat me, they never beat me at tennis. They started to push me at table tennis when they were about 15. "

"Mum and dad always joined in the games in the backyard," said Steve. "They were just another couple of people to play sport with a lot of the time. Dad was always keen to put us away. If we played tennis he'd want us to lose 6-0 6-1. He might have given us a few points to keep us interested but he would want to put us away pretty smartly."

Even as children Mark and Steve had focused their competitive drives as inward emotions. "They never outwardly showed that they would run through a brick wall," said Rodger. "They just tried so hard all the time. There was no outward emotion, they didn't get upset very often. The only time I've seen Mark upset was when he was given out in the Adelaide Test against India in early 1992."

The entry of the twins into organised sport was a bumpy one. Their baseball team struggled and Mark and Steve's first game of cricket was definitely not a fairytale beginning.

"That was a nightmare," said Steve. "We were seven I think. I don't think we had a proper coach that year. So it was mum and a couple of other mothers. They were padding us up and they didn't know which leg to put the pad on. I think we got bowled out for three. Mark got out first ball. He got bowled by a full toss, first ball, and mum was busy trying to get the pad on my leg and she put it on the wrong leg. Eventually she got it on the right leg and I went out to bat with the box on my bloody knee behind the pad. As I was walking out it felt a bit uncomfortable. I can't remember where I put it in the end. Probably wouldn't have mattered too much at that age anyway. I think I blocked my first ball and was cleaned bowled the second so it wasn't a real good start for us. Three balls between us and the team out for three. Things didn't look too rosy at that stage."

The twins' first cricket coach was Alan Dougherty. He had them from the time they first played organised cricket at the age of seven until they were 14. Dougherty never played top grade cricket but his love of the game saw him play 20-odd years in the Moore Park competition. He was regularly late getting to his match from the boys' game and won the trophy for the competition's best allrounder a number of times, playing until his late fifties.

When the Waughs started registration had been delayed by rain so the boys were split into two groups and headed off in different directions for practice matches. Dougherty's son Neil took the second team and at the end of the day reported back to his father with an enthusiastic: "Get on to these two little blokes. They can really catch a ball".

From big things do little acorns grow and as far as cricket went the Waugh acorns started off pretty small. Mark and Steve took quite a while to develop their talents and were very much bit players early on. They were playing three years out of their age group in the under-10s and there were bigger, older kids who were the stars.

The one area the twins shone in from the very start was in the field. Their backyard play had honed their ball sense to a sharp edge and, given the fact that other players were hogging the limelight, it was what they got most practice at anyway. "They were exceptional fielders for their age but they were nowhere near our best players for two or three years," said Dougherty.

"There were nine guys in the side who went along and did nothing except field," recalled Steve. "The highlight was getting picked up in the morning in the back of a ute and getting to the game and fielding balls for a couple of hours. But that never worried us too much, we were just happy to be there. It was good fun with all the other guys and, as I said, half the fun was getting picked up and driven to the ground in the back of the ute with the rest of the guys and getting a free drink and maybe on the way home stopping off to get something to eat, an ice cream or something. Occasionally we would get a bat, I think we batted four or five, but these two other guys used to do everything."

"I can't remember it worrying us," said Mark. "I thought that was just run of the mill. It wasn't your right to get runs, whatever happened, happened. I wasn't too worried. We had a good team. We used to win the comp.

The twins were pretty easy to please in those days. Everything is relative. When you're little even the most minor triumphs loom pretty large and that is as true for the Waugh twins as it is for any little bloke. "I can't remember how that first season ended up so it couldn't have been too good," said Steve. "I think my top score was 28 and I thought 'jeez, I'll never get higher than that'. I thought that was the highest score I was ever going to get. We both got picked in the under-10 reps when we were seven and we batted 10 and 11 in that. I think I got six not out in one game and I was pretty happy with that as well. It's funny. I was just happy to get one run when I went in to bat in the reps."

But it wasn't too long before the Waughs overcame their lack of experience and height and started to assert themselves."They picked up the important things quicker than most,"

Steve and Mark learned all they wanted to know about bowling by just watching fiery Test, and Bankstown, quicks Len Pascoe (left) and Jeff Thomson. Pascoe ran his eyes over the young Waughs and quickly concluded he had nothing more to offer them.

said Dougherty. "If you showed them once they could do it. They were very good thinkers of the game and very good team kids. There wasn't anything between them as far as batting was concerned. They were different. They were both aggressive. Early on they were limited by their physique but they overcame things very well. Steve was the harder hitter of the two at the time. He was more unorthodox but more dangerous.

"Mark showed terrific promise with the ball. He bowled good-length medium pace. When Steve picked up the ball all he wanted to do was bowl bumpers. Those were the days of Lillee and Thomson and, especially with Thomson and Len Pascoe being locals, every kid wanted to be a fast bowler."

It could have been so different for Mark. He dabbled with leg spin when he was 12 or 13 and showed terrific promise. Dougherty is still upset that he didn't stick with it and when Mark is pressed he'll admit as much too.

"He was potentially the best I'd ever seen," said Dougherty. "He had good control, bowled a terrific wrong 'un and turned the ball really fast off the wicket. We didn't have a keeper who could handle him sufficiently to get the full results. He was mad to give it up. He could have been as good a leg-spinner as you'd get."

"I don't know why I gave up bowling leggies," said Mark. "I only bowled them for a couple of seasons. I can remember getting nine wickets in a game. I regret giving them up. These days, because there aren't many leg-spinners around, you don't have to be that good to make it to the top. If you can bat as well then you're there. That's what I keep telling Daniel. If you can keep bowling spinners and you can bat you've got a big, big chance of playing first class cricket.

"I've tried bowling leggies in the nets but I'm hopeless now. I can bowl off-spin all right. I thought of bowling off-spin when I had stress fractures in my back. I remember bowling off-spinners at the start of that season in the nets and I got a wicket at the SCG bowling off-

Fast bowling legend Dennis Lillee, an inspiration to all young cricketers in the 1970s.

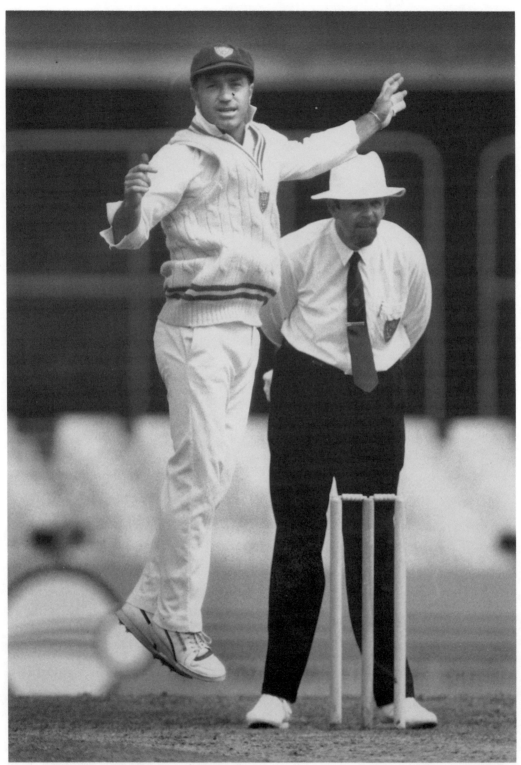

Even the most talented need a lift and Test allrounder Greg Matthews has been a true friend to the Waughs throughout their first class careers.
(Gregg Porteus)

spin. Mark McPhee (of Western Australia). I bowled him. But then I just went back to medium pace again. I suppose it just takes so long. You can tell a bloke you can bowl spin but it is going to take four or five years, isn't it, before you get a chance in a game. So because I bowled medium pace before for NSW I just went back to that.

"But I think one day I might bowl a few offies. When I get a bit older. It's a bit hard in a side like NSW because there are so many guys who do it. You've always got two full-timers and then a couple of blokes who can roll their arm over. I remember Greg Matthews got a bit worried that year I bowled them in the nets. Thought I was a bit of a danger I think."

More than just educating them on the technical aspects of the game and sportsmanship Dougherty deserves a little credit for keeping them in the game. In keeping with Bev and Rodger's desire for the twins to experience a broad range of sports one morning Bev approached Dougherty and suggested that as the boys weren't doing so well they might give tennis a try. A quick-thinking Dougherty suggested a poll.

"It was all very friendly. She was just sounding me out," said Dougherty. "I said let's have a talk to the boys and see what they say and they said, 'No, no we don't want to give up cricket'."

It is all too common for the stars of junior sporting teams to get big heads. Still, it's hard to be too critical when you consider the example that is set by so many parents. Mark and Steve were fortunate that both their parents and coaches had things more or less in perspective. As a result the twins never viewed team sports as a solo pursuit. Not only were they sharp enough to realise that it is hard to win if you've alienated your team-mates by your selfishness and egotism, they naturally enjoyed the success of the other players. To them it was not important that you did well but that you tried.

"What I liked about them was their attitude towards the other kids, kids of less ability," said Dougherty. "Kids that age are worried only about themselves but they used to get a great kick out of one of the lesser lights taking a good catch or scoring a few runs. They were genuinely pleased. They were good kids."

Dougherty may have played down their abilities as seven and eight-year-olds but that doesn't mean he couldn't see the potential they possessed. And before too long he couldn't keep his opinion to himself. "At nine or ten I told people at work that I had two kids that were going to play for Australia for sure," he said. "They had that stamp on them. They weren't scoring hundreds or taking lots of wickets but they had an eagerness to learn and the athleticism to go on. Even the kids around them you would have considered better cricketers. Dean was bigger and stronger as a nine-year-old. I had him for a year and he dominated. If anyone had seen him they would have thought he had all the potential in the world compared to them because they developed gradually."

"Alan rang when Steve made the Shield side and said 'I'm looking pretty good. People aren't laughing at me now'," recalled Bev.

While many would question the wisdom of letting young children play so far out of their own age group, something they continued to do while they were with Dougherty, he believes that it only had a positive affect on Mark and Steve. "In the long term the fact that they were meeting older opposition had a big bearing."

Brian Freedman, father of the Waughs' Canterbury and Sheffield Shield team-mate David, coached David's South Bankstown junior side from the under-8s to the under-10s. He said the twins were so dominant that sides would hope to draw them in the first round of the season because the Waughs usually took holidays then and the boys would be missing from the Panania side. He was also struck by their precocious talents in the field.

"Their ability to catch at eight was far superior to kids many years older and that's a skill they've never lost," said Freedman. "And their ability to run between wickets and judge a run was freakish, especially when they ran together. They were so quick that if they weren't batting together there was always the opportunity for a run out because the other kids couldn't keep up."

Mark and Steve soon realised that they were better than their mates. Perhaps the reason they didn't get big heads was because success crept up on them. They didn't just put on the pads and become stars. They knew how the also-rans felt as well.

"It took about two years before we started to contribute anything to the team," said Mark. "When we were nine I think we started to get a little better at it. Then in under-10s we played in a rep team. We weren't very good though. I mean we were just average sort of players. And then from there we must have improved a fair bit. In under-12 reps I was captain and got the most number of runs in that competition. I suppose that was the start. Then we made the NSW Primary Schools team at about the same time. And from there we just sort of leapt ahead of everyone else, became the outstanding players in the team."

"It was at primary school that we started to kick away from most of the other guys," agreed Steve. "There were always one or two other good players but we were the main players in the side. So it was at that age we started to realise we could be really good at sport if we put our mind to it."

Getting picked in all the representative sides may have also tipped them off. "We were always touring somewhere," said Steve. "That probably got us keen. That was half the fun, going to places like Lismore and Wagga on the train. We had a great time then. We started to get into it and make a lot of friends. We got up to all sorts of mischief on train trips of 15 hours. It used to be great fun just staying awake at night and playing tricks on each other. It was an adventure. It was all new to us."

Steve was a little bit hazy on the exact details of the shenanigans he and his cohorts got up to but eventually compiled a shortlist which included wandering around town after curfew "trying to find things to do", putting frogs in sleeping bags, spraying people with whipped cream, throwing rocks on roofs and "stuff like that".

One area where they still lagged behind was in confidence. They may have been growing in stature on the sporting field but they were just as timid and embarrassed off the field whenever anyone turned the spotlight on them.

"They were terribly shy early on," said Bev. "When they started doing well at sport I can remember they had to stand up on stage down at the YMCA. They got an award when they were six years old for participation in sport. It was a combination of athletics and soccer, and representing the area at all those things. They gave them a twin award and they both had to go up on stage. They hung their heads and they were just so embarrassed. They were like that for a long time."

That's not to say they didn't enjoy their success and let their emotions run away with them every once in a while. Dougherty recalled an under-12 double wicket knockout at Padstow which the 10-year-old Waughs won ahead of about 20 other pairs. "They couldn't get home quick enough to show mum the trophy," he said.

That was just the beginning. They won the Torch-Roselands Sports Star award at 12. They spearheaded a win by Panania Primary School in the 114-team Umbro International Shield schools soccer knockout, Panania beating Cardiff South from Newcastle 3-1 with Steve scoring two goals and Mark one. While they were representing the school Panania were runners-up in the State soccer carnival in 1975, and won in '76. They won the State cricket carnival in 1976 and '77 and were runners-up in the State tennis carnival in '77. Mark was captain and Steve vice-captain of the NSW Primary Schools cricket team which won the national cricket carnival undefeated. Queensland had won six out of the previous 10 years and Mark and Steve combined for one partnership of 150. Mark also captained the tennis team to victory, and Steve was skipper of the NSW soccer team.

However much they might have objected when dragged to centre stage there is no doubting they had made up their minds very early that they wanted to be the best. "They didn't go around bragging," said Bev. "They wouldn't go around saying it to anyone else but you could hear them in the backyard. 'Oh, I'm going to be such-and-such some day. I won't have to work. I'll be playing for Australia'. Only to each other. They certainly weren't precocious enough to be saying it to anyone else. Actually, looking at the way they were co-ordinated when they were really young, 18 months old catching balls and connecting with balls, I always thought unless something went drastically wrong they were going to reach the top level. I wouldn't have been thinking Australia, I would have been thinking NSW. I thought whatever they did, whatever sport they went to, they definitely had the ability."

Given the burdens of such a large family at such a young age the Waugh household was never awash with cash. That's not to say that the boys walked around with the seat out of their pants, but just being comfortable was a bit of a struggle. The boys' many sporting commitments only added to the burden. The honour of representing their state in primary school and jetting off to places like Adelaide was all very well but Bev and Rodger still had to find the money to send them. It is yet another tribute to them that they not only provided for the boys but provided the right gear.

"We were pretty lucky. We were always up with the trends and always had the best gear so we never missed out there," said Steve. "I think we were 11 when we won our Slazenger bats off the *Sunday Telegraph*. We thought it was great winning those bats. I think up to that stage we might have been sharing one and to have one each was great. But in under-10s there were always one or two guys who had a bat and they used to share it around. It's funny how it always used to be the No. 11 who used to have the good bat and never got to use it. At the end of the season his bat would be worn out and he had probably scored 10 runs with it but he always used to buy a new one the next year. You could always rely on him to bring a new one."

SIX

For The Love Of Sport

ONE OF the reasons Stephen and Mark had begun to shoot ahead of the other children was the pressure they put on themselves to perform well. As they moved into their teens that pressure became external as well as internal. Now firmly the stars of their teams and responsible for their week-to-week fortunes they carried the burden not only of their own expectations but those of others as well. Not for the first or the last time in their lives, it was a point where things could have turned sour — or even ended all together. There is a shocking attrition rate of child sports stars. It is due in no small part to the pressures placed on them by parents, coaches and team-mates. Winning becomes everything, and because it is the end rather than the means that counts, all the fun disappears. And when winning is expected and therefore not pleasurable there is no reason to play anymore.

Fortunately, enjoying themselves is something that the Waugh twins never lost sight of. Thanks to their parents and coaches they have been able to temper their fierce competitiveness with an appreciation of the game itself and the people who play it. They have always busted a gut to win but how they win is just as important as the win itself. Given Mark's adult elegance and style and Steve's steadiness, strength and aggression, it would surprise many to learn that it was Steve who stood out stylistically when they were growing up. "Stephen was always a little bit more flamboyant in everything," said Bev. "Mark was always very, very steady and totally reliable."

It was more obvious at soccer because they played such different roles. "Steve was the one up the front who went for all the glory and Mark was as solid as a rock at the back," said soccer coach Ron Mannell. "Steve loved to score goals, he was always up the front busting his little boiler. (But) I always had a lot of time for Mark. A striker can make 10 mistakes and score a goal and be a hero but a back can't do that. Mark was as reliable as a Swiss watch. They seemed to complement one another, when one was in trouble the other was always there to help out. They were never affected by anything that was bestowed on them. They were always matter of fact about their ability. That was a reflection of their home life.

"They never stopped trying. They weren't quitters, you could never say that, they never gave up at all. They were always aggressive but in all the time I knew them they never took out their aggression on any one individual. They were well-behaved. In the end they haven't done anything more than the average teenager and I can't say they've given anyone any trouble. I'd only be too proud to call them my kids.

"At times I felt sorry for them. They had a hell of a load to carry, there was so much expected of them."

Mannell was the coach at the centre of the storm when Mark and Steve were deregistered by the Bankstown Association. They were playing in the Bankstown under-12 rep side when they were picked in the NSW Primary Schools cricket side that was selected to contest the Australian titles in Adelaide. Unfortunately that clashed with the final of the soccer and when the Waughs told the Association that they would not be available they were deregistered. As a result they changed clubs to Auburn. Mannell holds no grudges though he understands the feelings of parents whose kids may have been playing the only final of their lives. Still, he said for the Waughs the cricket was the most important thing at the time.

Len Quested, a professional for 10 years with English clubs Huddersfield and Fulham before emigrating to Australia in 1957, was the twins' coach for a couple of years at Auburn. Steve said Quested, who played three or four times for Australia, was a great coach. He, like cricket coach Dougherty, was unafraid to gamble on their talent and heart.

"I was of the opinion if you're good enough you're big enough so we always played them out of their age group," said Quested. "They were that good. I always said that Steve showed the better skills and techniques. Mark was more of what I call a plodder. Although he was a good player, he was the first one picked in the side every week. If you drew a graph Steve could be brilliant one day and not so good the next whereas Mark's would be a nice wave. He never really did anything wrong. Mark wasn't such a great ball player but he was a very effective defender. He was a natural defender. Mark had a lot of skills. He just wasn't as flamboyant as Steve.

"It was a pleasure to coach them. They knew what they could do but you could never accuse them of hogging the ball. Football lost something when they turned to cricket. I thought they might have kicked on in soccer. They could have done another Botham, they definitely could have got a game in England quite easily. They were exceptionally good at whatever they did. You didn't really have to teach them, just point them that way.

"Steve used to get hacked around quite a bit because he was such a brilliant ball-player but he never lost his temper. He always had that surprised look when he was fouled, like 'that's not the way to play the game'. He was a well brought-up boy and that came through in the way he played and everything he did."

Quested has a good yardstick by which to measure Steve's ability as a striker. Playing in the same team was Robbie Slater, the former Socceroo and NSL striker who is now playing with Lens in France.

"There was a bit of rivalry between him and Steve," said Quested. "They were both forwards. All Slater wanted to do was score goals. It didn't matter how badly he played if he could score a goal, he'd think he'd played well. With Steve it was more how he played, and how much of the ball he got." When asked who was the better player Quested was blunt: "Steve killed him, there was no comparison."

He has no doubt Steve and Mark were, and maybe still are, both capable of playing first division soccer in England, and even representing Australia.

"Steve had fluency." he said. "He could run at you and have you going the wrong way with a cock of his shoulder. When he had the ball you got excited. Soccer's lost excitement these days. Players like Len Shackleton and Stanley Matthews could excite a crowd through sheer ability and Steve had that ability. The boys relied on him to win us a game. When he got the ball something was going to happen."

Another measure of Steve's ability is a piece written by former Socceroo and soccer expert Johnny Warren which appeared in the *Sydney Morning Herald* on July 15, 1983: "I have not seen a better goal this year than the one scored by East Hills High School's Stephen Waugh in the Commonwealth Bank Cup at Mt Druitt Town Soccer centre last Wednesday evening. It was a goal of which the legendary Franz Beckenbauer would have been proud. Waugh began a 50m slalom run well inside his own half and beat seven opponents before smashing a 20m drive past the Springwood goalie. Waugh, who plays for Croatia's reserve team, was one of the many talented youngsters on view, and his goal enabled East Hills to beat Springwood 3-0 and so advance to the quarter-finals."

Despite their love of soccer neither Mark nor Steve had a favourite team or players that they followed. They watched the FA Cup every year and the World Cup and the English soccer on TV, but the most either will admit is an interest Steve had in Liverpool. He did say he loved watching Pele and Maradona perform: "They were probably my two favourite guys to watch because they were really exciting. They could always pull something out of the bag where no other player could do it."

The pair were able to maintain a rough balance between soccer and cricket for a long time but in their mid-to-late teens it all got too much and soccer went the way of tennis. Previously, whenever there had been a clash, they favoured cricket and it hadn't made a great deal of difference. But once they started playing professional soccer the club, Sydney Croatia, was not so understanding or flexible. Steve was on the verge of first grade and when his new coach put it on the line Steve walked — but not without regret. Mark, on the other hand, wasn't enjoying the same amount of success and one cold winter night pulled the plug of his own accord.

"I wasn't too keen on soccer training, to be honest," said Mark. "But cricket training was no problem. I used to enjoy that. I suppose I didn't like the running in soccer. There was a lot of running involved and it was cold, too, in winter. Actually I might have ducked training once when I was playing with Sydney Croatia. I was playing second grade but I wasn't getting much of a go, wasn't getting much of a game. We were training two or three nights up the back of Fairfield and then on the weekend I wasn't playing so I just didn't go one night. And that was it. I stopped playing.

"I think I was always going to play cricket. I don't know how good I was at soccer. I don't think I was quite as good as Stephen."

The decision to jettison tennis in favour of cricket was just as easy for Mark. "I don't think it was that hard a choice," he said. "For some reason I liked cricket more. I can't explain why. I suppose it was the Australian sport for young kids. Cricket was the big thing to play for your country. It was the real Aussie sport. Although I enjoyed tennis, too. I was probably better at tennis than I was at soccer. But the thing is in tennis you play in tournaments and you have to wait around all day for your game. I didn't like that too much."

Another of the many sporting talents the twins possess is mastery of that most frustrating of games — golf. Golf is a major part of their recreation these days. They will often play once or twice in the lead-up to a game during the summer, but, like soccer and tennis, Mark has no regrets about not exploring his potential there.

"It's hard to say," he says. "If you put your mind to do something there's no reason to say you couldn't succeed but I wouldn't like to say I could have been a professional golfer. I would like to play more golf.

"I don't miss soccer at all. I enjoyed it but I've got no regrets. I still play social tennis, golf and squash. That's enough. There is just one condition. It's got to be competitive. There's nothing worse than a real uncompetitive game of tennis or golf. It's just something that's in-built. It's still relaxing, I still enjoy it."

Mark, in his casual manner, has enjoyed and moved on but Steve still yearns for the joy of physical combat. The only thing holding him back is his present occupation.

Mark on the golf course with NSW and Australian team-mate Michael Whitney.

"I loved playing soccer and I'd love to play it again but it's just too hard at the moment," he volunteered. "If you get injured all your contracts are null and void because you're playing another sport. So you really can't take the risk. But one day I'm sure I'm going to play again. Soccer was a big part of our lives. The same as cricket. We would be training three, four days a week. We would be in State Primary Schools and we would play for Bankstown on the weekend and our junior sides as well, so we would be playing probably four games a week. I suppose I liked the physical part of the game as well. I ended up playing Australian Schoolboys. Brisbane asked me to play for them when I was with the Australian Schoolboys and Sydney Olympic asked me as well. There were always plenty of offers there but I had to make a decision one way or the other."

When Steve says he enjoyed soccer as much as cricket he is not kidding. Mark always preferred cricket but Steve would sign up again tomorrow if circumstances permitted. He admits to having pondered a career in soccer on more than one occasion when he was younger.

There is still a soft spot in his heart and Steve maintains a link, however tenuous, to the game.

"I normally take a soccer ball on tour. A few of the guys like kicking the ball around," he says. "Mike Veletta is a good soccer player and Simmo was a good player in his day. I still practise juggling. I still do that OK. But I would hate to think how I'd go after not playing for seven or eight years. I think I would be a fish out of water."

It was in their teens that things started to get serious on the cricket front for the Waugh twins. They were being selected in all the junior representative sides and developing into the pillars of whatever team they played in. Even at 13 and 14 the breadth of their talents, and singular personalities, was becoming obvious. Ian Gill coached the twins in the Moore, Watson and Green Shield representative teams between the ages of 13 and 16. He had known them since they were six because he was coaching a rival soccer side. He recalled one game where the eight-year-old Waugh twins kicked off and scored before Gill's team had touched the ball. "Mark and Steve did it on their own," he said. "Later on in cricket they virtually ran the side on their own. The other kids were good cricketers but Mark and Steve dominated all the time."

Before landing the job of coaching them Gill gained an appreciation of their talents through being on the receiving end of a number of very special performances. In the under-14s Gill's Villawood side scored 124 in a 15-over match against the Waughs' Panania East Hills side and thought that would be more than enough to win. But Steve scored 112 and guided Panania to victory in the 10th over. "He put us all over the ground, the kids just didn't know where to bowl. He took 24 off the first over. But we got revenge the following year when we beat them in the under-15 final. We scored 140 and Mark opened and when he got out they were 1-100. But Steve was out without facing a ball and they fell apart."

Gill said neither boy was a particularly quick bowler and admitted surprise at the pace they can generate these days. "The other kids were just as quick. The Waughs were more aggressive because of their outlook. They were there to play the game and play it properly. Other kids would muck around but Steve and Mark never would because they were there to play the game and give it their best. The players around them benefited from the way the Waughs played the game, the competitiveness and the way they always were striving to do better. Quite a few of them are playing grade cricket now."

Having recognised their talents Gill had the good sense not to ride them too hard, thus the twins enjoyed more freedom than would have normally been the case. "Steve was the

Steve during the '89 tour of England.   (Philip Brown)   Australian coach Bob Simpson.   (Gregg Porteus)

captain and I tried to let him run the team. I just advised him," Gill recalled. "He had the knowledge to set fields and make his own decisions. Steve captained aggressively, he read the game and made changes accordingly. If he was unsure he would ask me."

Many outstanding players become tyrannical captains because they make the mistake of expecting their team-mates to measure up to their own lofty standards. They confuse ability with effort. It was a mistake the two Waughs did their best to avoid. "As long as players in the team give one hundred per cent you know they're doing their best, that's the main thing," said Mark. "I'm happy with that. The only time I got upset was when I was captain of a few teams if I thought the other blokes weren't trying 100 per cent. I like to see other people do well."

As a captain Mark wasn't reluctant to give his young team-mates a blast if he thought they deserved it. "Oh yeah, usually at that particular moment when they had misfielded a ball or something. Especially if it was off my bowling. I got a bit upset if I thought they weren't trying. It might have upset of few of them but that's how I play the game." Mark said he had no problems with a player making a mistake if he was giving his all. "If he was doing his best and his best wasn't good enough then so be it. I've got no problem with that. If he tries."

Not that he felt such an attitude was particularly praiseworthy. "If you're a decent sort of person it's a natural thing to give everyone a chance to do their best. I don't think it is anything particularly outstanding. I've found most people are like that. In cricket teams, anyway."

But such charity and fair-mindedness went only so far. Mark was definitely not an affirmative action employer. "I always like to win. I'd try to satisfy most of the team but the bottom line was I liked to win. Most of the players in the team were good enough anyway. They had their chance. I always thought the good players would come through regardless. Blokes who weren't interested would drop out anyway."

Gill modestly admits that he had little direct influence on the twins technical development. "Steve and Mark were just so far ahead of the other kids that they just tried to improve their own games without getting too much advice from other people. But they were very keen to learn. They were always looking to improve their game. Steve didn't have a very good technique but he had a great eye. If the ball was there he'd hit it but it wouldn't be textbook stuff. Whereas Mark was textbook style." He said that while Steve hit it hard and Mark was more inclined to work the ball they both had all the shots and could pick up the weaknesses in the opposition bowling. He recalled one occasion at Padstow Park where Steve cut a ball for six over point. "It wasn't a short hit either. That's the way he was, he could do anything.

Gill was another who remarked upon their freakish ability to judge a run. It was a talent with which their team-mates were still having trouble keeping up. "They were awesome running between wickets," Gill said. "Because they had an understanding. They didn't talk, they just ran. When they weren't batting together there were quite a few run-outs. They would pick a fielder's weakness and run whereas other kids would hold back."

He also remarked upon the positive aspects of their parents' behaviour. In other sports, particularly tennis, the parent has become coach, manager and confidant by this time. "Bev and Rodger never stood in Mark or Steve's way; they tried to help as much as they could. They always let them go out and enjoy their sport. They weren't over-dominating, never pressured the boys. They stayed right away."

The twins were getting all the cricket they wanted at 14, 15 and 16 because they were playing with their junior club in the morning from 9-11 and skipping the final hour so they could play grade in the afternoon. Every Saturday they were playing from nine in the morning to six at night.

They took this demanding schedule in their stride as if they had been preparing for it all their lives — which, of course, they had. The twins' extraordinary capacity for work just expanded to accommodate the extra demands. And their run-scoring grew at a similar pace. "It happened quite a bit. I think there were a few times when I got hundreds in the morning and hundreds in grade cricket," said Steve. "They were the golden years. Getting runs every morning and then every afternoon. We used to really enjoy the cricket, look forward to every Saturday. It was a different challenge."

In the 1980-81 season, when the twins were 15, Steve had scored more than 1500 runs by January in Green Shield and grade cricket. Among that mountain of runs were five hundreds, four of which were unbeaten. He scored 143 in 110 minutes against Waverley in the Green Shield competition, an innings that included 96 runs in boundaries, and topped that off with hauls of 5-45 and 7-126. He was averaging 104 in grade cricket at the time. In one fourth grade match he scored 123 and Mark 124.

The peculiar demands of squeezing in two games in one day emphasised their remarkable indifference to statistical yardsticks. "I don't remember worrying about averages," said Steve. "I suppose at the end of the year we looked at them (but) we never really went out for our averages. A lot of times we had to throw our innings away because we had to go and play grade cricket. It was just a matter of doing as well as we could in the amount of time we had. In juniors we obviously won a few of the bowling averages and batting averages. It was always good to get a trophy at the end of the year but it wasn't our primary motivation, whereas for a player like Dean Jones this is one way he motivates himself to succeed. Good luck to him. That's his way of doing well."

Their self-confidence meant they were not seduced by the religion of technique as they progressed through the ranks. Too many players complicate the game by exploring and, too often, getting lost in the maze of ways to play what is a very complex game. Former Test spinner Ashley Mallett always stresses in his Spin Australia clinics that the simple approach

An ecstatic Dean Jones embraces Steve after Waugh hit Curtly Ambrose for six in a World Series match at the SCG in 1988-89. Jones and Waugh shared a partnership of 112 in the last 10 overs and the six came off the last ball of the Australian innings.

is the best. While not wishing to condemn coaches or the pursuit of good technique, there is a difference between doing things properly and doing things well and sometimes the two are mutually exclusive. Look at Max Walker, Mike Procter, Jeff Thomson, Michael Bevan, Steve Small, Ian Botham, Froggy Thomson and further back to "mystery spinners" Johnny Gleeson and Jack Iverson. All these players shunned the textbook but scaled the heights of cricket. While not as obviously eccentric in style as players like Walker and Procter, the Waughs remained true to their code of aggression, though that's not to say they knew exactly why they were doing it and why there were successful.

"I can't remember actually watching anyone and copying them," said Steve. "I can't really put my finger on it. Maybe we were just lucky. We might have seen the ball better than other guys. Or had better reflexes. I don't know what it was. But we used to go out there and it would just come naturally. You would hit the ball and away it would go. You never thought too much about it, why it happened. We were never really taught too much. We never really had too much coaching. We used to go to Barry Knight's during the week but that was more a confidence thing. He'd give a bit of advice, but not too much. We would go into town and I think half the fun was going to McDonalds afterwards. It was just exciting going in the train to town on Thursday night for an hour or so and getting a bit of coaching. It was more of a novelty than anything else. He was pretty good because he never really asked us to change too much. He told us we were naturals and to stick to the way we were playing."

"We never worried too much about technique," Mark agreed. "We had the occasional lessons but it was mainly all natural. Just the way we worked it out for ourselves. Obviously if we were doing something badly then our coaches would have pointed it out to us but they didn't really. As we went along they just let us go. I think it's good that we weren't over-coached. I'm not saying you don't need any coaching but I reckon too often coaches tell kids too many things. Cricket is using your eye to hit the ball. It's a natural thing. If you do well and score runs without all the coaching, then you don't need coaching."

"It was pretty good. We never had too many people sticking too many theories down our throats," Steve offered. "If you want to do better you've got to change your game a little bit. But I don't believe in coaches who try to change kids when they are 12 and 13. You've got to let them go then and just let them use their natural talent. That's all we ever did. And I think you'll find most players who made it to the top have done that. Mark Taylor might have been held back for that reason. People thought he was an opening bat and he had to play a certain way and it wasn't until he realised that he could play all the shots that other guys could play that he really changed as a player. I think when he played League cricket in England he went over there and just relaxed and played all these shots. And once he knew he could play them he was a completely different player. That's one example of a bloke who was told to play a certain way because he was an opening bat and didn't realise his potential until he got a bit older."

Ian Davis, the former NSW and Australian batsman known as the Wiz, is more than qualified to endorse the Waughs' approach. Davis first came in contact with them through his work in the sporting goods industry when the twins were 13 or 14. "I'd heard big wraps about them; they were probably the best two young cricketers of that age," Davis recalled. "We gave them a couple of bats. I'd heard a lot about them but I'd never really seen them play. Dion Bourne asked Lennie Pascoe to go and see them play and give them a few lessons. I can remember Lennie saying to me during a Shield game — and this is when they were about 13 or 14 — that he'd gone out to give them a lesson and he reckoned they could have taught him a few things. He said he couldn't teach them anything."

Unfortunately not all junior coaches and selectors were such free thinkers and the twins had the odd character-building experience. Steve in particular was criticised for his aggression and suffered the consequences.

"I think I always tried to score runs quickly; we always did," he said. "I can't remember playing a defensive innings for too long. We used to go out and try to whack it from ball one.

Great mates Mark Taylor and Steve Waugh share a beer and a laugh after their maiden Test centuries against England in the First Test at Leeds in 1989. (Philip Brown)

In those days the bowlers bowled enough loose balls for us to get away with it and our talent got us through. I think it cost me once or twice. I remember missing out on an under-15 state squad when I had scored the most runs in the rep competition and done really well. I remember the old man got a bit cheesed off that Mark got picked and I didn't when I was No. 1 scorer so he went up and asked the coach Peter Horwitz and selector Peter Spence why I wasn't picked. And Spence said I had scored my runs too quickly and that was the reason I hadn't been picked. I still haven't worked that one out to this day. So I suppose that's one way it cost me but in the long run it hasn't affected me too much. At the time it was a bit hard to swallow. But there was always going to be ups and downs as you find out later on."

A more amusing run-in Steve had was with South African Test great Barry Richards' at a coaching clinic Kerry Packer ran through the *Women's Weekly* during the World Series era. Fifty boys were selected in regional trials and congregated at Cranbrook School in Sydney for a week's coaching. Steve had already gotten off to a good start on the first night. "The first meal I walked into the hall and dropped my tray in front of about 100 people. I didn't know where to look."

More was to come when he went into the nets. In his youthful exuberance he began thumping balls out of the net and quickly earned Richards ire. "He dragged me out of the nets and said 'Get out of there. If you're going to bat like that you might as well not play'. That was a bit of a comedown. I thought I was pretty good and then I got booted out of the nets." He mischievously noted that he had failed to mention it to Richards in recent years during the South African's stint as executive director of the Queensland Cricket Association.

The World Series Cricket camp wasn't all doom and gloom though. "It was a great experience," said Steve. "All those coaches and different techniques and looking at video

Former Test opener Ian Davis.　　Australian batsman Mike Veletta.　(Gregg Porteus)

and seeing how you were batting and just getting involved with a lot of other good cricketers. It really improved your game."

Although both Waughs are, not surprisingly, firm believers in natural ability and claim to have never fallen prostrate at the feet of the great god technique, that's not to say they ignored it.

"Up until 15 or 16 you could get away with natural talent," said Steve. "You were good enough to see the ball and the bowlers weren't good enough to get you out, or not regularly. But after that bowlers improve and once you get into grade cricket you can't really rely just on your natural ability. You have to brush up on your technique, your defensive technique, so that was mainly what I tried to improve on. I suppose it was when we made grade cricket and state under-16s where you saw other very good players and you knew you had to keep up with them or try to be better than them."

Not that the changes were drastic. "We were basically still natural players but we just had to fine tune our game a little. Even then, we sort of had reputations anyway and a lot of people were, not in awe, but scared of playing against us and it probably helped us a fair bit. We always seemed to score runs against that sort of opposition so I think it was basically natural talent that got us through to there. I think it can get you through until virtually first grade. And then you can still do OK."

The outstanding quality of their contemporaries was another factor that, although not crucial in making the Waughs what they are, undoubtedly played a part. Mark Taylor, Andrew Jones, Brad McNamara, Scott Hookey, Brett and Jamie Williams, Richard Stobo, Phil Emery, David Freedman, Tony Fort and Gavin Robertson were all in the same group at high school and running into them certainly forced the twins to lift their game a notch or two. McNamara was the first and came as quite a surprise to the Waughs who had grown accustomed to having things their own way.

"This bloke would come along and clean us up," said Steve. "He had a bit of pace. Brad was a rude shock, probably the first guy we'd come across who could actually match it with us and take us on.

"It was just one of those age groups that for a couple of years was really strong. They picked two NSW sides in high school and Mark Taylor, Mark Waugh and Andrew Jones were in the second side. It shows how good the first side was. And that was when we were 18-year-olds so we weren't unknowns in that age group. I was in the ones and I think the second team might have been stronger than the first team. But for those players to be picked in the second team there must have been a lot of good players around. Even people you talk to now say that was one of the freakish years for sport. Teachers still say it was a very strong age group."

Steve stayed with Tony Fort, who he and Mark had met when they played in the NSW Primary Schools soccer and tennis teams, during the CHS regional tournament one year in Maitland because the championships were being held in the Hunter region. For once Steve let himself get a little cocky and tempted fate. "After each game he would meet me at the front door with a cheeky grin on his bloody dial, asking how we had fared," said Fort. "I'd say, 'well, we won and I scored 70, 80 etc' and he'd say 'not good enough, I just scored 110 etc'. He would then proceed through our lounge room telling my family how weak I was (in a cheeky manner) and make his way to the pool where he would paddle about, very content that he had won again. He was about to fall flat on his face though. The final between his side and our 'country hicks' was played at the Newcastle No 1 Sports Ground. We won comfortably but somehow he forgets about that game now. He is one of those lucky types who has a selective memory."

The Waughs have been the centre of remarkably little controversy given the aggressive way they do battle and their constant occupation of centre stage. One incident Steve recalls in which his competitiveness raised some hackles occurred during a Davidson Shield match at school. It was a quarter-final against a school from Sydney's northern suburbs and the game was approaching a thrilling climax. One of their batsmen hit the ball into the covers and was looking for a single. The fieldsman retrieved the ball and quickly returned it to the bowler's end where the bowler took the bails off with the runner well out of his ground. He claimed he was not running but Steve, the captain, believed he was and declined to recall the batsman. In the end it didn't matter because East Hills went down in a close finish.

But that wasn't the end of it. When the players left the field one of the opposing parents stopped Steve and gave him a piece of his mind. "He said he had something to do with the Cricket Association at the time," said Steve. "He said 'it's the most disgusting thing I've ever seen on a cricket field. You should be ashamed of yourself. You will never play for NSW because of that'. I really thought he did the wrong thing and deserved to be out. But this bloke saw it the other way and he said he was going to make sure I never played for NSW. Six months later I was in the State side so I don't think he had too much power."

While they may have escaped most of life's nasty illnesses their love of sport made them pay when they shot up during adolescence. Bev said they had aches and pains in all their growing places. Knees, elbows, backs, everything. But despite the physical and mental pressure of playing for so many teams in so many sports, the twins never got sick of sport. Both claim they never felt like missing a match.

Mark says he rarely felt the pressure of being the team's star player for so many years.

"I think I handled the pressure pretty well. I didn't think of it as that much pressure in those days I suppose. I never really worked that hard. I never missed training but I didn't spend five hours in the nets. Whenever I went to training I did my best and that was good enough for me."

"We loved it," said Steve. "I think we just thrived on it. As soon as we had a week off we were keen to get back into it. That was all we lived for in those days, sport. We never knew anything else. School was only a way to play more sport. I don't think we took school too seriously. I could never see the point of going home and studying for two hours or doing two hours of homework when you could be out playing sport or getting into some mischief somewhere. I'd much rather be having fun than sitting down with my nose in a book or trying to make my running writing neat. There were better things to do than that.

"I can never remember being tired or really ever getting injured. I don't know whether I had a lucky run or not, but considering the amount of sport we played, we should really have had some sort of injury along the way, but we never seemed to.

"I never got sick of it. Even now I could play a different sport every day and be happy with it. I think sometimes it can get frustrating when you're only playing cricket . I like to play tennis a lot, and golf, and I love to play soccer and all those other sports. But you can really only play one sport. And I don't like playing too many social sports. I can't have a hit of tennis without trying to win. I don't like hitting a ball back just for the fun of it. If I'm going to have a game of tennis I like to try to play my best and beat someone."

There were regular school trips to Jindabyne each year but the Waughs had cracked first grade at Bankstown and couldn't go. It is one of the few regrets Steve has about the choices he has made. "In a way I regret not going but at the same time we had just got picked in first grade. We thought it was more important. But the guys would come back with stories about how they'd had a great time. I suppose in the end we did the right thing. They're the sort of decisions you've got to make if you really want to make it in sport. You've got to be keen and dedicated. But maybe we missed out on a bit there.

"I think over the years we missed out on a lot. When we were young we did because sport was everything. Weekends, night time. We never really went out while all our mates were going out and had girlfriends. They were doing different things to what we were doing. Just full-on sport. We never really thought we were missing out, but I suppose looking back we could have."

A case in point is their 21st birthday party. They didn't have one. Mark was away and Steve wasn't keen on a big celebration so the family just went to a restaurant for dinner. "I don't like a fuss being made of my birthdays," said Steve. "I like going to other people's parties but I don't like going to my own."

It is no puzzle to Mark that he and Steve did not fall foul of all the teenage temptations which might have caused them to forsake sport. "I enjoyed it and I was quite good at it, and mum and dad encouraged us all the time to play sport," he volunteered. "I never liked the beach much anyway."

Top: NSW celebrate winning the McDonalds Cup in 1984-85, the first half of a historic double. At back: Steve Waugh and Greg Dyer; centre: Murray Bennett, Greg Matthews, Imran Khan, Wayne Seabrook; at front: John Dyson, Dirk Wellham, Phil Marks, Dave Gilbert, Peter Clifford.

Right: Allan Border (far left) and Merv Hughes (far right), with Steve and Mark during the Australian tour of England in 1989.

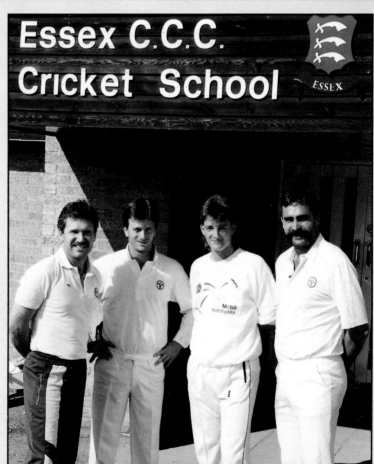

Essex C.C.C. Cricket School

ESSEX

*Champagne flows
following the 1984-85 Sheffield Shield
final, won by NSW after a desperate finish against
Queensland. Back row (left to right): Geoff Lawson, Bob Simpson (coach),
Murray Bennett, Wayne Seabrook, Dave Gilbert, Steve Waugh, Imran
Khan; seated in centre: Bob Holland, John Dyson, Greg Matthews;
at front: Steve Smith, Dirk Wellham, Phil Marks, Steve Rixon.*

Steve pushing nervously forward in his debut Test, against India in Melbourne, December 1985.

Mark hooking during the second innings of the 1989-90 Sheffield Shield final in Sydney, against Queensland. He scored an unbeaten 78, helping NSW to a decisive 345-runs victory.
(Live Action)

SEVEN

Schooldays

Hᴵɢʜ school was a time for further growth and definition for the twins, in the directions both their lives and personalities were taking. Their commitment at school, always exercised more out of duty and their natural inclination to tackle everything they had to do with vigour, began to lose its unequal battle with their love of sport. Though they both are far from stupid they quickly accepted that school did not have much relevance in the pursuit of their dreams. If they had enjoyed study it might have been different. Their attitude could have been a problem but East Hills High was very much a sport-oriented school, from the principal down. And while they got offside with the occasional teacher they generally enjoyed friendly relations with the teaching staff — no matter how flippantly they might have treated a subject. East Hills High had always boasted more of a sporting tradition than an academic one. Apart from the four Waugh brothers, leading sporting products of East Hills include Olympic swimmer Graeme Windeatt and Australian Rugby fullback Laurie Monaghan as well as Mark and Steve's NSW team-mate Wayne Holdsworth.

The school area as a whole produced a remarkably talented age group of cricketers. Apart from Shield team-mate Brad McNamara, also playing at the time were some-time first class batsman Scott Hookey, Australia Institute of Sport graduate Jamie Williams, his brother Brett and fellow first grader Mark England. "It was one of the strongest zones in the state," said school cricket coach Ron Perrott.

Such was their status that the twins were used in the promotional brochure that schools turn out now to attract students. Steve even rated a full page photograph and details of his sporting successes in the 16-page booklet. In Year 12 he earned school blues at cricket and soccer and won the school's prestigious Presidents Award while Mark received a cricket blue. Steve was captain of the East Hills cricket team the last two years at school, and he shared leading roles with his brother. Mark would open the batting and bowl first change while Steve would open the bowling and bat No. 3. They had made the First XI at an unusually tender age in Year 9.

The twins' school reports offer some interesting insights into their character. In Year 8 one teacher wrote that Mark "is a student who can be relied upon to do his best", and a year later, "Mark's public speaking has not proven to be of an adequate standard". It was in Year 11 that the comments on both Mark and Steve noted a downturn in performance. At the end of that year a teacher noted: "Sport is affecting his biology, but Mark has made a genuine attempt to keep up".

In the final year of school one teacher felt that Mark was "too quiet, should seek help" and another noted, "steady improvement. Needs now to alter his present silent outlook by actively seeking answers to the problems he has. He must use both his time and resources to the fullest by making mature appraisals of his progress" and "must ask for help with his studies rather than wait for the solution to gradually emerge".

Early in high school Steve attracted comments like talkative, enthusiastic, keen, interested, active class member, capable and well-mannered, polite and co-operative. And perhaps as a reflection of his good relationship with the teachers it was noted at the end of year 11 that "Stephen is capable of balancing his life to include success at school as well as on the sporting fields. Providing he continues to balance the demands on his time he should continue to do well".

But at that time the balance tilted heavily in favour of sport. Both missed their Year 11 finals because they were absent at the CHS regional carnival. This disappointed quite a few

(Gregg Porteus)

of the teachers. When the time came to discuss their futures with Ron Perrott, who doubled as their careers adviser, there was no doubt about what they wanted to do. Play cricket. But they still went through with the charade of work experience. Steve worked as a greenkeeper at the Picnic Point Bowling Club while Mark tasted life as a lab assistant at British Paints. As far as their career advisor is concerned they pulled the right rein. "In Year 12 I asked them one-on-one what they wanted to do," said Perrott. "Their answer was play cricket in England. I think they got their priorities right."

The boys themselves had no doubt and have had no cause to second guess themselves.

Steve later returned to the school and was interviewed by a student at school assembly on speech day. He was asked if he was sorry he didn't spend more time on his studies and the answer was a simple "no".

Steve's on-field image as a dour and intense competitor is refuted again and again by those who know him well — particularly his schoolmates. All, including Steve, admit to being card-carrying members of the larrikin clique at school, a group focused on fun rather than study. Not only was Steve a fully fledged troublemaker in class — he was one of the ring leaders.

Long-time friend Todd Crameri said Steve was always good for a fruit fight. Crameri recalled one occasion when Steve raided a fruit tree and brought a bootful of fruit to school. He armed his mates with plenty of ammunition and organised a bombardment of the girls school across the road. Crameri said the large group of teachers that eventually swooped was only outnumbered by the casualties resulting from the raid. A number of mates also mentioned that Steve was pretty handy with a water bomb, too.

Another favourite trick was to stop their car in the school gateway on the way home and block the departure of the rest of the school. It's a wonder their popularity survived. Mark denies being a central figure in any of these pranks though. "I was one of the hangers on. Steve had a higher profile. I was a bit of a scaredy cat."

Crameri agreed: "Mark was pretty quiet, unassuming. Steve was always the centre of things and Mark took a back seat. It's funny because there's been a total reversal in recent times."

Having decided that schoolwork was an unnecessary distraction Steve took a very relaxed attitude to his studies. He knew he was gambling with his future but he had the courage of his convictions and took the risk. "I wagged school a bit," said Steve. "I never went to too many maths lessons in Year 11 and 12. I think I only went to two or three in the whole two years. You take 12 units and only 10 count towards the HSC. I gambled on throwing out those two (maths). So I had a few spare periods. We used to go down to one of the guys' places for a cup of tea or go to the beach or go for a drive down the coast somewhere and come back a couple of hours later and lob into school.

Long-time friend Andrew Wyres remembered wagging more than one period of English. "These periods were usually spent catching possums at the 'duck pond' along Henry Lawson Drive. If wagging school wasn't risky enough then driving there and back with Steve and Danny Stanley sure as hell was. Now that I think back it's a wonder that we passed the HSC at all. I have memories of the night before our HSC maths exam laughing at the fact that based on the previous two years' maths exams we would not be able to answer more than three questions. As it turned out it wasn't too far from the truth."

With all his sport and practical joking and lack of enthusiasm for certain subjects there was very little time for Steve's schoolwork. Therefore he had to resort to extreme measures. There was much surprise when he got more than 300 in the Higher School Certificate.

"I was surprised when Stephen got a better HSC mark than me," said a still incredulous Mark. "I couldn't believe that. He copied off me all year. I think they got our papers mixed up. It's not that he's dumb but he shouldn't have got more than me. But it doesn't really matter what we got. We're playing cricket now."

Cars were a feature of many of the Waugh's adolescent adventures. One that has become a little scrambled with time is when the car was crammed well past the recommended limit. Some say it was just a spur-of-the-moment trip to the mud flats and others a Guinness Book of Records attempt, but Steve and Richard Lane agree that a passenger who was travelling

Blues fast bowler Wayne Holdsworth is one in a long line of East Hills High students to grab the headlines.

(Gregg Porteus)

on the outside rather than the inside took a tumble after an indignant occupant of the car struck his grasping hand a couple of times or opened the door. His spectacular roll in the gutter earned the car's occupants an audience with the school principal.

Mark Grant said Steve was a hoot to be with in a car. It was a regular practice of his to call out to people when the car was stopped at lights or stop signs or in traffic. He'd call them Dot and give them a wave and often the pedestrian would give a bemused wave even though they had no idea who Steve was.

But Bev and Rodger often found it hard to see the funny side of Mark and Steve's car crises. Because neither was willing to fill the car up in case his brother used all the petrol they would either not bother or put just enough in for their journey. As a result they were continually running out of petrol. And, because they were mechanical morons whose knowledge of cars was limited to correct use of the ignition, foot pedals, steering wheel and petrol cap, whenever anything went wrong, as it often did, they had no idea what to do. And who did they call? Good old mum, that's who. Rodger didn't have much patience in this particular area and usually wanted to leave them to their own devices. But Bev was too much of a softy and regularly rode to their rescue. On one occasion the car would only go in reverse. Next time out the gear box stuck in second. The list goes on and on.

If, as so many teenagers did and still do, the twins had measured their self-worth by their success in the areas of cars and girls then they would have turned out very sad cases. Because one area where they lagged well behind was girlfriends. Both say their love for sport meant they didn't give a lot of thought to the fairer sex but it also seems that their shyness, like most blokes their age, was particularly acute in the game of love. Steve has only ever had one real girlfriend, his wife Lynette, and he met her on muck-up day at the end of Year 12. She was a student at sister school East Hills Girls.

They had been introduced by Richard Lane about six months before. Lane, a friend of Lynette's, had grabbed her at a school dance and told her he had a "really shy, really sheltered bloke" for her to meet. Steve said she came over and talked to him for about two minutes before flitting off back to the dance floor. Then out of the blue he rang her and asked her to the school formal. "I didn't know who it was," said Lynette. "I had to ask 'Steve who?'. I was actually waiting for another guy to call me." After the formal there was a party so Lynette changed at a friend's place and Steve did likewise. When he finally emerged she asked him why he had taken so long. "He said he'd been watching the one-day cricket match," said Lynette. "I told him that I hated cricket and he said 'well that's the end of you then'." Steve claims she is making up that story.

Lynette recalled the first time Steve came over to dinner at her house. "We had left school and were studying for our HSC exams," she said. "I had my cousin and his wife over for dinner. At that stage I knew Steve played cricket but I didn't know he had any ambition. My cousin asked Steve what he was going to do for a living and he said 'play cricket for Australia'. The whole table just went silent."

Mark also started to go out with girls around the end of school and after three reasonably serious medium-term relationships has settled down with partner Sue Porter. But he said that such a slow start was not unusual. "A lot of the blokes didn't have girls because of the fact it was a boys school. Oh, we used to fancy the odd one (but) I wasn't really that interested. When I was 17 or 18 I gave it a bit more thought. I was fairly shy with girls, I still am though I'm a bit better now. I wouldn't talk to them, they'd have to talk to me if they wanted conversation."

EIGHT

Working Lives

FINDING fame and fortune in their favourite sport is every child's dream. Quite a fortunate few get to live their dreams but for the most part Australian sports people must combine their sporting career with a second job or live hand-to-mouth through odd jobs or the generosity of others. A handful do nothing but play their chosen sport all year round. Not only did Mark and Steve break into this privileged inner circle, they have had very little cause during their 27 years on this earth to enter the day-to-day battle to earn a crust. The 12 months after they left school represents their entire stint in the world of normal "work". Here are two wage slaves who escaped well before the bosses could break their spirit.

Having finally left school and chosen his career, neither Steve nor Mark was interested in playing it safe. Mark did not even bother applying for a place at university while Steve attended the teaching course he had enrolled in at Milperra Teachers College for the grand total of 90 minutes. He explained that he had already failed three subjects after missing the first two weeks of term while playing for the Australian Under-19 side against Sri Lanka. He went to drama and then music and it was during that lecture, sitting there with 50 girls and three guys, he decided he had made a mistake. "I thought if this is what it's going to be like I'm out of here," said Steve. "A couple of girls tried to stop me. They told me to make sure I knew what I was doing because I could wreck my whole life."

"Lynette and both our mums thought I was mad. Looking back it was a gutsy move but I knew it wasn't for me."

Steve noted with a wry smile that the college kept his fees, and also put him on the honour board that lists the Milperra students who have gone on to represent Australia in sport.

He went on the dole for a couple of months. His gainful employment included an unhappy stint as an indoor cricket umpire — "It was freezing cold and you'd cop abuse from every Tom, Dick and Harry" — and one day a week for a year on Bankstown Council work gangs. He would get up at 5am and help mulch trees that had been cut down.

"It was a nightmare job," said Steve. One day he was sent to help mow a local oval. It was there he learned a lesson about life. "I was mowing away and the other blokes were just sitting around," said Steve. "One bloke came over and asked me what I was doing. He told me they wanted to take two days to do the job." Waugh joked that the council workers' motto was 'lazy but obedient'.

Steve also worked at a sporting goods company but was never too down about the job situation. "I never thought about the future, I made enough money to get by," he said. "Fortunately Shield cricket came along and it became less of a worry. When he started playing first class cricket, Steve had $100 in the bank. Neither of them really had any money until they started playing cricket.

Steve knew he was really on the way when he was offered a contract on his first trip to England by a woman representing Kerry Packer. Steve had played a handful of games for

Gregg Porteus

Allan Border and Merv Hughes
have turned their celebrity status
on the field into money off it.

(Philip Brown)

NSW and was the replacement Esso Scholarship player at Somerset at the time. He couldn't work out what was going on. He even rang Brian Freedman back in Australia to ask his advice. The situation in a nutshell was that with a large chunk of the Australian side defecting to the South African rebel tour, Packer wanted to ensure the side wasn't gutted for years to come by protecting the best of the young stars. Five up-and-comers, including Steve, were approached and offered three-year contracts, paying five-figure sums annually, that would stop them going to South Africa. "A lady came up from London," said Steve. "I didn't know what the hell it was about. I hadn't even thought of going to South Africa." That's not to say he declined the kind offer. "I was very keen to get the pen out of her hand. It was big dollars. I did nothing over the three years, just collected the cheques. It enabled me to buy my block of land. I was really lucky in a way."

Except for the Packer windfall, Mark's story is much the same. He decided, though, to give tertiary education a miss all together. "I didn't like doing homework too much, or study," said Mark.

Mark's major source of post-school employment was the sporting goods company where Steve worked. "I worked in the sales department on the phone for a couple of months, then I ended up out the back in the warehouse, packing deliveries. I used to go to sleep in this huge, big box. I used to curl up and have a little nap in there. All up I did about a year's work. Far too much, too."

He also umpired indoor cricket to raise some pocket money but he didn't enjoy that too much either. "I used to cop a bit of stick from the players. It was a bloody hard job. A lot of the players were very aggressive. I remember a couple of times players threatened to come up the ladder and belt me. It's certainly not an easy job being an umpire." It appears that memories of his difficult time adjudicating have faded, but more of that later.

Mark was never worried that he had nothing to fall back on if his cricket career went belly up. "Not really, it never crossed my mind," he said. "I was just confident I was going to be good enough. I don't know whether I was living in a fantasy world or not, I probably was, but I was never keen on the idea of studying any more or getting a job."

Neither did he believe that he missed out on things growing up because of the huge demands sport placed on his time. He certainly has no regrets." Not considering the things that sport has brought me, travelling around the world and that sort of thing."

Both are vague about the direction their life will take once they finish their cricket careers. It is a reflection of the focus that has got them so far that both have given the subject little thought. "I haven't really thought what I'd like to do after my career is finished," said Mark. "I think it would be something to do with sport. Promotion or something like that. But I haven't had a long think about it. There are plenty of openings. You meet a lot of different people along the way, so I don't think it is a major worry at this stage. Hopefully I've got another 10 years left in cricket."

Given their stature in the game, their youth and good looks and the unique promotional advantage they enjoy being twins, they attract many offers to endorse products. But their natural inclination to avoid putting themselves in the public eye means they have taken up relatively few. The pair did a drink driving television advertisement, and Mark had a non-speaking role in a Just Jeans ad. But their low profile is just as much a result of cricket's traditionally staid advertising image. Relatively few players have made large amounts of money endorsing products, Allan Border and Merv Hughes being two of the more high-profile performers in this area in recent years. Most others are restricted to cricket equipment contracts. Their brief exposure to the advertising industry has already helped take the edge off their shyness. "I wasn't a few years ago but I'm comfortable now," said Mark, who can see product endorsement as a profitable area. "I'm not very good at guest speaking and that sort of thing so if I can do an ad, a TV ad, or represent some company I think that'd be the way to go."

"It's a bit scary," said Steve. "We're sports people so it's a bit daunting — millions of people watching you make a fool of yourself. It's never easy but it gets better every year. I'm not too keen to get into that side of things."

One intriguing offer the pair received was to cut a rap version of Ian Dury and the Blockheads' hit single *Hit Me With Your Rhythm Stick.* "They were so keen, they kept asking us," said Mark. "We were a bit worried because we can't sing — that's for sure. Then they sort of lost interest and they didn't get back to us." Steve believes someone in the cricket establishment had the good sense to refuse official accreditation for the project, thus pulling the plug on the whole deal. "If it had come off we probably would have pulled the pin ourselves. Doing it might have ruined our careers."

Steve, like Mark, has no firm plans for life after cricket. His love of travel opens up a few possibilities but he feels the most likely areas are sporting, leisure and promotions. "I've had a think but nothing's cropped up. I'm not really too fussed. I don't mind coaching and I'd like to run a business but I'm not sure what that's going to be."

Both Waughs have had their fair share of managers but have also looked after a good portion of their careers themselves. "It's pretty hard to find a manager you can trust," said Steve. "There are a lot of sharks out there. One guy wanted to get us on *Neighbours.* He wanted to turn us into movie stars, something we're not. Most of the time you use common sense and you get by. Lynette is a pretty good judge of character. She sees a lot of things that I don't."

"I've always been a bit wary of managers," said Mark. "Mainly I've done things myself. I negotiated with Essex and Slazenger, who have been good to me. I find out from other players roughly what sort of money they're getting and then I work out myself what I think I should be getting.

"The important thing with both of us at this stage is that we haven't established ourselves as cricketers, so that's what we are mainly concerned about at the moment. If we're not playing cricket for Australia we're not going to be worth two bob to anyone. So our first priority is to play cricket and to do well at that and hopefully the other things will follow. The opportunities will come. But we don't want to get too involved with commercial things that might affect our cricket. Cricket comes first ... if we play well then the money will come. But at the same time we can't look a gift horse in the mouth. If there is a good offer then you would be stupid if you didn't take it."

NINE

The Silly Things
Young People Do

As WELL as the discipline and example of their parents, sport largely was responsible for the twins' wholesome image, and the fact they kept on the straight and narrow. But it was also sport that enabled them to begin the natural teenage exploration of life's more adult pleasures. Their partner in crime was NSW allrounder Brad "Buzzard" McNamara. The three first met as stars for their respective Bankstown and Canterbury junior representative sides and the friendships blossomed when the three started playing in the same teams and eventually began touring together.

McNamara is a fine example of that classic Aussie expression, "a good bloke". While his determination and dedication have rarely wavered in his pursuit of higher honours in cricket, he would be the last to deny that he loves a good time. Brad didn't just come out of his shell on those early cricket tours, he exploded, and the relatively naive and previously sport-obsessed Steve Waugh hitched a ride. In the intervening years the pair have shared a succession of adventures, but first an example of how close the two have become.

Steve was married to Lynette on August 16, 1991, and had asked Brad to be his best man. Unfortunately the English league side with which McNamara was the professional in that northern summer, Oldham, was scheduled to appear in the Lancashire Cup final that very weekend. That put him in a ticklish position. Given the importance of the occasion, McNamara decided the most convenient solution for all concerned was a little white lie. He told Oldham that his grandmother had died and that he wanted to go back for the funeral. Such was his popularity, or maybe it was the importance of the Cup final to the locals, that sympathetic articles appeared in the area's papers. "It was bloody hilarious," said McNamara, who still has the clippings to prove it.

"I probably would have told them the truth if things were a little different but the club was going fairly well and it was hard to get away," said McNamara. "It was one of those things, you're best man and it's one of your best mate's wedding — you've got to make an effort. It was something I didn't want to miss." But he didn't want to abandon Oldham either so he hatched a plan that would see him fulfil his obligations on both sides of the globe.

Humorous the funeral headlines may have been, but not so funny was the excruciating travel schedule he had to follow in his quest to keep everyone happy. There is little doubt that flying from England to Australia and back again in the space of four days is no joke. "It was an absolute nightmare," testified McNamara.

In keeping with his harsh schedule, McNamara had to do the right thing by Oldham, on the day he arrived back in England. "I actually got back on the Sunday morning and had to play that day at Old Trafford." Fittingly the saga had a happy ending, McNamara scored a century and took five wickets to lead his side to victory against Blackpool.

Modestly he says he was just doing his job. "It's what you're expected to do. They don't settle for anything less when you're the professional over there." When asked how he felt after the game he replied: "Absolutely stuffed". But he still managed to drag himself out for a few celebratory drinks afterward. "I kept up but I slept for two days after that — it wasn't as if I didn't have a few celebrations here in Australia for the wedding."

Although it would seem practically impossible to keep such an audacious stunt secret McNamara said the club still was not aware of what went on.

Such devotion was born of a bond developed through years of touring in under-age cricket teams and then the NSW senior cricket team. Their first escapades came in a trip with the NSW under-16 side to Tasmania. "That was the start of our touring career," said McNamara. "We did some silly things down there, things that normal kids would do. Throwing garbage tins on roofs and all sorts of stuff like that."

But from little things do big things grow and things certainly escalated on subsequent trips. It was on tour that the boys discovered alcohol and developed a taste for gambling.

Interestingly the twins opted for different vices, Steve opted to wrestle with the demon drink while Mark nurtured his life-long love of punting. The trio's relationship has mirrored that. "I'm fairly close to both of them but in different ways," said McNamara. "Mark and I both love the races, we both love a punt. We got to the races a fair bit or just find a TAB somewhere. But I probably see Steve socially more. If I want to go out for a beer I ring Steve but if I want to go out to the track I ring Mark."

Alcohol first reared its ugly head on their first under-19 tour with NSW which they made as 16-year-olds. "The under-19 trips were fantastic, we really had a ball," said McNamara. "Everyone played up. It was our first real taste of getting away."

Steve's schoolmates by now were joining him in all the silly things young people do when they are celebrating the freedom and heady possibilities of their teenage years. Focused and committed he may have been when it came to cricket, but when it came to alcohol Steve could be as dumb as the rest of them. "A couple of us used to drive into town," he said. "We'd got to a pub and the two guys who weren't driving used to scull as many nips as they could in half an hour and get absolutely smashed and we'd drive home. That was our idea of fun in those days. Looking back it was pretty stupid. You woke up crook the next morning, a bit of a mess in your bed, no dollars in your pocket. But it was something to talk about at school I suppose.

"I remember the first time I got really smashed. I went away for the Indoor titles in Perth and I had never really drunk before. We had a party one night and someone got me on the Scotch and got me on a drinking game and nearly killed me. About three hours later I couldn't move, couldn't even get out of my chair. I was crook for about three days. So I've never really touched Scotch since."

Party-time peaked at the under-19 titles in Melbourne after a night out with the Victorian side. Again Steve allowed himself to be drawn into a drinking game. He may be an all-round freak at sport but experience should have taught him by now that this is one game he should give away. The particular sport was called Colonel Puff and the drink was beer.

"I had never drunk beer at that stage but I got caught in the game and had a few sculls. And once I started sculling I couldn't play the game properly, I must have sculled 20 beers in half an hour. I was an absolute mess. Myself and four or five of the other NSW players went back to the hotel and caused havoc. I woke up in the morning with my clothes in the hallway and spew all over me. That was when the coach sort of kicked me and said 'better get up, we've got a cricket game in about an hour and a half'. We were to play Tassie that

Gregg Porteus

Best mate Brad McNamara has been through thick and thin with the twins on and off the field.

day and I didn't feel like playing but one of our fast bowlers was injured so I had to fill in as opening bowler.

"We lost the toss and had to bowl so it was nightmare stuff. I was stretching at fine leg and falling over. It was an absolute shocker. In between overs I had to pretend to be doing up my shoelaces and threw up on the field. I must have had 15 chunders that day on the field. Thankfully no Australian selectors were watching and I got away with it. I remember I bowled 10 overs and took 0-12. As I came into bowl the first time I wasn't really sure I was going to land it on the square at all. Steve Funnell, the footballer, he was in the side as well. I had to get him to carry my bag into the dressing room I was that crook. I couldn't even carry my bag! He saved me that day. That was probably the worst experience I've had on the cricket field with a hangover and feeling crook. I don't think I'll ever be that bad again. I promised myself I would never get that bad again."

"It was stinking hot, 35-40 degrees," said McNamara. "And we lost the toss and fielded. I wasn't too bad, I was stuck away at mid-on. Stephen had to open the bowling, I'll never forget it. He's bowled the first few overs and said to me 'I don't feel to good'. He's walked back to his mark, dropped the ball and turned his back to everyone and pretended to tie up his shoe lace and let fly with this huge bloody chunder. I don't know how many people were watching the game, all the selectors and those sort of people. Actually he did it beautifully, no-one noticed it. Unfortunately I got a real good view of it, it didn't make me feel too good."

Despite that minor aberration both Mark and Steve performed brilliantly, Steve being named player of the tournament with Mark not far behind. But the pace did not slacken off the field. McNamara shifted the blame to the senior members of the side. "There were quite a few big drinkers in the side and every now and then we'd go out and try to match them. One time we got picked up by the police for wrestling in the middle of the road at three or four in the morning. We used to play stupid bloody drinking games. We used to have to scull a jug. There were a few horrendous drinkers in that side, blokes who would scull jugs. We weren't in their class but we'd give it a go.

"Occasionally we liked doing runners from restaurants. I don't think Mark was involved but Stephen and I definitely were. If we were caught doing that sort of thing it would have been the end of us. We were absolute idiots." Steve said this happened just the once, agreed that Mark definitely wasn't involved and suggested he was an innocent victim himself.

On Steve's first lonely trip to England as an 18-year-old he was fortunate to have the support of McNamara who was playing league cricket just south of London. Unfortunately they had still not exhausted the youthful inclination to crash through the barriers that define the sensible use of alcohol. "We used to get into some horrendous drinking sessions in England. It was just ridiculous, all the Poms would egg you on," McNamara recalled. "Steve and I would be the only Aussies there and they'd be saying 'Come on you Aussie wimps, drink'. And being young and stupid, we'd end up paralytic."

McNamara's patron at the Teddington club was a bon vivant by the name of Michael Welch. Welch's house was known as the Grove Club and he played host to an imposing line-up of Australian cricketers over the years — McNamara, Waugh, Geoff Lawson, Peter Taylor, Tom Moody, Phil Emery and Dave Gilbert to name a few. Welch said a Grove Club XI would be a formidable side when you throw in other houseguests like Mike Gatting. Steve never played for Teddington but he did turn out a couple of times for a midweek side Welch runs called Thames Valley Gentlemen. It was certainly a lively atmosphere, merriment being the main preoccupation and featured a homemade concoction called a mudslide, which consisted of Kahlua, Baileys, vodka and crushed ice, among other things. "I think I lost the

NSW celebrate reaching the Shield final in 1989-90, after defeating Tasmania at the SCG. Mark is far right in the back row and Brad McNamara is to his immediate right. Steve was in New Zealand with the Australian team and missed the match ... and the party.

plot for a couple of months. I blame Buzz and the mudslides. We've learned our lesson since then," said Steve.

Mark was more or less spared from these tales of juvenile excess. While he does drink he is the perfect example of moderation. He rarely loses control simply because he doesn't want to.

"It's never been Mark's cup of tea," said Brad. "He's never been interested in going out on the drink. He's never been keen on nightclubs. It's funny, Mark's probably a little more outgoing but less sociable, in terms of going out. In his younger days he was very quiet."

NSW and Australian team-mate Mark Taylor, concurred. "Mark could make 300 in a Test match, take 10 catches and five wickets in each innings and have three beers and be happy while other blokes would have a big night out," he said. "He enjoys going out and having a lemon squash and having a night out at the bar with the boys."

Mark started late in the drinking game and while he can't remember the first time he had a drink he thinks it was probably at Christmas when he was 17. He certainly has no trouble remembering the first time he went too far. It was at the national indoor championships in Melbourne when he was 17. He struggled to attend the presentations at the end of the championships after putting too much bacardi or bourbon, he can't quite remember which, in his coke the evening before. "I had to keep going to the toilet to be sick," he admitted.

But that was really the end of it for Mark. Moderation has been his habit ever since. Steve says that whereas Mark could have a couple of drinks a night every night he himself is either a none or plenty man. He won't often have a drink but if he does he likes to enjoy himself. Mark's reason for his moderation is that while he likes having the odd drink to wind down after a game or relax with his friends he does not enjoy the sensation of feeling drunk.

"I don't like it," said Mark. "I haven't really been drunk too many times. I don't like feeling sick the next day, it's not worth it."

Over the years cricket has taken the Waughs and their various compatriots all over the country and in and out of various pubs, restaurants, clubs, theatres and assorted entertainment establishments. In amongst the rapid changes of modern life one thing has remained constant. On the under-19 trip to Melbourne the boys visited a blue movie theatre called the Shaft Cinema and it's been on the itinerary ever since. "It's kind of tradition that every time we go to Melbourne we have to go to the Shaft and have a quick look and a laugh," said McNamara. "At Steve's wedding we sent a phantom telegram from the Shaft wishing him all the best and thanking him for his patronage."

Neither Waugh has ever been in danger of emulating spiritual mentor Doug Walters in the area of cigarette smoking. "I tried it once or twice and didn't like it." said Mark. "I don't particularly like people smoking near me."

But Mark Waugh does have a vice. The punt. The unfair and unkind have actually referred to him as a desperate. Mark blames his father for his gambling habit but there is no doubt that McNamara was a willing accomplice. The twins' gambling had been small time but things changed yet again on a cricket trip. This time it was a Combined High Schools tour to Brisbane.

"I think we got there on a Monday night and the Albion Park trots were on," said Brad. "At that stage we didn't have any money so our parents would kick us $200 or whatever it was for the week. So we go to Albion Park all cashed up and I think the lot of us lost every cent we had so we spent the next week without a cent."

It wasn't the last time that was to happen either. "I remember the first time I was selected in a state side," McNamara recalled. "I was 12th man for a one-dayer in Perth and we were staying at the Burswood (hotel casino). I think at the time the game fee was about $800 and we were there five days. What usually happens is the manager comes around on the plane on the way home and gives you a cheque. I think I played my first game for minus $200. You walk into the Burswood and you can either go right to your room or you can go left to the casino. Junior and I used to take the left option unfortunately, usually to our demise."

TEN

Making The Grade

CRICKET is the life, lifestyle and livelihood of Mark and Steve Waugh. That they didn't give it away after their many successes as juniors owes perhaps as much to their genes as their personalities. You don't have to clamber far back up the family tree to discover a signpost to the skill that has defined their lives thus far and promises to bring them many more rewards in the future. Dion Bourne, Bev's elder brother, was an outstanding cricketer for Bankstown. An opener, he holds the club run-scoring record and was unlucky not to represent NSW. His mother still has a clipping of a schoolboy innings that hinted at things to come — both for him and his sister's off-spring. Dion was attending Tumut Intermediate High School when he produced an innings of remarkable dominance, scoring 177 out of a total of 190. There were 11 sundries and just one other batsman scored with a single shot — two to fine leg. There were eight ducks and a 0 not out.

The echoes sound even stronger when the last few paragraphs of the newspaper report are read: "Bourne is an unspoilt lad, proud of his achievements but humble to acknowledge his great talents; a quietly spoken lad who is anxious to learn and advance."

Dion Bourne captained Bankstown when they boasted two of the wildest quicks in town — Lennie Pascoe and Jeff Thomson. It is a measure of his integrity and the quality of his cricket that both had enormous respect for him. Both made a name for the wild-and-woolly way they behaved as youngsters and it was that raging fire in the belly that made them such feared opponents in the Test arena. To have harnessed their talents in grade cricket AND earned their respect is no mean feat. He exhibited the same light and sure touch with his two young nephews. Like Bev and Rodger, Dion was able to offer the right amount of encouragement and help without spoiling things by interfering.

"I might have said to him as a brother 'could you come and have a look at them and maybe coach them' and he just took one or two looks and said they don't need anything," said Bev. "He said they've got natural talent. He might have given them a few hints as they got older but his lack of coaching or guidance was, in a way, because he appreciated the fact that they would be better without it at that stage and enjoying most sports. He couldn't see that they were doing anything particularly wrong. A lot of people wanted to coach them but Dion said: 'No, just let them go. Someone might try to change them dramatically and maybe take away the natural talent they have'."

Bev and Rodger themselves had realised long ago that the only use they would be was as dispensers of spiritual and material support. "I could have coached them at tennis, squash maybe," said Bev. "But Rodger and I couldn't really give them any clues with cricket other than just general knowledge and practicing with them, throwing the ball. I bowled plenty of balls to them. And all my pantyhose used to disappear. They'd be hanging in the garage with a ball in the foot. But it was a good idea, it would swing all over the place. They would put the ball in the foot and tape it up with insulating tape. I think maybe they'd seen it on somebody's clothes line but I got hit with enough balls on the head without having one on the clothes line."

Despite the passage of time and the increasing age of the Waugh clan the threat to Bev's lingerie is still very much a reality. "They still do it," said Bev. "There's probably one out there right now. You'd think I'd be safe wouldn't you — a female in a house of boys. I remember one night I was going out and thought I had the choice of three or four pairs. None! They were all out in the garage."

There aren't too many aspects of their childhood that the Waughs will admit directly affected their cricket but Steve says "the ball in the stocking" is definitely one of them. "I used to spend hours in the garage. I think that was one of the things that helped me improve my cricket. Just hitting the ball up into the roof non-stop made you play straight. I used to spend ages in there just hitting the ball up and down if there was no-one to play with. I never found it boring. It was always sort of interesting and you could always work on your technique. Other people must have thought we were crazy, in there banging a ball up onto the roof of the garage."

Now there's a promotional possibility, a chance for some far-thinking company to blaze a path away from the traditionally sexist stocking advertisements that inevitably feature stunning models with long, long legs. The Waugh twins and pantyhose — there's a lot of razzamatazz potential there.

The twins experienced quite a bit of overlap in their transition through various development levels as cricketers. Although barely in their teens they were called up to grade cricket and thus spent a number of years playing junior, school and senior cricket all at the same time. Steve said that coming up against players of equal or better ability was at first a rude shock after years of unchallenged dominance. But the shock was brief and it didn't take long for the Waughs to again put a gap between themselves and the field. Steve's first experience of grade cricket was a rude shock for another reason. He was called into Bankstown's fifth grade side as a replacement late in the season and, although expecting modestly to bat in the lower middle order, was placed in the very lower middle order — No. 11 — because he was a bowler and, according to the captain, you didn't do both.

"I started from the bottom you could say," he said. "I think we were all out for 55 or something and I was 16 not out. So the captain learned from that and the next game I batted 11 again and got another 16 not out when we were beaten outright. It was a bit of a comedown. I thought I would bat six or seven at least. I didn't expect to be in the top four or five because I was a late replacement. I was just called in to gain a bit of experience. By the same token, I didn't think I would be slotted into No. 11 — before the roller."

But there was no chance of the young cricket hero putting the old skipper in his place. "No, I wouldn't have said anything to him at the time. I was too scared. I would have just sat in the corner and accepted it. I probably still would now. I just took it as it was and tried to do my best, show him up."

The following year he got 100 the first game and finished the season in second grade.

Whether it's because there were so many that few stick out in the crowd or because he's not a guy who values scores for themselves, Mark is difficult to pin down on his most memorable youthful achievements on the cricket field. One that does stand out is a lower grade hundred he scored for Bankstown when he was 15 and still playing junior cricket. It came against Penrith at St Marys in quite difficult circumstances.

"I always remember that, coming in on a hat-trick," said Mark. "I was batting with a fellow called Mike Stephenson. He was about 35 years old. I reckon I could have made 200 if he could have run between the wickets. I got about 105. I came in at six, Steve was out first ball. It was a stinking hot day. I remember going straight from junior cricket to play in the game."

After testing the fifth grade waters as 14-year-olds their rise to first grade was swift. Both debuted in the same game. It was at this stage that Ian Davis renewed his acquaintance with them. He was captain of the Balmain side and got a first-hand look at Mark's blossoming ability when the two sides clashed. But it wasn't just pure ability that the Test veteran noticed.

"They were obviously outstanding cricketers," said Davis. "They both played pretty well on the day, they bowled well and batted well. Mark played beautifully, I thought he just oozed class. It was undoubted that they had huge potential and the thing I noticed about playing them was how competitive they were. They were extremely competitive for such young blokes. Especially with the cricket ball in their hand, they were really aggressive and they didn't seem to be worried about the fact that I had represented Australia. They got stuck into me just like they got stuck into everybody else."

Davis said that all the senior players at the time respected the twins' ability, realising how dangerous they were. It was a subject much discussed between the old pros in the competition. "They could turn a game. They were aggressive in the way they bowled. They didn't bowl to contain. They bowled so they could knock a side over. And when they batted they were able to bat within themselves, and then if the situation required they could turn around and attack.

"They were so aggressive in their manner, the way they played the game. Which meant they could do anything on the day. A bit like a footballer, a Steve Mortimer or a Peter Sterling or someone like that. They just had that ability to turn the game around in no time."

They may have had minimal respect for big reputations on the field but they were the same withdrawn souls off it. The confidence that enabled them to throw everything but the kitchen sink at a man who had opened the batting for Australia was not there when it came time to have a beer and chat about cricket with him. "They were just so shy, it was just a hello and goodbye," said Davis, who nonetheless found something to admire in their demeanour. "They weren't skylarky, confident kids. They were very shy and withdrawn. You see a lot of kids these days at 18 or 19. They think they've made it and are as cocky as hell, full of arrogance. You'd swear they'd played 25 Tests. But they were never like that, I think that's why they've done well. Because they've been brought up with a fairly level-headed attitude. Deep down there'd be no doubt that they thought they would play for Australia but they didn't really let that out and I think that was to their credit."

After years of having done it easily against boys his own age Mark got a rude shock when he padded up at No. 3 for Bankstown in the final against Penrith in his first season in first grade. Opener Steve Smith had been scoring double hundreds but Penrith quick Graham Pitty knocked him over early and Mark, just 17 at the time, had to negotiate the final half hour before stumps. He got there with 20 runs to his name despite the fact that Pitty was bowling at "150 miles an hour".

"That was my first real test," recalled Mark. "I thought I was a bit out of my depth that day. I'd actually done quite well coming into that game. He was the first real fast bowler I'd seen, I thought he was too quick for me." He was out not too long after play resumed the next day and Bankstown were well beaten.

Veteran opener and past Bankstown captain Gary Crowfoot was impressed by Mark's effort. "He showed his class in that game," said Crowfoot. "It was probably the quickest spell of bowling I've faced."

But just because the twins were playing with the bigs boys didn't mean they were ready emotionally. A number of team-mates have said that Mark was too shy to shower with the older blokes after the day's play had finished. "We thought he had wooden legs," said team-mate and close mate Andy Divall. "I don't think we ever saw them. He always had tracksuit pants on."

Another team-mate and regular punting partner, Bill York, said that Mark claimed he didn't shower because he didn't sweat. But York caught him out on an indoor cricket trip to Melbourne. The team was being put up in a hotel and each player had their own room. After a couple of days York said Mark knocked on the door and said: "Yorkie, any chance you'd know how to work the showers?" "He hadn't had a tub for three days," chuckled York.

Crowfoot said the difference in maturity between Steve and Mark was startling. It appears that later press allegations of softness was well warranted early in Mark's grade and Sheffield Shield career. "It took Mark longer to mature and go on as a player. Steve always had a determined attitude and knew exactly where he wanted to be. Mark had a lot of time when he batted, a lot of elegance and grace, he just didn't have as hard a character as Steve at such a young age. The first time Mark was dropped from the Shield side he came back but he couldn't make up his mind where he wanted to bat whereas it wasn't a question with Steve. I chastised Junior about that. It was just like a job to Steve and Mark probably took a while to find his feet in that area."

Mark these days has got that particular area of his house in order, and at the same time his brother has progressed too. "His personality just seems to get stronger and stronger every year," said Divall.

One man who has had the opportunity to study the Waughs in depth over the years is Bankstown president Brian Freedman, whose son started as an under-10 opponent of the twins and went on to become a Shield team-mate. "Steve is much more determined. He has that fierce, unbending determination as far as I'm concerned," said Freedman.

He recalled a match at Waverley Oval just after Steve had started playing first grade. Steve received a vicious ball and was caught after desperately fending it away from his face. Freedman was sitting in a stand and soon received a visit from the disappointed young cricketer. "He came up to the stand and quizzed me for about half an hour," said Freedman. "Steve found it difficult to accept that he hadn't done anything wrong, and he was in agony trying to find out how he could better himself."

Another indication that the step up in class was making an impression on the Waugh psyche was Steve's developing habit of making copious notes about his game. "When I first played first grade I kept a record of every innings I played and how I got out and why I got out," said Steve. "I did it for about a year or so and then I thought 'oh, stuff this'. But I was pretty keen there for a while. I used to write everything down — bowling, batting, fielding, everything." This is the young man who had spent his entire junior career exercising enormous confidence in his natural abilities and for whom the highlight of a trip to cricket lessons was the after-training session at McDonalds.

Despite all the success the Waughs have enjoyed and the enormous demands placed upon their time, they still give all they can in time and effort to their grade club Bankstown. Their

Canterbury-Bankstown rugby league
champion Steve Mortimer, a footballer who
could turn a game. The Waughs can have
a similar impact on the cricket field.

The Bankstown team that won the Sydney first-grade premiership in 1987-88. Back row, left to right: L. Holdsworth (manager), G. Lovett, W. York, P. Talbot, S. Prestwidge; D. Mitchell; T. Crameri, Dean Waugh, D. Freedman, A. Couper (scorer); front row, left to right: S. Waugh, D. Thompson, S. Smith , T. Davies (captain), G. Crowfoot, S. Small, M. Waugh; insets: W. Holdsworth (left), and T. Sullivan.

enormous workload with NSW and Australia means that they are rarely able to play with their old mates but they will never dodge a Bankstown game or training session if they are free to attend. Far from getting inflated opinions of their talents, both feel they owe the club a huge debt for having given them the opportunity to play first grade so early.

"It's where we learned how to play the game," said Mark. "Whenever I get a chance I always play and I go to training whenever I can. Bankstown weren't scared to give us a go really young which was quite good. We were fortunate because a lot of clubs don't do that, they stick to the old tried and tested way."

NSW team-mate and current Bankstown club captain, Steve Small, refers to the popular and hard-working Steve as the Mayor of Bankstown. That's not to say he lords it over his clubmates. Not only do he and Mark show up but they refuse to swan around like superstars and have everyone treat them like royalty. They will run training drills, counsel younger players and even involve themselves in the thankless, and often mundane, work of the club's management committee. Neither do they demand compensation for giving so freely of their time. That is no small consideration given the fact that clubs in Sydney's unofficial second division, the Shires and Municipalities competition, are paying players $6000-7000 a season to captain-coach. "It's really important to the young players that they're there and show their faces," said Crowfoot. "It gives the club a lift."

For Crowfoot their loyalty to the club was epitomised by the performance AFTER the 1987-88 first grade final against Petersham. Mark and Steve were only able to play the Saturday of the game because they had to play for NSW in a McDonalds Cup limited-over final the following day. They threw the bat in the afternoon after a rain delay and scored enough runs for their team-mates who knocked Petersham over in about four hours on the Sunday. NSW had also won but they didn't forget their mates. "They were back at the club 'bandroom' at 7.30pm and they stayed there all night celebrating with the club," said Crowfoot.

"They've never refused a request from the club and they've never asked for money," said Brian Freedman. "They're absolutely loyal supporters of the club, the game and the community. When Steve is playing for Bankstown he couldn't play any harder if he was playing for Australia. Mark is almost obsessed. He gets so uptight because of a rough trot over the last couple of years he's probably less chance of scoring runs for Bankstown than he is for NSW or Australia. They never use the state cap or jumper when they play, it's never an issue. They just slip back into Bankstown."

"I get more nervous batting for Bankstown than I do for NSW or Australia," admitted Mark. "There's a lot more pressure. Everyone expects you to do well and I want to do well. I think I'm trying too hard. I always get out stupid ways — caught and bowled off a leading edge or I hit a long hop to square leg. It's usually the bad balls that get me out. I enjoy it and I do relax but I haven't got any runs. I'm relaxed until I go out to bat."

Whenever they're away on tour or playing in England club secretary Martin Klump writes to them to keep them up to date with what's going on in the club.

"They're the first to get people off their bums and moving at grade training now," said former juniors coach Ian Gill. "Especially with the young people. They like to help. They've got a lot of time for the kids. If I ring them up and ask them to attend a presentation or do some coaching, as long as they've got nothing on, they'll be there. They help whenever they can. The majority of the guys went elsewhere but Steve and Mark were very committed."

Three players Mark credits with influencing him early in his first grade career were captain of the time Bob Vidler, wicketkeeper Les Andrews and Crowfoot. "Bob saw us as having a lot of ability and gave us a lot of chances. He was the one who wanted us in first grade. Les was helpful, very encouraging. And Gary was real tough, very determined, always gave 100 per cent. I always looked at the way he played."

Steve said things were a little different for him in those early years because he had passed quickly through the first grade side on his way to the Shield side. "I was still good friends with them but it wasn't the same as it was for Mark. He was closer to them because I made the state side pretty quickly. I wanted to play State cricket and that was all I was worried about. Rather than worrying about being comfortable in the group I was looking further down the track than they were." He also feels they made a special effort to help Mark because they could see that he was also good enough to play first class cricket.

The focus that drove Steve on was actually documented at the time. He did a motivational course that he had bought off the NSW and Australian spinner Murray Bennett when he was 17 or 18. As part of the course Steve had to list goals for 10 years time, which incidentally is right about now. Recently he and wife Lynette stumbled upon the list. "Every one I listed I've achieved," said Steve. "There were about 10 things," said Lynette. "Building his own house, being married, playing for Australia, maintaining contact with family and friends."

Despite that intense focus Steve had not, and has not, lost his talent for teamwork and feel for the morale of fellow players. "Steve is very good to bat with because he goes out of his way to make you feel good," said Divall. "He always tries to build you up, make you feel as if you're doing a good job." He said just having them on the field pumps the rest of the players up. "It brings out the best in players. When they're around everybody lifts themselves because they know what Steve and Mark expect."

For years their competitiveness had powered the Waughs to victory but a cluey opponent could still knock them over if they played their cards right. Divall is proud to report that he

A dream fulfilled ... Mark flies the flag for English county Essex in the Australian off-season.

got the better of Mark on the tennis court about the time he broke into first grade. "We organised a game at East Hills High, " said Divall. "They were always big-noting themselves about how good they were and I don't know how it happened but I managed to beat him 6-0 in the first set. I decided that I was never going to get another chance to beat a Waugh 6-0 so I made up some excuse that I had to leave and took off. I was a real good champ, I've never given him another chance at the title. I haven't gone within 10 kilometres of a court since then."

By now all the backyard skiting was appearing possible. Playing for Australia wasn't just a dream anymore. Mark said he had a fair idea that winning a baggy green cap was a reasonable goal in his late teens. He had made first grade at 17 and played both NSW under-16 and Australian under-19. "Playing first grade at 17 is a fair sort of start. I had an idea then that I might do all right at cricket. I mean, people say when you are playing junior cricket that you are going to play for Australia but you don't really know. A lot of kids drop away don't they, the blokes who are stars in junior cricket."

"I think it was when we were picked in the Australian under-19 side," said Steve. "We toured around playing Sri Lanka, we played in a couple of different states and had a really good time there as well as playing for Australia. People were starting to whisper in my ear that I was close to State selection. And at that stage the coach at Croatia called me into his office and said: 'I want you to play first grade but you won't be able to play unless you give up cricket'. So that was it. I had to go one way or the other. My cricket career was starting to take off and I thought I could make a fair go of it, so that was the reason I took cricket up."

Steve showed just how capable he was of making a go of it when he played the Sri Lankans in the third Test of that under-19 series. Coming to the wicket in the midst of a collapse that saw Australia 4-181 chasing 356, Waugh smashed 187 off only 216 deliveries. When he was out the Australians were well on top at 7-470 and in fact the home side lost their last three wickets for only six runs.

The twins made their first very tentative steps overseas when they were 18, signing to play

The supposedly dour Steve shares a joke with a NSW team-mate at training.

with Bolton League club Egerton. Steve, who had played a handful of Shield matches for NSW including the Shield final the previous Australian summer, was to be the side's professional and Mark, who would debut the first game of the following Australian summer, was to play as an amateur because each club was only allowed to pay one player. They got off to a rocky start but fate intervened and they went their separate ways — for better and for worse. The rebel South African tour had gutted the Australian side and NSW quick Dave Gilbert, who was playing with Essex on an Esso Scholarship, was called up. Steve took his place at Essex and Mark became the Egerton professional. While it was probably a key factor in catapulting him ahead of Mark you can be reasonably sure that Steve would rather the memories were a little bit more positive.

"That was our first trip away and I don't really think we knew what we were doing," said Steve. "I drew the short straw on the plane and a bloke about 40 stone lobbed next to me and he sat there for the whole trip. Mark wouldn't swap. He sat there, nice and comfortable, going to sleep with his head on the window, and I was stuck in the middle. The flight was late and we didn't know what we were doing. We were wet behind the ears. We were trying to find out where our connecting flight was, and we ended up running and catching the plane just before it left. Our bags were left in Amsterdam and when we eventually got to Manchester the people who were supposed to pick us up got the time wrong so we were at the airport by ourselves and knew no-one. Mark was useless. He was just sitting around doing nothing while I was trying to organise how we were going to find someone. It was freezing cold and we had the wrong clothes on for a start. We had short-sleeved shirts on and it was about minus five. And we had no bags and no-one to pick us up. So it was a good start. We had no idea of what was going on in the real world.

"The South African tour had just been announced and half the team who had been picked for England didn't go. Dave Gilbert got called up to the Australian side so when we got to England I went down to Essex and Mark stayed in Egerton. So we were separated for the first time. I was down on the outskirts of London, it was a whole new experience, and I got very lonely. I sat there by myself for four months. I had just met Lynette at that stage so we were writing virtually every day.

"Mark was okay because he was with a family up there but I was stuck by myself down in London. I was with one of the other players and his wife but I never really saw them. I don't think they wanted me there actually. I think they got 800 pounds for having me there for four months, and they actually told me the only reason they took me on was so they could get a new kitchen. There was never any food in the fridge so I had to fend for myself. It was pretty hard coming from home where you got looked after all the time, all your washing and ironing done and a feed always on the table. I wasn't much of a cook at that stage. I survived on takeaways or I'd go around to a team-mate's place for a bit of a feed. I can't remember cooking too many times. I've never been big on curries so I gave them a bit of a miss. McDonalds copped a workout, Kentucky Fried, Pizza Hut, fish and chips, hamburgers. Some sort of fast food. I wasn't too fussy in those days."

Mark had the good fortune to fall into a situation light years away from Steve's predicament. "Once I got used to the surroundings and the people I enjoyed it. No problem at all. I was lucky because I stayed with Peter and Iris Greenhalgh. They were really good people and spoiled me. They were like a second mum and dad. They used to give me pocket money. If they couldn't give me my lunch they used to give me money to go and buy some. I think their daughter got a bit upset because she wasn't getting the attention she normally got."

Steve and Mark after the Australia v Essex match in the 1989 tour. Both scored centuries.

Steve was also having a little bit of trouble fully fitting in at Essex. That was less because of Steve or the Essex players and more because of the larger-than-life figure that had preceded him at Essex. "I wasn't really their idea of an Aussie," he said. "They had Merv Hughes there the year before me so it was a bit of a tough act to follow. He used to hang guys off the balcony and do all sorts of things like that. It was a bit of a shock when I turned up. I was quiet. I didn't drink much. I won't say I hadn't discovered drink but I wasn't a big drinker then. I was just sort of an occasional drinker. I wasn't like the normal Aussie who would throw four hundred beers down his throat and act like an idiot. So they thought I was a bit strange in that regard. I didn't really go out too much. I went home or to the movies.

"I think they found me a bit boring to begin with but that's just the way I was. It's pretty hard to compete with Merv at the best of times."

All the off-field woes and homesickness weren't affecting Steve's cricket. The highlight of his time was a double century in a 50-over match. It was an under-25 game against Sussex who fielded Australian allrounder Tony Dodemaide in their attack. Steve scored exactly 200 not out in the total of just over 300. "It was just one of those days. I think I got dropped first ball at first slip and didn't miss one after that."

Of all the awards, trophies and prizes Mark has received from cricket none is more unusual than the incentive award he clinched when he was at Egerton in his first English season. Two of his teeth had been knocked out at the annual cricket barbecue when he was 16, and although he'd had them capped the Waugh family was still looking at a big bill sometime in the future to have them properly repaired. The captain at Egerton, who just happened to be a dentist, told him that if he scored 1000 runs and took 50 wickets he would crown his troublesome teeth for nothing. Mark duly accomplished his targets and the dentist-come-captain kept his word. But the Englishman wasn't quite as manipulative as he appears. "I think he was going to do them anyway," said Mark. "But it was a bonus because they are pretty expensive."

Following his stint at Egerton Mark returned for a season with the MCC groundstaff. He described it as a level below county cricket, with the staff playing matches against teams like Army and Navy and county second XIs. "It didn't improve my cricket but we had a good time, young blokes the same sort of age can think of a few things to do when they're together every day."

Unfortunately, on a number of occasions that wasn't a good thing for Mark. "I remember England were playing a Test match against New Zealand at Lord's and they told me I was going to meet the Queen because I was an overseas player. So during the week I sent all my stuff to the dry cleaners, my blazer and trousers, and had a haircut. I got to the ground that day and wandered around for about half an hour trying to find somebody to tell me where to meet the Queen. Eventually I went downstairs to the bloke who runs the groundstaff, and he told me it was a hoax. I was so excited for about a week."

That wasn't the only time they took advantage of the young Australian. The ground staff consists of about 25 players and different combinations are selected for the various matches. That makes it very important to be aware of when you're playing and when you're not. The man who had been so worried about getting in trouble as a youngster was the perfect target for the staff jokers. "A couple of times they rang me up and told me I wasn't supposed to play that day when I was and twice they told me I was playing so I rushed to get a taxi in and found out I wasn't playing." Still, Waugh acknowledges that he got off very lightly.

"Fortunately I didn't get whitewashed. If they don't like someone they strip them, take them out to the Nursery Ground, which is the practice ground at one end of Lord's, and stake

The great West Indian Viv Richards.
Steve more than held his own against
Richards while playing for the
Lancashire club, Nelson.

(Gregg Porteus)

them out on the ground with nothing on. Then they get this bucket and put whatever they want in it, spit, urine, water, grass, food, anything, and they throw it all over you and they paint you white with shoe cleaner as well. That was a regular occurrence. It happened to one of the guys when I was there. As far as cricket was concerned it didn't teach me much at all. But it did teach me not to trust anyone."

Unfortunately he didn't learn too many lessons from his delayed introduction to the realities of housekeeping. The lack of a second, or third, mother and father at the flat he shared with a couple of other members of the ground staff should have been enough to shock him into some sort of proficiency around the house or kitchen given the way that young bachelors are prone to live. But Mark, as is his manner, muddled through largely unscathed. "It was a rude shock having to do a bit of cooking and washing. In fact Neil Smith, who was one of my flatmates and now plays for Warwickshire ... his mum used to do quite a bit of our washing. And another one of the fellas, Paul Bently, used to be chief cook. I don't know what my job was."

Steve spent the 1987 English summer with Lancashire League club Nelson as its professional and during that time he became fast friends with current captain Michael Bradley. It wasn't a raging success statistically for Waugh because rain played a big part in the summer's schedule. In the end he scored about 800 runs and took 70-odd wickets. There were at least five games rained off and if they had been played Steve could have reasonably expected to score more than 1200 runs.

"Steve was at a disadvantage because we had a terrible summer," said Bradley, who pointed out that Waugh scored roughly the same amount of runs as Vivian Richards, who was playing with Rishton at the time. "Steve's innings tended to be match-winning performances." Bradley can only remember one time when Steve blew a match. Ironically it was against Richards and Rishton. Steve was 98 and tried to get the six needed to win with one hit but was out stumped off Richards.

"Steve was bowling to a tailender once and hit him on the pad three times in an over and each time asked the umpire why it wasn't out. The first time it pitched outside leg, the second time it was just going down the leg side and the third hit just outside off-stump. The fourth time he hit him on the pad he turned to the umpire and said: 'where did that go, underneath?'."

Brad McNamara advised taking an Englishman's words on that subject with a grain of salt. "I think they'd say that about any Aussie guy. They've always both been very, very competitive. When things don't go their way with umpires they're quick to let them know about it. They don't stand there and mouth off, they just hit the ump with a quick one-liner. But you can say that about most players. It's funny over there. When you're getting paid to play obviously you want to perform for them and there's some bloody bloke who can't see up the other end. Sooner or later you're going to give him a gobful. They've always been very aggressive on the cricket field. And not just towards umpires. They don't mind having a word with the opposition."

Despite the run-ins with umpires and the occasional mischievous attention of the national tabloids Mark, who has spent a large portion of his adult life playing in England, enjoys his time there. "I think England is a pretty good spot. I don't mind it at all. The only thing I can't understand about England is the way when it's hot they have no air-conditioning in cars and the drinks aren't cold. Hotels are always hot. They just can't cope with the hot weather which is stupid because the last three or four summers have been really warm. Yet they've got things like pork pies and sausage rolls that they eat cold."

ELEVEN

Testing Times

Whether they were conscious of it at the time or not, the Waughs had spent their whole life preparing for their ultimate reward — Test selection. The countless innings, the thousands of hours in the backyard or the garage, the interviews and presentations, the pressure and the politics, all gave them the equipment and experience to make a go of it in the big time. But excellent as their preparation was, they were still quite unprepared for the breath-taking rollercoaster ride they would be forced to endure in international cricket — particularly Stephen. Which is a good thing really because while the shock of the sickening downward swoops of poor form and ill-fortune have been that much harder to come to grips with, it has meant the successes have been all the more sweet.

Doubly ironic is the fact that although long acknowledged as heirs to the throne, their final ascension came as a surprise to both of them. The announcement of Steve's inclusion in the second Test team against India at the MCG in December 1985 came at the last minute so the Waughs were caught unprepared. He had come into the 12 in place of first Test 12th man Robbie Kerr after just 11 first class matches and had been considered unlikely to play. But an injury to Greg Ritchie pitched him into the side. When Steve won Test selection for the first time it was an exciting moment for the Waughs, but they handled it in their own understated way. "We only had a small celebration," said Rodger. "Nothing lavish. We never had big parties. We just had a small congratulatory drink and a few people came around, not all that many." The late announcement meant that Rodger, who made a frantic dash down to watch his son's first Test, didn't get a chance to see Steve bat.

"It was only announced on the morning of the match," said Rodger. "Dean had a rep game on that morning so we had to watch that. We were out at Hawkesbury listening to him bat and I was very nervous. I went down to Melbourne the next day so I saw four days."

Steve himself admitted to suffering from a curious shortage of his trademark confidence at the time. "When I was picked I was excited but scared," he said.

Selection woes or reprimands from unsympathetic adults had been mere hiccups in the speedy ascent to the top of cricket for Mark and Steve. Neither believes he really did it tough until he started playing with the big boys. Everyone is aware of Mark's lengthy battle to crack the national team, but in Steve's case he went all the way to Test cricket before things turned really sour.

"I hadn't really done it tough until then," recalled Steve. "In grade cricket I had done it easy all the way through and then I came in to Shield cricket and started off pretty well. But when I got thrown into Test cricket it was a different ball game. It was a bit of a shock my first Test. Walking out into the middle of the MCG and I'm facing guys like Gavaskar, Vengsarkar and Shastri and they've probably got 500 Tests between them. The wicket turned square and I thought 'God, if this is what it's like I'm not going to last too long'. But I managed, one-day cricket helped me there for a while. I came to terms with it a bit better, the publicity and what was expected of you. But to start with it was a bit of shock, people ringing up and wanting interviews and TV interviews. I didn't really want to be a part of that. I just wanted to play cricket. But you can't, these days you've got to do both. You can't have one."

While not a media performer of the calibre of a Border or a Hughes or a Mark Taylor, Steve has been able to come to grips with the demands of his role and is now an accomplished interviewee. That's not to say he enjoys it. "I don't think you ever really do get comfortable with it unless you are a natural. Even today I am not totally comfortable with it but I've come to accept it. I know it is part of the game and it doesn't worry me now whereas in the early days it probably did. People expected big things of me and I was sort of pulled out of nowhere and expected to do miracle things. I wasn't quite up to it at that stage. I wasn't ready for it. I was grateful I got a chance and would never swap what happened but ideally it would have been better to prepare with a couple of more years in Shield cricket. But at that stage they didn't have too many choices."

The grim circumstances that gave Steve a chance to crack the big time at a much younger age than would normally have been the case only added to the difficulty of grasping that chance and making a go of it. "It was pretty hard because the side was struggling and they probably had more important things to worry about than me. I didn't really have a lot of guidance until Greg Matthews and Dave Gilbert helped me in my first Test. But apart from that there wasn't a lot of help forthcoming because everyone else was worrying too much about their own game and doing well. They were all still trying to cement a spot in the team themselves. I mean the first time I met Geoff Marsh it was a centre wicket conversation during my first Test match. The day before the match I'd really just said hello. A bit of small talk and then you're out in the middle in a Test match and you don't even know the guy you're batting with. That sort of thing never happens today. So it was a whole new experience and I wasn't really ready for it."

That he wasn't quite ready showed in his results. He found it difficult to score runs and kept himself in the side with a few wickets, his brilliant fielding and the promise of things to come. For the first time the unshakeable Waugh confidence was well and truly rattled. "There were times I sat back and thought 'jeez, am I good enough to play with this side?'" said Steve. "The first 12 Tests I think I only averaged 12 or 13. People were starting to get on my back. Early on it was okay, I was the new guy and I was given time to settle in, but once I didn't start doing that well after a couple of years I think people started to talk. It was hard because you start to doubt yourself. I got the odd 50 but I never kicked on. I started to get a few wickets but I was just hanging on, I wasn't really cementing my spot. I knew deep down I was good enough but sometimes you doubt yourself when you are up against quality opposition like Richard Hadlee and you're thinking 'it's going to be tough to get runs'.

"That's why Allan Border is so tough. He is so tough mentally. He puts it in the back of his mind and goes out and backs himself. You've got to do that and treat it like any other game. But I suppose I was treating it like a different game. I was putting too much pressure on myself. I was telling myself that I had to come good because the whole country wanted me to do well and if I didn't they were going to be on my back. It made me think about more things than cricket."

It was a time when Steve leant heavily on his family and girlfriend Lynette. With poor form and defeat splintering the side the young rookie needed support, and he got it from those close to him. There had been a daily exchange of letters between him and Lynette during his first lonely trip to England, and the telephone was his lifeline during the horrific tour of Pakistan early on. Such is the bond of his friendships that his close mates even rang

Steve battling against Mike Gatting's Englishmen during the Third Test in Adelaide in 1986-87, his first full season of international cricket.

Two images of cricket in the West Indies. Above: Steve batting on the beach at St Vincent. *(Gregg Porteous)* Below: Mark (far right) watching some unconventional work by the Sabina Park groundsman in Jamaica. The other Australian cricketers looking on are Mark Taylor (next to Mark), Dean Jones (in white cap), Mike Whitney and Craig McDermott (to Jones' right) and Bruce Reid (far left). *(Gregg Porteous)*

Mark acknowledges the Australian dressing room after reaching a hundred in his first Test innings, on the first day of the fourth Test against England, in Adelaide in January 1991. At left is Greg Matthews, who batted with him through most of the afternoon. (PBL Marketing)

Whether scoring runs, taking wickets or grabbing catches, Steve was rarely out of the limelight during the 1989 tour of England. This photo was taken during the sixth Test, at The Oval. (Philip Brown)

him in Pakistan to offer their support. That was a time when he needed all the help and understanding he could get.

"Long tours can be lonely sometimes, especially when the side is not doing well, because most blokes tend to lock themselves away and try to think about their own game and try to work out ways to improve it. When the side was going bad it was like that. NSW players would go out together and Queensland players would go somewhere else for a feed. That's completely changed now. That's one of the reasons the Test side is so much better than it was when I first came into it. That comes with being more relaxed and the side doing well. But when you are doing poorly you tend to stick with the guys you know and feel comfortable with and can give you support. That's why, I suppose, the guys were a bit segregated. But it is a vicious circle. Once you do that in a team you haven't got any team spirit, then your performances suffer again and there's no real way of getting out of it."

That 1988 tour of Pakistan was perhaps the lowest point in Steve's career. Personally it was a disaster for him in every way possible. He suffered through a horrendous batting slump courtesy of a mixture of poor decisions and bad shots, he was ill for much of the time, the team itself was struggling badly and the tourists were at the centre of a vicious storm over umpiring standards. He scored just 92 runs at an average of 18.4, which included a face-saving 59 in the final Test in Lahore. What made it worse was the apparent insensitivity of people back home. The Aussies were doing the best they could in difficult circumstances and people who had no idea what they were going through were criticising their sportsmanship.

"It was just a really frustrating tour and things weren't going well for the team — we talked about going home a few times. And *Sixty Minutes* put their nose in and made us look like a bunch of bad sports when we weren't. It was a tough tour and we got back and people gave us stick about the way we behaved over there. You can't really say they were cheating, but I think you know when you're not getting a fair go. You are trying to represent your country and trying to give your best and you're being ripped off. That was probably the lowest point in my career."

That's not to say Stephen spat the dummy. The slamming of doors, throwing of equipment and scattering of furniture and fixtures is as old as the game itself. For instance, there is an air-conditioning unit mounted on the wall at the entrance to the visitors dressing room at the WACA ground in Perth which bears mute testimony to the frustrations of more than a few batsmen over the years. The cooling grills are riddled with gouges where a bat guilty of a false stroke, or the property of a batsman victimised by a shoddy decision, has thumped into it. There have been numerous stories of doors that have come off hinges and glass that has shattered after an angry entrance. While not claiming to have waltzed through the tour with a big smile on his face, Waugh said he rarely indulged in dressing room histrionics.

"I might have taken it out in the dressing room once or twice but not too badly. I very rarely have thrown my bat, I might have thrown it once or twice over there, knocked a few cups off the table, but nothing too major. I tend not to. I think it looks pretty bad if you come into the dressing room and start throwing your gear around. I think that's a cheap way of showing you're cheesed off rather than going out and doing your best on the field. I think it's the easy way of getting out of it."

One area Steve is happy to admit letting his anger and frustration run loose is bowling. He believes it is a vital ingredient in his quest to get wickets. "I don't bowl well unless I get aggressive. It's taken me a few years to work out but if I just go out there and bowl and try to be friendly I bowl a heap of garbage."

Steve wasn't sure he was the right man for the job after receiving his first ball in Test cricket, from the Indian left-arm spinner Ravi Shastri

He certainly had plenty of motivation when he returned home. Lynette, who is a compulsive compiler and chronicler, had kept a record of the tour's press reports. Steve may have thought they were copping some stick while he was in Pakistan, but Lynette's little file certainly opened his eyes. "That's the only time I've seen him angry," said Lynette. There have been benefits, if anything that disastrous can be described as positive. "I'd be a lot better next time because I know how to handle it," said Steve.

Australian coach Bob Simpson was a great help to the shaken young man in those early dark years. "It was pretty hard at first coming into the side. I felt a bit on the outside, I didn't think I was quite good enough. Bob Simpson was good, he gave me a lot of confidence. He always used to tell me I was good enough, that I could make it at that level. Then I finally came through with a couple of good scores and I was on my way."

The first time Steve struck a blow for both himself and the team was at the 1987 World Cup in India and Pakistan. Australia entered the tournament as 16/1 outsiders but the team mood was surprisingly upbeat.

Above: The victorious Australian camp celebrates after its thrilling World Cup win in 1987.

Left: Geoff Marsh (left) and Allan Border congratulate Steve after Waugh took the key wicket of Phillip DeFreitas in the final.

"I just fancied our chances," said Steve. "We had a feeling we were going to do well. It was similar to the Ashes tour." Another similarity was the mood of the pre-tour press.

"Zaheer Abbas wrote that we were no better than a schoolboy side. A lot of people were saying it was one of the worst Australian sides ever. There was no real pressure on us to do well and I suppose in a way that helped us. We could relax a bit more. We had two trial games and blitzed the opposition. We had good teamwork going. The bowlers were going well, the batsmen were hitting the ball well and we were fielding well. We just had a feeling that we were going to do well. Then we won by a run in Madras. We had the biggest party of all time that night. It was as if we had already won the World Cup. It was just a great team atmosphere. We knew then we were a real chance. No-one fancied us, but I really thought we were going to win it from that moment on."

Waugh was one of the stars of Australia's Cinderella win, playing a pivotal role in each of Australia's victories and emphatically forging his Ice Man reputation with some nerveless spells in the final overs. In the opening one-run win over India he bowled Maninder Singh, who incidentally was the batsman dismissed by Greg Matthews in the Tied Test, with the second-last ball of the match. Steve was thrown the ball in the match against New Zealand for the final over with the Kiwis needing just seven runs to win and ace bat Martin Crowe 58 not out and on strike. He had Crowe caught first ball of the over and shattered keeper Ian Smith's wicket with his next. Tailenders Martin Snedden and Willie Watson grabbed quick singles before Watson was run out by Waugh in his follow-through. After the match he attributed his success to watching the way Indian great Kapil Dev had bowled at the death. In the final Steve grabbed the crucial wickets of the lethal Allan Lamb (45) and a rampant Phillip DeFreitas (17) in the 47th and 49th overs to restrict England to 8-246 and give Australia the World Cup by seven runs.

Steve thrived on his new-found role as Australia's key man in a climax. "I like to bowl the last few overs," he volunteered. "I tend to think I can win the game rather than lose it. You've got to be positive. I think there is more pressure on a batsman than a bowler when they are trying to win a game. If you keep your head it is going to be very hard for a batsman to hit fours or sixes to win the game. So I've always fancied myself in that situation. I really enjoy it. For me it is the best part of one-day cricket. It is the biggest challenge. You've got to back yourself. You can't go into those last few overs not thinking you can do it. If you're scared you're not going to do well — you've got to be positive. I really enjoy it so if there is a chance I always say 'give the ball to me. I'll give it a go. I'll back myself'. I think over the years I've probably come out in front. Bowling-wise I never feel under too much pressure. I'm not the world's greatest bowler but if it gets down to the last couple of overs I'll back myself against any batsman."

Apart from shatter-proof nerves Steve's most famous weapon has been his slower ball. That, like his Ice Man role, came about more by accident than design during a training session before a match against Western Australia at the WACA. "It was a long session in which I had been bowling for a fair while and Greg Matthews wanted a few extra minutes," Steve recalled. "I was mucking around a bit and bowled a slower ball out of the back of my hand. He was stunned. "That was a winner that ball," he said. "I couldn't pick it. You want to bowl that in a game, it's going to be a winner for you. I tried it the next day and got a wicket with it first ball (Mike Veletta) and I've stuck with it ever since. And really it came about by accident. Now I just try to work on a few variations because the guys are always looking for it."

Super-competitive Steve thrives on the challenge of bowling the pressure overs. (Gregg Porteus)

NSW team-mate Greg Matthews summed up Waugh's World Cup when he said: "Steve carried that Australian side during the World Cup in 1987. The resurgence of the team as a one-day side dates back to then."

As pivotal as his performances in Australia's World Cup win were, there is no doubt that the 1989 Ashes tour of England remains the high point of his career thus far. Having battled for years to fulfil his promise after being thrust prematurely into an embattled Test team, Steve burst into full flower with dazzling brilliance. He had been considered a little unlucky not to have made the 1985 tour despite his inexperience and received the perfect going away present in 1989 when *Wisden* named him one of its five cricketers of the year for 1988. He was the 55th Australian to earn the honour and the first since Bill Alley in 1962 to earn it solely for performances in the English County Championship. Both played for Somerset.

Steve received the honour because of his batting for the English county side the previous English summer. Somerset was floundering in the wake of the acrimonious departure of Viv Richards, Joel Garner and Ian Botham, and a serious back injury to Martin Crowe only made matters worse. Steve's appearances had previously been confined largely to limited-over games by a rule that restricted counties to just one foreign player in championship matches. But in 1988 he stepped into the breach with eight centuries in his first 30 county innings – – neither Crowe nor Richards had managed such consistency. He scored 1314 runs in 24 innings at an average of 73, finishing a close second behind the brilliant Graeme Hick in the national averages.

Captain at the time, and now respected cricket critic Peter Roebuck said Steve was of immense value as both a batsman and a tactical ally as well as being very popular with the players. "The players still talk about him," said Roebuck. "Even now you'll hear 'it'd be good to have that Aussie bugger back'. It was a young side and he was only 22 or so, but he was very mature. He mixed with them and joined in their entertainment, but at the same time he managed to be a father figure. He was very highly regarded as a cricketer and a team-mate. He didn't say much but when he spoke people listened. I valued him immensely. I thought his assessment of other players was very good. He would assess them very quickly and very coolly. There were things that weren't very obvious to me at the time and he would spot them very quickly."

Roebuck rates Waugh as a better buy for Somerset than prolific South African opener Jimmy Cook. Despite the regular avalanche of runs from Cook, Roebuck said that Somerset finished at the foot of the table the three years he was there. "Jimmy was not an outstanding overseas player for us because although he scored a mountain of runs he didn't win many matches. Steve scored less runs but won more matches. We thought he was a nervous starter but when he counter-attacked he played some absolutely dazzling and memorable innings. It was brilliant batting — often against pace and often with the tailenders — rather than a greedy accumulation of runs. Give him a situation and he'd react to it."

Roebuck finds it interesting that in a recently published book *"The Bedside Book of Cricket Centuries"*, by Terry Smith, Waugh nominated a hundred he scored for Somerset and not one of his breakthrough Ashes centuries. The innings in question occurred with Somerset down for the count against a rampaging Sylvester Clarke. Australians have not seen Clarke at anywhere near his best but his ferocious reputation is widespread in England. "The like of it has not been seen in Sheffield Shield cricket," said Roebuck. "When you get a West Indian angry on a green wicket it's something else. It wasn't an average county game, it wasn't an average county attack and it wasn't an average situation. Here was a West Indian smelling blood, the team eight down and Steve Waugh standing between them." Allan Donald is the reigning pace ace in England but he does not possess anywhere near the menace of Clarke. "Clarke is a nastier bowler," said Roebuck, who can afford an opinion like that, now that he is retired. "Name me any 20 batsmen in England and give them a chance to choose between the two and they'll pick Donald to a man. He certainly went for Steve that day."

If that innings was not extraordinary enough Waugh repeated the performance against Windies Test quick Courtney Walsh at Bristol. Again Somerset had crumbled to eight down for not much more than a hundred when Steve was joined at the wicket by useful but not particularly threatening tailender Neil Mallender. "It was a wonderful counter attack," said Roebuck. "I declared 20 runs behind because I thought I had to open the game up and Steve

English players and fans became sick of the sight of Waugh's classic back-foot drives by the end of the 1989 Ashes tour.

(Gregg Porteus)

The Waughs live for moments like these ... the Australians celebrate their Ashes victory as the winning runs are hit in the fourth Test.   (Philip Brown)

was absolutely furious. He threw his bat down on the field and when he returned to the dressing room he basically said 'what sort of game's this?' Luckily for me we got them 3-10 and in 10 minutes he'd cooled down and apologised. In fact we bowled them out and would have beaten them if Steve hadn't dropped a sitter at slip. It was interesting to see how hot he was and how involved he was.

"I played 19 seasons of first class cricket and I've played with Viv Richards, Sunil Gavaskar, Martin Crowe and Ian Botham and I would rate those two innings in the top 12 or 14 I've seen."

Waugh also scored a remarkable hundred in a 40-over one-day match against Northamptonshire. "It was a total back-to-the-wall innings," said Roebuck. "We were way out of the game and he won it from nowhere."

Roebuck feels that Steve has played his best cricket in England. "I think it's partly technique. That backfoot slash is Steve's signature and also his downfall. It's hard to play fast bowling on a bouncy wicket with an open face. But the ball doesn't rise quite so quickly or quite so sharply in England. I feel he should straight drive more and be more willing to leave the ball alone. If he played straight at the start of his innings we knew he'd get a score and if he was slashing or playing across the line we knew he'd miss out. I sometimes think he doesn't work hard enough. He's fit and trains hard but I don't know if he works hard enough on his technique. I personally believe that Steve has to keep an eye on how he is getting out, and work out whether it was necessary."

Steve kicked off the Ashes tour of 1989 with a Test average of 30.52 but not a single Test hundred. Given the pressure that had built up over the years it is no surprise that when the drought broke it did so in thunderous fashion. And neither Steve nor the anxious Australian public had to wait long. Just one innings. That elusive century came in his 42nd Test innings in the First Test at the Headingley Ground in Leeds. His chanceless hundred was brought up off just 124 deliveries in 160 minutes as Australia chalked up an incredible 373 runs in the day. He went on to score 177 not out.

He feels the time with Somerset provided a valuable grounding despite the step up in class. "I averaged about 80 playing county cricket so I knew I could score runs over there. But Test cricket is different to county cricket. I went in with a pretty positive attitude and had a little bit of luck early in that first innings. From there my confidence just grew. I was a different player after that first innings. I suppose before that I had a few doubts as to whether I was good enough to make it at the top level. Things changed after that hundred.

"I think I nicked the first ball and it fell short of first slip — I was a bit lucky there. And I was scratchy early on and then I had a couple of fours. A couple of nice shots and from that moment on I knew it was going to be my day. Everything hit the middle after that and I was very confident, relaxed. I don't think I could have played much better than that. Up until 50 I hadn't thought too much about it but once I got to 50 I thought 'you better make the most of it today'. I had got to the situation where I had probably 10 or 11 fifties under my belt going into that match so I really needed to convert one of them. I made a special effort to really concentrate and try and get a hundred in that Test. Because I knew if I didn't get one then I'd keep putting more pressure on myself and the press would keep hounding me. Things just came naturally that day. I hit 11 fours and the score just kept ticking over so I didn't have much time to think about it."

Underneath that unflappable demeanour was a turbulent whirlpool of emotions as Waugh crept closer to shaking the monkey off his back. "I had no saliva. I though if I don't get it now I'm going to collapse." When the moment of truth arrived the climax was more Python than Hollywood. Waugh said he tried to smack his chewing gum away with his bat in celebration but when it came to the big moment the man who had just flayed the best bowlers in England was not up to the task. "I spat the chewie out and went to hit and missed," he recalled sheepishly. "It was about the only thing I missed after the first couple of balls. There was one thing I always wanted to do when I got my first hundred and that was kiss my bat but I never did it. I forgot.

"Jonesy was the main partnership. We always seem to bat pretty well together. I'm pretty relaxed when I bat with Jonesy so that helped too I guess. He's good to bat with. He's always confident and he gives you a few raps at the other end. I think we both knew it was going to be our day. We just said, 'let's bury them, let's really nail them'.

"Foster was by far their best bowler. It wasn't a great attack but it wasn't an easy one either."

Waugh denies being superstitious but a change in routine seemed to do the trick that day, so not wishing to question fate, or whoever it is in charge, he adopted it as a good luck charm. "On that Ashes tour I shaved before the first Test so I was out there clean-faced and did well in that game. I stuck with that for about seven or eight Tests and then I started failing so I quit that idea."

The hundred snuffed out one of Australian cricket's most engrossing sagas of the time — or as far as the media was concerned anyway. Steve's resume had endured repeated scrutiny over the dearth of centuries, and 1989 settled that question once and for all. While he denied not scoring a hundred was affecting his game, there is no doubt about his feelings concerning the press fascination with the subject. They certainly coloured his emotions in the wake of the momentous occasion. "I had mixed feelings. I was relieved and obviously very, very happy. I was proud to score a hundred for Australia and also very happy for myself that I had proved that I could do it. I think I was more happy for myself to get the hundred just to show a few people up. I knew I was good enough to get there but sometimes something stops it. I don't know what it was. Maybe fear of success or doubting my ability. I'm not sure. But a couple of times I got in the nineties and threw it away.

"I think the press was more interested in it than I was. I knew that I should have scored a hundred before that but I'd been fairly consistent for about 10 Test matches, so I wasn't too worried. I think too much emphasis is placed on getting a hundred. It's more important to be consistent for the side when the team needs it. A good 50 when the side is 5-100 is more important than a good 100 when you're 3-400."

Despite his feelings about the press' misplaced enthusiasm, he does not deny that he let himself down in his near misses. "They were disappointing. I did the hard work, especially against the West Indies in Brisbane. It wasn't an easy wicket to bat on plus they were going in for the kill in the second innings. I only got four in the first innings and I thought that if I didn't get runs then it could be my last Test for a while. So there was a lot of pressure on that day and I got dropped when I was about 20. I suppose that was the turning point in my career. If I had got out for 20 then I might not have been sighted for the next five or 10 years. The odds were stacked against us. The ball I got out off I hit the sweetest of any shot I played that innings but it went straight to the guy at cover point. I was disappointed with that but I was more disappointed with the next 90 in Perth. I batted well again but the shot I got out to was disappointing. It was a real weak shot. You don't get the opportunity to get many hundreds against those blokes so I suppose I blew two of them."

The occasion of Steve's breakthrough in England was complicated a little by Rodger's being in hospital. Steve's father had been hit by a mystery illness shortly before the Test match began — hardly the ideal preparation. "I was in hospital for two weeks," he said. "It wasn't a stroke, they couldn't find out what it was. I went in the first of June, it was the boys' birthday on the second and Steve got his hundred on the third. Steve rang up on his birthday and I said I was in hospital and not to worry and the next day he got the 177. It was fantastic."

There is no doubt in the celebrations that followed, big and small, that Steve was not the only relieved one. His father spoke for all those who had sat anxiously on the sidelines, agonising through each step of his painful progress. "He'd struggled to get it. He batted well a lot of times, got a couple of nineties. He got out to two great catches against the West Indies. Steve's always got out to unbelievable catches. He's been unlucky in that respect."

And there is also no doubt that, despite his protests, a tremendous weight had been lifted from his shoulders. "I probably enjoyed my cricket more than I had previously. The press was off my back. I was more relaxed and confident to play my own game. I know I can score a hundred every time I go out to bat."

It certainly seemed that way at the time. Waugh walked out in his next innings and flayed the England attack for another hundred, this time an unbeaten 152 at Lord's. He came to the wicket with the score at a worrying 4-221 and was still standing when the innings was finally terminated for 528.

"Scoring a hundred at Lord's was a dream come true," said Steve. "It is the home of cricket, you can feel it. The second innings was also more valuable for the team. Neil Foster bowled a really good spell and I had to bat well to overcome that. The innings was a bit more subdued. I had to work harder for my runs. I put on a couple of hundred with the last three or four batsmen which put us in a winning position so it was more of a team innings for me than the first one. But I think the second one I was more relaxed and when I got it it wasn't the same feeling as the first one, that's for sure. I knew once I got a hundred I had to get another one just to make up for all the hard times."

In his Headingley hundred Steve had enjoyed the company of Merv Hughes, who scored his second successive Test 70. At Lord's he was joined by NSW skipper Geoff Lawson. He

Steve and Dean Jones, Christmas 1990.   (Gregg Porteus)

also notched 70 but in the end the excitement got too much for old Henry. "He said, 'I wonder who was the last batsman to get a hundred in a session at Lord's," said Steve. "Of course the next ball he got caught. I think he got a bit cocky, the big fella."

Lawson may never have made it that far but for a bit of luck. Waugh's ton was also consummated in less than dignified fashion. "I nearly ran Henry out getting it," Steve admitted. "It was a suicide single. I wasn't too concerned about him. Geoff would have been run out by five yards."

Such was Waugh's form that the English press, about the only section of British society apparently not constrained by the reticence and decorum that is so much a part of being British, really went to town after his Lord's century. Headlines such as "The new Aussie ace", "The new Don Bradman", Run-machine Steve", "Declaration of Waugh", "All out Waugh", "Post Waugh Depression" gushed forth. And, to be fair, they didn't spare their own team when they ran out of martial puns: "England's Flops Face Another Shameful Shambles" and "Gower's Losers", to name just a couple of tasteful samples.

Having already endured similar praise when he burst into first class and Test cricket Waugh found it relatively easy to cope with all the hype. "It is nice to have those comments made about you but you know yourself what you can do and what you can't do and who you should and shouldn't be compared to. You can't start to believe it or you're gone. They were writing me up as the new Bradman but that's bull. You know in your heart how you are going so you don't worry about what the press is saying. You've got to back your own ability."

When Waugh was finally dismissed in the first innings of the third Test at Edgbaston in Birmingham he had scored more runs (393) without being dismissed than any other player in the 112 years of Ashes battles. At the end of the series he had become only the fifth Australian to score more than 500 runs in a Test series and average more than 100, scoring 506 runs at an average of 126.5. He wasn't keeping bad company either — Sir Donald Bradman, Neil Harvey, Doug Walters and Greg Chappell.

In 1930 Bradman scored 974 runs, including the then-world record of 334 thrashed at Headingley, at an average of 113.12. Amazingly Waugh scored his at a faster rate, 3.76 runs an over to 3.70 by The Don.

Even now Steve is not too sure about what went right in England. "I think I was just in a confident mood. I suppose my shot selection was good looking back. I didn't play too many rash shots and defended well. When you're going badly you pick your game to pieces but when you're going well you don't worry about it."

The atmosphere in the touring party may have had something to do with it.

"It was a perfect tour. A great bunch of blokes. There wasn't an argument in four and a half months. There'll never be a tour like that again."

Rodger Waugh was visiting his parents when Steve was dropped for Mark at the completion of the Third Ashes Test against England at the SCG just 18 months later.

"I was up with my parents at Ballina at the time," Rodger recalled. "Bev rang up and said: 'Mark's in the team'. I said 'that's great' and she said, 'well Steve's the one who's made way for him', so that put a bit of a damper on the situation. I didn't know whether to feel happy or unhappy or what. I was happy for Mark of course. But it was hard to get too excited and feel sorry for Steve at the same time. Steve took it very well. I think it was a bit unfair, he was a bit stiff. It always irks me to think Dean Jones gets such a good run."

The fall of the axe was more of a disappointment than a shock to the man who had been crowned Ashes hero little more than a year previously. "I half expected it," said Steve, who thought he may have gained a reprieve with an impressive first innings effort in that Test.

Steve batting at Old Trafford in 1989. England captain David Gower has dived at the ball, the keeper is Jack Russell.
(Philip Brown)

"I batted well the first day for 48 and thought I was on my way before I got a good one from Devon Malcolm. I played a bad shot in the second dig and got out and thought 'that's it, I'm going to be dropped'. I was disappointed, I thought a few blokes would go with me, but it doesn't really sink in until the plane's ready to leave and you're not on it. But there's no point in feeling sorry for yourself. In a way it was a bit of a relief because the longer it dragged on the worse it would have been. I was feeling the pinch."

True to the Waugh ethic of personal integrity and strength Steve delivered the twin bombshells to Mark himself. "He just came around to mum's place and said: 'Congratulations, you're in the team'. I said 'Oh, what, the Test team. Who got dropped?' and he said 'me'. I just said 'oh, bad luck' and he said 'don't worry about it'. There was a stunned silence for a couple of minutes. It was sort of tense. Mum congratulated me and sat there not really saying too much. Stephen was the one who actually spoke the most."

On the surface it is an almost banal exchange. The impact comes when you think of what was left unsaid and what must have been felt. Bev's maxim "actions speak louder than words" never rang truer than it did that night.

Chris Madden, a former junior representative team-mate, said he was stunned by Steve's composure when he rang the night his axing was announced. Not even the derailing of his dream could disrupt Waugh's natural tendency to turn the focus of a conversation on his mates. Steve rang Madden, whom he had not spoken to for a while, and asked him to come and look at some tiling work he needed done on his new house. "That night he rang me up and said, 'well, I've got plenty of spare time so do you want to drop around and have a look at it?' It wasn't, 'I'm dirty on the bastards for dropping me'. And all he wanted to know was how I was and what I'd been up to."

Yet again Steve needed support but it is a commodity he has found as plentiful as the tough times he has had to endure. Apart from his family he has counted former greats Bill O'Reilly and Hunter "Stork" Hendry among his supporters as well as fast bowler Dennis Lillee and media personality Alan Jones. Then there are his NSW team-mates.

"NSW is pretty good," said Steve. "You all help each other out, but early on in my career Greg Matthews was good. He tends to take new blokes under his wing and show them the ropes and stuff. He was good, he gave us a lot of advice. He was always good with encouragement. But you always had good mates who would help you out. When I got dropped from the Test side I had probably eight or nine guys from the Australian side ring

Mark celebrates with Greg Matthews after he had scored a century and Matthews starred with 95 not out and four wickets against Jamaica on the 1991 West Indies tour. (Gregg Porteus)

me up. Lynette kept a list of who rang. That way you find out who your friends are. It gives you a bit of a guide, anyway. People always hang around when you are doing well but you soon find out when you're not going well who are your supporters and who'd back you."

While his wife is amazed at the loyalty Steve gives and receives from his friends he doesn't believe he deserves any special credit for the way he treats them. "I don't see that as strange," he says. "You get to find out who your friends are when you play top-level sport." Lynette remarked that they had lost friends since Steve broke into the big time. "They haven't been friends," said Steve. "That's why we lost them. Most of my friends, I know are good friends."

Waugh admits to being surprised at the reaction of his Australian team-mates. "It did surprise me. A lot of other guys have been dropped before and I don't know if they had the same response. It's nice, I suppose. It's a mark of respect, and a sign that people hold you in pretty high regard. It's nice to know you've got good friends."

He briefly returned to the Test XI on the subsequent tour of the West Indies and after waiting patiently was given his chance in the Third Test at Trinidad. That meant, of course, another milestone. The Waughs became the first pair of twins ever to play in a Test. The pair combined for a half-century partnership before Steve was dismissed for 21. Again it was more of a media event than a special event for the twins, and Steve played down its significance. "I didn't think about it. I don't think either of us thought it was special, wasn't any big deal. When it happened I thought it was nice but at the time I was just concentrating on the Test."

Steve's fight to win back his Test spot has been hampered by a back injury in recent seasons. It restricted his bowling for quite a while and there are some NSW team-mates who feel that he has not been able to regain the zip he once showed on a regular basis. Still he is not complaining about his unlucky run. Neither is he asking for any applause for the way he has fought to overcome the injury.

"I've had a pretty good run really," he said. "I think you've got to put up with a lot of injuries if you want to play. I mean, if you want to pull out you can probably pull out of 80 per cent of the games through an injury, but you've got to take them into the game if you want to play. You can't afford to let some guy jump in your spot. Some injuries spur you on to play better. If you have a sore finger it makes you concentrate much better. So sometimes it can even help but you don't pull out because of a niggling injury."

One of his few regrets is that he did not train diligently as a youngster. "I'm obviously better in the last two years. I really had to change. I coasted along when I was young. We got along on our fitness because we played every day and we trained every day. I think when I started bowling it affected my body. I really had to change my attitude in the last couple of years. Now I think I'm up there with the best trainers going around. I train pretty regularly now. Injuries take a lot longer to heal so you've got to become more aware. Guys like Mike Whitney and Geoff Lawson played through to their mid-thirties while other guys have fallen by the wayside because their fitness hasn't been up to scratch or they haven't trained hard enough. So it's just a matter of looking at those guys and seeing what they have done.

"I've had a bit of help the last couple of years from a bloke who has looked after me, Nigel Websdale. He's done a lot of good work for me over the years. He rang me up when I had the back problems and said 'I've been reading about you in the papers, has anyone done anything about it? I'm willing to help. I can get you a training program'. A lot of people don't like his methods because he's not really qualified but you've really got to find out who is

Steve and Mark take a break during their historic first Test innings together. (Gregg Porteus)

best for you and if they work you go ahead with it. I've found he's been good for me so I'm happy with him. I think without him I wouldn't have made it through the last 18 months. I would have broken down at some stage again."

Having seemingly beaten his career-threatening back injury Steve is now facing squarely up to the challenge of winning back a Test batting position. "That's the next big test, to see if I'm good enough to get back. It's harder than first being picked. I've got to stick it up a few people this year."

Next to an Ashes tour of England the West Indies, Australia's opponents for the 1992-93 summer, are the ideal opponents for a Waugh comeback bid. "I like playing against the West Indies because you've got to be really competitive against those guys," he said. "You've got to be aggressive and that's how I like to play cricket. I don't like sitting back and letting things pan out. I like to try to make things happen and get in there and do my fair share."

But doing his fair share and scoring prolifically may not be enough if the Australian

(Philip Brown)

batsmen can hold the line and prosper against the West Indies pace attack. The perception that Steve has struggled since he was dropped from the side is in danger of becoming as weighty a burden as was his supposed inability to score hundreds earlier in his career. While there was at least a statistical basis for those hypotheses and question marks, the current "weakness" is pure fallacy. In the 1991-92 summer, when he did not play a Test match, he scored 448 runs in nine Shield innings at an average of more than 50. Included in those nine innings were two hundreds and two fifties. Added to that were his consistent performances for the Australian one-day side in the lower order.

"For people to say this guy is scared or technically deficient is grossly off the mark," said Matthews.

Waugh was happy with the contribution he made in Australia's unhappy World Cup defence. "I felt I batted well. I might only have averaged 25 but I got 20s all the time. I felt I was one of the better Australian batsmen in the World Cup and one of the best in the whole competition batting six or seven."

He is just as confident that he will make it back. "Looking at who's in the side now I know that I'm as good as anyone and if I put my mind to it I know I can make it back there. It is frustrating watching a Test match knowing that I could be there doing the job as well as they are. I don't particularly want to watch too many more Test matches, I want to play them. There is only one way you can do that and that's play hard and do well on the field. I like playing for NSW, but the ultimate is to play for Australia.

"I don't want to be labelled as a one-day cricketer. That's a bit of an unfair tag. Simon O'Donnell and Peter Taylor have probably suffered a bit from that. O'Donnell's had some pretty good performances over the last couple of years but he is never really talked about as playing in Test matches. I think you can get labelled pretty quickly if you don't do something about it. I don't think it's happened to me but I think I'm in danger of it. I haven't missed a one-day game in seven years. I might have been 12th man once but I've played in every other game Australia's played in the last seven years. But I think a lot of people forget I've played 44 Test matches and I'm still only 27. I don't want to be considered just a one-day player. I don't want to end my career having played 300 one-day games and 44 Test matches.

"I also wouldn't like to finish my cricket career and have everybody talking about the 1989 Ashes tour. The World Cup in 1987 stands out for me as well as the Shield finals. I don't want to be remembered for one tour, as the bloke who went well overseas and failed in Australia. I hope to rectify that. Hopefully there'll be plenty more tours and plenty more opportunities to do well for Australia."

(Gregg Porteus)

TWELVE

Twin Ambitions

WHILE Steve was finally enjoying his day in the sun in 1989 brother Mark was laying the foundations of his successful entry into Test cricket. His had been a long wait and when the time came it would be in circumstances completely the reverse of Stephen's. While his twin had been rushed into the Test side as a callow rookie Mark was forced to compile 7501 first class runs before the door opened. During Steve's wondrous 1989 English summer Mark was sharpening his skills with English county side Essex. A hit-and-run visit the season before, when Essex gave Mark a trial at the end of the summer on Allan Border's recommendation, had enabled the two parties to sound one another out. Mark then came back and did the business in 1989. He scored more than 1500 runs in the county championship, averaged 43.91 in first class cricket, and he topped the Sunday League averages.Most satisfying would probably have been his 100 not out for Essex against the touring Australians — a score which Steve, of course, matched for Australia.

As impressive as his performances were that season, he was still not able to step out of the shadow of his brother. During the English summer Mark had clawed his way to the top of the first class averages but the satisfaction was dulled somewhat by an error that saw them published with the initials S.R. rather than M.E. More was to come upon his return to Australia — and from people who should have known better. NSW Cricket Association president Alan Davidson, the great Test allrounder, was speaking at the official launch of the new season and during his speech acknowledged the personalities present. After mentioning Geoff Lawson and Peter Taylor he said: "I saw Steve Waugh earlier ... I'm not sure if Mark's here". In fact it was Mark sitting a few tables away and Steve was nowhere to be seen.

He enjoyed a tremendously successful Australian summer, scoring 1009 runs at 77.61, and was named NSW Cricketer of the Year and Sheffield Shield Player of the Year — a double honour he had also taken out in 1987-88 with 833 runs at 64.08 and four hundreds. Now it was off to finishing school. All the old criticisms still hung to Mark like so much old baggage and he was determined to dump them once and for all. He couldn't have done it in more emphatic fashion. So successful was he with Essex in 1990 that Mark equalled his twin's achievement when he was named one of *Wisden*'s cricketers of the year. He scored 2072 first class runs for Essex at an average of 76.74 which *Wisden* said, "even in a summer of indulgence for batsmen, showed him to be a performer of the highest calibre".

Highlights of his rampage were 204 against a Gloucestershire side featuring Windies veteran Courtney Walsh, 125 against Walsh's fearsome young team-mate Ian Bishop and Derby, 125 against Windies great Malcolm Marshall and Hampshire, and a limited-over century against a Lancashire attack spearheaded by Pakistan's talented Wasim Akram. All up he thrashed eight hundreds, including the first two double centuries of his first class career.

"It was the best thing he did, going to England, it really turned his game around," said NSW team-mate Mike Whitney. "Graham Gooch helped him in that respect but he doesn't talk about him much. He has said to me that Gooch, Neil Foster, Derek Pringle and Paul Prichard all helped him at Essex."

Gooch, Essex and England captain, is unstinting in his praise of Waugh. In his own gentle, no-nonsense way he has nothing but good things to say about Mark.

"I think he has the potential to be one of the best players of his generation," said Gooch.

Neil Foster, the Essex and England fast bowler, has seen both Waughs develop their extraordinary talents in English county cricket. He rates Mark the better batsman and Steve the better bowler.

"He's got his best years to come as a batsman. You learn a lot, I think, from your early twenties until about 25, 27. Once you get to that age I think you've got a bit of maturity, a bit of experience you've gained in those years before, and you're still young and fit. You've got your best seven or eight years in front of you. I'll be very surprised if he doesn't end up with a very, very good Test record.

"He was unlucky to start with in that he had to wait a while to break into international cricket. And that was, obviously, no fault of his own. It was just that Australia had, and still has, a very powerful array of batsmen to select from and there was a lot of competition there.

"We were very lucky here in Essex to pick him up on the recommendation of one or two people in Australia, Allan Border included, and we've been delighted with him. I think he's a top-class batsman, he's got classical technique, and he's a very nice fellow as well. He's very important to us here at Essex. And coupled with that he bowls a bit and he's as good a fieldsman as I've ever seen. So as an all-round cricketer I've got nothing but praise for him.

"Mark got off on the right foot cricket-wise with Essex, scoring a hundred in his first match, a Sunday League fixture at the county's Chelmsford home ground. "It was obvious then that he was a class player, a good fielder," said Gooch.

The England captain, despite the influence he has undoubtedly had on Mark's maturing as a Test-quality player, was unwilling to claim any of the credit. He said the opportunities to learn provided by the English system have simply speeded up Mark's development, just as they have helped many other imported cricketers.

"With overseas cricketers playing as many matches as they do here, it can't help but improve their game," Gooch said. "You get to play 20-odd first class matches a season and probably 30 one-day games. So the learning process is speeded up. And you learn in all sorts of conditions. You play on slow wickets that turn, green wickets that do a bit. I think he has improved a lot over the last two or three years. I wouldn't say coming here has made him a class player. I think that would have happened anyway, but I certainly think playing here has done him no harm."

Gooch dismissed any doubts about Mark's mental toughness. "He has been an absolute pleasure to play with. He's tried his bollocks off and he's done well for us. He's a nice lad and I don't think it is, personally, a fault. I like guys who are nice guys and fit in. We at Essex pride ourselves on the players we've had here. They're good in the dressing room and they're good with other players. We've been very lucky. And the success we've had at the club over the last 10 years has been helped no end by our overseas players."

Australian cricket has a much more aggressive ethic than English county cricket but the naturally competitive Waugh didn't have any troubles fitting in, according to Essex top order bat Paul Prichard. "I think he fitted in perfectly. I don't think he is an overly aggressive person anyway. He bats aggressively and he fields and bowls particularly aggressively but his nature is not one to upset people unduly. He's a very competitive cricketer with a very nice nature."

Prichard also scoffed at any suggestions that Mark lacks a little ticker. "Never. Not one game can I remember when he hasn't put in, batting, bowling or fielding. It's definitely not part of Mark Waugh's make-up not to do his best. I think everybody can look back to their younger days and say they were probably too soft. I think a lot of it is a lack of experience. Now that he has more experience he does seem to view situations differently which makes him a better player. I don't think he has ever been soft. I don't think it has ever been in his nature to be soft on a cricket field. I think 'pure elegance' would be a better way of putting it than saying 'casual'."

Mark sheds his easy-going tag when he gets the ball in his hand.

(Philip Brown)

Mark says the worst 'dummy-spit' he has ever done in a dressing room is to swear. He has never thrown his bat or gloves or smashed things and can't understand why other players do it. "If I ever got upset it would be bowling. I'm pretty aggressive. It helps me, it's just the adrenalin rush. I've said stupid things to umpires and players but I've never been fined. I didn't do it as a kid and I tend to do it more in grade. If I've got respect for a player then I won't say anything but if I don't think much of a player and he carries on I'll say something.

"If I was a fast bowler I'd be pretty nasty. I have got enough pace to stick it to batsmen. I can't stand when we get bounced and our fast bowlers don't give it back to them. I think it's important to show you're not intimidated. If a fast bowler comes in to bat I'll give him some."

That aggression means Mark has to watch himself in county cricket. And it also means he is uncomfortable with the attitude of many players on the circuit. "You're not allowed to swear; it's not expected, especially in county cricket. You just can't get away with it. Because it's a job they expect you all to be happy, you're all trying to make money. It hasn't been hard to tone down my aggression but I have been warned by umpires once or twice. The thing is they play so much, games run into one another, they just meander along. One of the problems is that a lot of players are happy just to turn up, score their 1000 runs at 35 and get paid."

"In the field he gets aggressive," agreed veteran quick Neil Foster. "If, for instance, we're not fielding well that niggles him; to see his team-mates letting themselves down upsets him. And he gets quite upset when he bowls. He's very fiery; there's a complete change around when he's got a ball in his hand. You throw him the ball in a situation where you want something to happen and he'll try to make it happen all right."

Foster noted improvement in Mark's bowling, feeling he wasn't so keen to roll his arm over when he first arrived at Essex because of a back injury. Still, he says Mark's potential remains largely unfulfilled.

"Every ball he tries something different instead of actually settling down to bowl within the limitations of line and length at the pace he can bowl," Foster said. "He wants to bowl somebody out with every ball and it doesn't work that way. Consequently he bowls too many bad balls. He's probably more talented with the ball than he often appears. I think the reason is he tries too much, he thinks he can do things he can't quite do. If he knuckles down he'll be able to do the things he's trying to do. He just hasn't given himself much chance yet."

Foster is well-placed to comment on both brothers, having played with each of them at Essex and against Steve for England. Foster is an intelligent cricketer whose experience of both cricket and cricketers makes him more than qualified to offer a view or two on the twins.

"I knew Steve as a youngster at Essex," said Neil. "He did bloody well; he obviously could play at that stage. He got 200 in a 50-over game playing Second XI. He was quite a quiet boy. He's had that sour look about him which isn't necessarily the way he really is. You always think to yourself there's something more to him; he's not a straight-up-and-down guy you can just sum up. Whereas Mark, who is still quiet, is much more a plain sort of guy. He's pretty much as you see him.

"Of the two I'd always prefer to watch Mark. He's got that certain flair and is a far, far better back foot player than Steve.

"Steve did particularly well last time he was here, we probably saw him at his best. He's also quite a flamboyant player. He's the sort of guy who once he gets in he's going to make you pay. Sometimes Mark just gets a little bit slack and plays a lazy shot and gets caught at mid-wicket or drags one on. That's the way he gets out rather than bowled out. Steve on the other hand probably has more technical weaknesses but you've still got to bowl hard at him to get him out.

"It's a crying shame really that whenever Mark's got in Steve's had to be left out because they're both great players and to be competing for the same spot is a bit cruel really. I'm certain Steve'll come back and in the years to come they'll play a lot of Tests together. Mark's a better batter and Steve's a better bowler and although they're competing for the same spot by and large I feel it's weakened the Australian bowling strength not having Steve there. He's done a good, steady job most of the time whereas I think Mark's a bit more hit and miss."

In addition to playing with him at Essex Foster and his wife Rom, and Prichard and his wife Jo-Anne, have become very close to Mark and companion Sue off the field.

"I think he was always very confident about his own ability but it was more deep down inside him," said Prichard. "These days he seems a lot more confident person on and off the field. A lot more confident with people he doesn't know. Just a little bit more outgoing. In the early days he wasn't too keen on wearing a tie and shirt and blazer to every game. It wasn't his cup of tea at first but that's also changed a lot. He's been transformed into one of the smartest members of the team."

Foster agreed. "Certainly since he's played Test cricket and become a Test star he's changed as a person, because he's become more confident," he said. "He's still basically a quiet fellow but the shyness he had when he first came here is gone. He's more than happy to stand up for himself. He's probably a slightly better player than when he first came here but he's more confident about his game. His whole persona has become more confident. He's got more ability to actually dominate attacks. When he first got here he'd play the bowling on its merits but wouldn't actually look to dominate. Now I think he goes out trying to make a point early on."

Foster agreed that Mark hasn't learned any magical secrets in England, also citing the benefits of simply playing more. For example, in June 1992 Essex had just six days off from the gruelling county championship, Sunday League and Natwest trophy competitions — and they got one of those days only because of their shock first round defeat in the Benson and Hedges Cup. And that does not take into account any matches they may have had to play for Derek Pringle's benefit year.

"Coming here and having a lot of innings helps an overseas player," said Foster. "Obviously they're good players when they come here anyway, it just gives them an opportunity to play more innings and generally experience the ups and downs of the game. Mark has definitely improved, probably in the sense that he gives his wicket away more dearly now. Like anyone he looks at his average but he's never going to let his average dictate the way he plays."

"His batting has probably become a lot tighter in certain areas, and coupled with his natural flair and elegance, it has made him a better player," Prichard offered. "Mark had cut out a lot of the shots that may have got him out in the past."

"The fact we've asked him back even though he's going to miss the last seven games of the season says something about the way we rate him," said Foster. "We could have gone for other overseas players and had them for the whole season. We've taken a gamble he'll do enough in the time he's here."

Peter Roebuck, through the links he built up over all those seasons with Somerset as well as his writing, has the opportunity to canvas a broad range of opinion and he comes up with an answer that may surprise the few people who remain unconvinced of Mark's credentials.

"Mark would be one of the best two or three overseas players in county cricket as a match winner, along with Carl Hooper and Malcolm Marshall," he said. "The thing overseas players need to do is turn matches which is why the Waugh brothers have been such outstanding characters. In England Mark is regarded as a very hungry batsman — hungrier than Dean Jones."

"It was certainly a good opportunity for me," said Mark of his time at Essex. "When I was picked to play for Essex I had played only a limited amount of first class cricket. It was pretty unusual for a county to sign an overseas player who hadn't played Test cricket. I was surprised when they asked me. I definitely think it helped my cricket. They've got the world's best bowlers playing over there. All the West Indians and South Africans. It was a good learning process because you play so much cricket in different conditions and different formats. It's like a job really — the more you do it, the better you get at it."

Mark certainly doesn't believe English cricket holds the mysterious key to better cricket. There were no special tricks he learned or secrets that were passed on by wise old county pros. "I just got more experienced in a shorter time. Because I've played so many games it's quickened up the process of learning how to play first class cricket and how to work my own game out. Stuff like learning to play the right shot at the right time. And there's a certain amount of pressure being an overseas player. The supporters expect you to do well all the time and having Allan Border there two years before was a fair pair of boots to fill. So I learned to play under pressure as well."

Whatever the pressure on overseas professionals Waugh escaped the worst of it at Essex because he benefited from support within the team. Essex is much like NSW, in an English sort of way. The dressing room is jovial and all the players, whatever their personal quirks, get on. They are not forcing themselves to be pleasant, they actually enjoy each others' company. Combined with the positive atmosphere is the influence of such level-headed old pros as Gooch, Foster, John Childs, Derek Pringle and coach Keith Fletcher. There were undoubtedly benefits to playing under England's captain, but Waugh said he did not get too much direct instruction from Gooch.

"Directly he was not a big influence. But just watching him go about his game is a bonus. A bloke at the age he is, and he's just so hungry for cricket. The way he practises and his attitude towards the game. He's an attacking batsman and a good sportsman. He always gives 100 per cent. He always plays to win but he plays fair. If we were chasing 320 to win in 40 overs he'd go for it. He's said a few things to me along the way but he hasn't actually coached me or tried to change my game or anything."

A lot may have changed for Mark but he still holds dear his distrust of coaches and the accompanying belief in his own ability. "You've got to work the game out for yourself. I've been fairly successful at first class level so I don't see a big need to change my game at this stage. If I just keep playing the way I have been playing the last few years hopefully that should be good enough at Test level."

Mark needed all that self-belief and strength to keep his game on track while waiting for a crack at Test cricket. The frustration of knowing you are good enough can be burden enough, but the accompanying press speculation has proved too much of a distraction for many young cricketers over the years. By simply continuing to score runs, despite going unrewarded, Mark delivered a silent, but nonetheless emphatic, message to those who thought he didn't deserve a Test cap because of doubts about his temperament.

"I tried not to let it worry me," said Mark. "I had a couple of good seasons with NSW but I saw it was going to be hard to get in and I had to keep scoring runs. I thought my chance

The twins have combined for many special partnerships over the years but none quite like their world-record rampage against Western Australia in December, 1990.

would eventually come if I scored enough runs. That's how it turned out. But I don't really know if I was ready for Test cricket two years before or not. They might have picked me at the right time. It's hard to say really. It was good in a way that I had so much first class experience, so many runs under my belt, first-class hundreds, when I did get picked for Australia. When I was picked I was a bit surprised actually. I didn't think they would choose me. It came as a shock even though I expected it at some stage."

Mark says despite the frustrations he never got discouraged. "I thought about it sometimes and was disappointed I wasn't getting a chance but I was enjoying playing cricket and scoring runs for NSW so I didn't really think about it that much to be honest. I knew in the end if I kept putting runs on the board they couldn't ignore me forever. But I knew if I wasn't getting runs for NSW there was no chance. So I just kept scoring runs."

The straw that broke the camel's back, or rather got him through the eye of the needle, was Mark's prolific burst of early-season form in Australia in late 1990. What was essentially a solid run of scores was capped off and overshadowed by a sting in the tail. He had started with 49 against Tasmania in Sydney and followed that with 15 and 12 for the Australian XI against England in Hobart and 74 and 65 against touring Kiwi champions Wellington in Sydney. That meant he needed just 150 runs in the final match of 1990 against Western Australia in Perth to become the 10th Australian to score 3000 first class runs in a calendar year. An indication of the difficulty of the task was the fact that the previous season NSW team-mate Mark Taylor (3092) had become the first Australian in 25 years to achieve the feat. A daunting challenge to be sure but one which the destiny-chasing Waugh brushed aside with contempt. He combined with Steve for a world-record fifth wicket partnership of 464 runs in just 407 minutes and finished 229 not out, hammering 35 boundaries and one huge six off Ken MacLeay.

Mark's 1990 total of 3079 placed him 10th on the list behind Sir Donald Bradman (4368 in 1930, 3838 in 1938, 3193 in 1948), Neil Harvey (3506 in 1953), Charlie Macartney (3147 in 1921), Victor Trumper (3130 in 1902), Bill Lawry (3122 in 1964), Taylor and Bob Simpson (3081 in 1961). Only Bradman (97.06 in '30, 112.88 in '38 and 99.78 in '48) had averaged better than Mark's 81.02.

That WACA innings was an absolute gem. A chanceless innings is rare enough but when two batsmen tear apart an attack the calibre of Western Australia's for almost seven hours and don't give one chance, that is a truly momentous event. Greg Growden wrote in the *Sydney Morning Herald* after the first day's play: "The best bowling attack in Australia was reduced to a gibbering rabble because of the pair's inexhaustible batting talents."

The swathe of records the twins cut down in their time at the crease bears eloquent testimony. It broke the world record fifth wicket partnership previously held by Don Bradman and Sid Barnes, scored against the Englishmen in the Second Test of the 1946-47 series at the SCG. It was an Australian first class record for any wicket, beating the previous mark of 462 scored by David Hookes and Wayne Phillips against Tasmania at Adelaide in 1986. When he got the nod to replace Steve at the end of January 1991 Mark had scored 487 runs at an average of 121.75 in Sheffield Shield cricket so far that summer. It was a genuine crossroads for the pair. Since then, allowing for the odd rise and fall, Mark has enjoyed an overall positive career path while Steve has battled to shake a variety of career-threatening perceptions, despite continuing to score prolifically. At the time of Mark's selection he had scored 7501 runs in exactly 100 first class matches at an average of 55.15 with 25 centuries and 33 fifties. Steve, in comparison, had scored 7086 runs in 122 matches at 44.57 with 19 centuries and 32 fifties. He had also taken 156 wickets at 31.99 to Mark's 64 at 41.50.

"It was a hard situation obviously because I took Stephen's spot," said Mark. "Naturally you've got feelings for your family. I was disappointed that Stephen was dropped. It took a little bit of gloss off it at the time. Mum and Dad were obviously upset for Stephen and happy for me so it was a bit of a tricky situation. But once I got over that I knew I had to do the job for myself and my team. I had waited so long to get a chance so I wanted to make the most of it. It's that sort of game. Unfortunately you can't feel sorry for even your brother for too long. It would be great if we were both in the team. That would be the ideal situation. But I think you realise that sometimes that's not going to happen."

Things didn't get any easier for the twins the next day. NSW was playing South Australia in a Sheffield Shield match at the Sydney Cricket Ground and despite appearing bound for outright victory the Blues succumbed to the weird, frenzied atmosphere that surrounded the Waughs that day and almost lost the match. Croweater quick Colin Miller did the damage, scything through the NSW batting with six wickets in 10 balls. "I remember the next day at lunchtime there were plenty of cameras," said Mark. "I couldn't concentrate on the day's cricket. People were asking us to stand next to each other and pose for photos. It wasn't very comfortable. One of them asked Stephen to smile and he said 'what have I got to smile about?' It was no surprise to see us not get too many runs that day. There were so many things happening. The phone in the dressing room was ringing every five minutes. All the media wanted to speak to us. It was a bit unfair on the team, we couldn't really concentrate on the cricket."

There was no formal celebration of Mark's long-awaited breakthrough. There wasn't any time. He and Sue shared a bottle of champagne with his parents at his house the night before he left to go to Adelaide. It was probably a mixed blessing because the lack of time and the media avalanche meant he couldn't stew too much about the coming challenge.

"I didn't have that much time to think because there was so much media attention," Mark volunteered. "It was all a bit much really. I didn't have time to think about my cricket at all. Once I got to practice it was just like normal. I wasn't that nervous. I took the phone off the hook. I was rooming with Merv Hughes. He thought he was my bloody secretary, my answering service. Actually it was good rooming with Merv. He was funny and light-hearted, always cracking jokes. He kept a good atmosphere in the room."

There were no special plans or goals that had been devised and revised during Mark's years waiting patiently in the wilderness. Interestingly, his experience meant he went into his debut in a markedly different frame of mind to Steve. "I was just going to play the way I had played for the last couple of years," he said. "There was no reason to change. After all it is only the same game of cricket. I didn't set any goals, just to do my best and see what

Opposite page: Australian captain Allan Border delivers a well-deserved pat on the back after Mark's marvellous debut century.

Left: Mark relaxes after the stunning opening to his Test career; top: Ian Healy; above: Greg Matthews.

(All photos by Gregg Porteus)

happens. But I was confident of doing well because I was in pretty good form. I think that helped."

Despite the trying circumstances of his elevation to the Test team Mark responded in inspiring fashion. He became just the 15th Australian to score a Test century on debut — the 13th against England and the first against any country since Wayne Phillips, who scored 159 against Pakistan at Perth in 1983-84. It was an innings forged in the most difficult circumstances, his captain Allan Border and leading batsman Dean Jones having just been dismissed in the space of four deliveries and the alarm bells a deafening clamour with the side 4-104. Soon the score was 5-124, but Mark went on the offensive with the help of Blues team-mate Greg Matthews.

He brought his half-century up with consecutive boundaries off English left-arm orthodox spinner Phil Tufnell, part of a sequence of five fours in just 10 deliveries, and his century with another boundary off the hapless spinner. The magic moment came 176 minutes into his innings. As if he had not achieved enough, Mark went within five runs of a century in the final session, but was denied that honour when a cautious Border called his batsmen off at 6pm with five overs still to be bowled. When English quick Devon Malcolm forced Mark to play a short ball onto his stumps the next day he had scored 138 runs.

Waugh received support from a surprising quarter when he entered the cauldron — England batsman Robin Smith. "Robin has always been a pretty good friend and when I went in to bat he said something like 'now's the time to release the handbrake, champ'. I can remember the team was in trouble but I never really thought about that. I just thought about batting normally. I didn't think 'we've got to get our heads down here and guts it out'. I just thought about playing my natural game and getting on top of the bowlers because it was a very good wicket. There was no reason why we should have been 5-124. It was a good day for batting. As the innings went on I got more and more confident. It's probably one of the best innings I have played in any sort of cricket, as far as hitting the ball really well. I can't remember mishitting a ball. Everything I hit went for four. I saw the ball clearly that day. It was like a dream come true I suppose, getting a century on your debut and getting it — I don't know whether easily is the word — but without too much fuss."

Former Test great and respected commentator Richie Benaud described Mark's debut as simply magnificent in Sydney's *Daily Telegraph Mirror* the following day. He said he found it difficult to recall a better innings on debut in Test cricket. And there is probably no-one better qualified to make that remark.

English expert Henry Blofeld said in *The Weekend Australian*: "It was an incredibly impressive first Test innings. From the moment he straight drove his second ball from Phillip DeFreitas for three he really looked the part. One can pay him no greater compliment than to say he made the art of batting look absurdly easy. His footwork was good, the placing of his strokes was excellent and he has a marvellous natural sense of timing.

"The only other first Test innings I have seen which compared to the authority of Waugh's and also matched it for power and elegance of strokes was played by West Indian Lawrence Rowe. In the first Test of the 1971-72 series against New Zealand — played at Sabina Park in Kingston — Rowe made 214 in the first innings and 100 not out in the second of a drawn match. I have never seen a much broader or straighter bat than Rowe's in those two innings."

Waugh himself backs up that imposing accolade with a comparison of his debut hundred with the one he scored on the harrowing 1991 tour of the West Indies. Despite the awesome opposition and the physical and psychological battering he and the team had endured, Mark's 139 not out was the epitome of aggression. His hundred came up off just 113 balls and included nine boundaries and three sixes. The second 50 was even more furious — scored off 39 balls with six boundaries and two sixes. He finished the series with 367 runs at an average of 61.17. "The Windies are a better bowling side so I suppose you would have to say it was a bit more difficult to get a hundred against them, but being my first Test I thought my innings against England was a better innings. The one against the West Indies I just played a lot of risky shots. There was a fair amount of luck involved, whereas the first one was a bit more calculated. I suppose it was a more pure innings for a batsman. Technically it was better than the other one. Not as many risks and I didn't need any luck either. It was just one of those days when everything went right."

Gooch admits to conflicting emotions about Mark's outstanding Test debut against the Englishmen at Adelaide. "I kept ribbing him a little bit jovially before, you know 'you can't

Steve batting during the Benson and Hedges Challenge, a one day tournament featuring Australia, England, Pakistan and the West Indies, staged to coincide with the America's Cup in Perth in 1987.

Mark bowling for Essex against the Australians in 1989, the first time the twins opposed each other in a first-class match.
(Philip Brown)

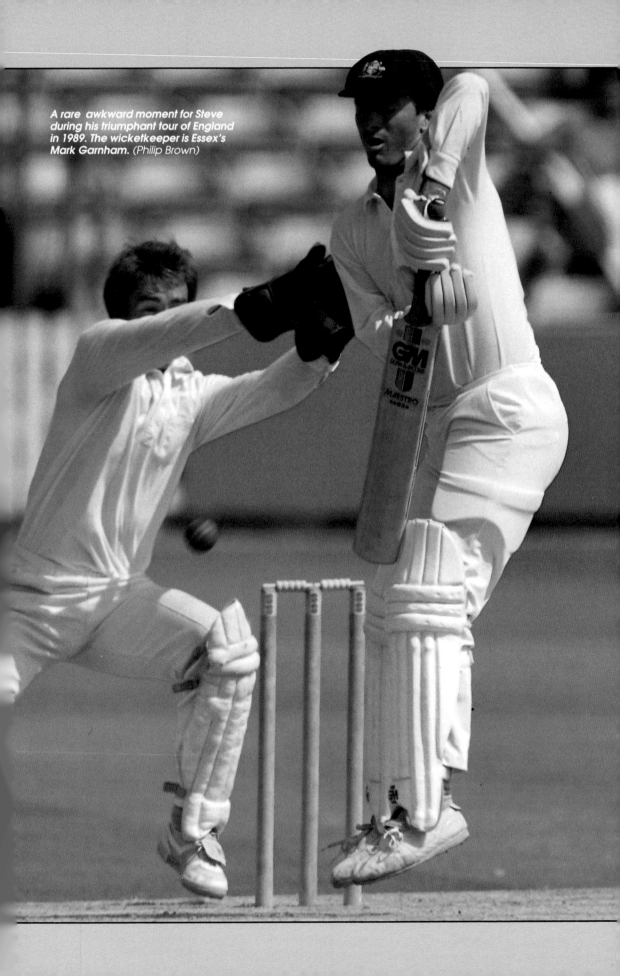

A rare awkward moment for Steve during his triumphant tour of England in 1989. The wicketkeeper is Essex's Mark Garnham. (Philip Brown)

*Mark square cuts a
four for NSW against
Victoria, in an FAI Cup
match at North Sydney
Oval in 1991-92.
(PBL Marketing)*

get in the team' and 'you musn't be a very good player if you can't get in'. When he got in obviously I was delighted for him but our ideal scenario would have been to win the game with him scoring a hundred. He played beautifully.

"It was the dream debut to score a hundred in the manner he did. I don't think any hundred is ordinary, but it was a really fine innings. I had mixed feelings really. I was delighted for him but disappointed obviously that we didn't press home our advantage."

Gooch, who congratulated Mark on his ton with a simple "well done" and shake of the hand, rated it as one of the best Test debuts he had ever seen. "I reckon that was one of the better ones. He was brilliant to watch. He took the bowlers on and played really superbly. And, what's more important, he dug his team out of a very difficult position."

Since Steve's debut Rodger had left the bank and invested in a newsagency. Commitments there meant he was unable to go to Adelaide and enjoy Mark's Test debut first hand. It was a tough day for him.

"I remember listening at the shop and being a nervous wreck," said Rodger. "I shut the shop early and he got his hundred just before six o'clock. It was great. Never in my wildest dreams did I think he would bat so beautifully first up. It was an unbelievable innings really."

Despite having watched two sons represent Australia, a third make the State squad, and have a fourth steadily work his way up through all the rep teams, playing the role of spectator has never been easy for Rodger. "I find it a little bit easier watching the youngest bloke (Danny), I don't know why. I can't watch Dean, he's such a nervous starter, he makes me nervous. I've always found it easier watching Mark than Steve. Steve's always a bit iffy early whereas Mark's harder to get out earlier. From the point of view of watching them both I've always been more relaxed watching Mark. It's a bugger of a game to watch."

Making it even harder for Rodger are the commentators. Adverse comments about the boys really get under his skin. "They must know I'm listening," laughs Rodger. "Ian Chappell's been after me for a game of tennis. I haven't had time but when I do I'm going to belt the daylights out of him to get back for all the little comments. They all have their moments these commentators. They're all for them and then they're all against them.

"I probably get more cheesed off than anyone and I'm not even playing the game. That's the competitive part of me."

And then there's his job, which is just about the worst you can have if you've got a thin skin because not only are there workmates to cope with but every Tom, Dick and Harry that walks in off the street can have a shot at you.

"A lot of people come into the shop and what they read is what they say. I bite like a big shark too. They tell me they're doing no good and I say just look at the averages," said Rodger, who added. "But a lot of people were disappointed when Steve was dropped. People regard them pretty highly around here."

Both the Waughs have enjoyed a good run with the media, and while there has been the odd hiccup, Mark acknowledges that fact. "There have been a few things along the way, some quotes have been written that I didn't say, but generally I've got no complaints about the media." Still he doesn't believe the good gentlemen of the press, and one Melbourne-based journalist in particular, did him any favours in the lead-up to his axing from the Test side before the last Test against India in the 1991-92 summer.

"All the talk around was that I was going to be dropped because I hadn't made a score," said Mark, who still couldn't quibble too much with the final result. "There was a lot of talk around about our batting during the summer; it was slow, it was negative and we weren't getting on top of the bowlers. There was a general feeling that we weren't batting well and someone had to pay the price. If you are a batsman in Test cricket and you don't get runs you've got to expect to get dropped.

"I didn't make a score in Adelaide but the selectors had stuck with players for a fair while and I thought I was still a chance, even if I didn't get runs, to finish the series at least. It was disappointing because a year earlier in Adelaide I had made my Test debut and made a hundred and a year later I was dropped. It just goes to show that you can't get too over-confident or blase about the fact that you are in a team. You've got to keep working all the time and don't take anything for granted, you have to be 100 per cent focused. I think after the West Indies trip I came back, played well and I thought 'we're playing India, it's going to be easy. It's just a matter of turning up and getting out there and scoring the runs'. But it didn't turn out like that. I think it has taught me a lesson."

His cockiness resulted in some poor play, some poor luck and, finally, an unaccustomed loss of confidence. The young champion who had plundered the world's best bowlers for the past two years suddenly hit earth with a thud. During his mini-slump Mark lost a weapon just as important, and tangible, as his bat. "I wasn't as confident as I normally am when I go out to bat. In the first couple of Tests in Brisbane and Melbourne I was hitting the ball really well and got out. I made one mistake in three or four innings and was out. It wasn't as though I was hitting the ball badly. It was just that everything seemed to be going against me and I had that in my mind when I went to the crease. I thought, 'I'm going to be unlucky today, something is going to happen', and it did. I lost my confidence. It is only natural when you're not scoring runs that that happens. But I was still determined. It was lucky I had a Shield game in the next couple of days. It was a good chance for me to get back into a bit of form on my home wicket in Sydney.

"Fortunately I made 158 and got everything back on course. Technically I was probably playing across the line more than usual and that brought my downfall a couple of times. But I was seeing the ball well, that wasn't a problem. It was just one of those things that happen in cricket. Fortunately it didn't happen that long for me. Four or five innings. Unfortunately it was long enough for me to get dropped.

"It's disappointing at the time but I think it makes you more determined to make it not happen again. I was okay about it. I mean, I must have been right. I got a hundred so it didn't affect me for too long to be honest. Sure you're disappointed but it was particularly hard to concentrate on the last day in Adelaide because Bobby Simpson came up to me and Geoff Marsh early that morning, before the day's play and said we'd been left out of the next Test. It was hard that day but life must go on. It's not that I lost my ability overnight, I still had my ability to do well."

Greg Matthews has no doubt that Mark has a golden future as does Steve. "Mark Waugh and Mark Taylor are going to be playing Test cricket for as long as they want, barring injury," he said. "And Steve will definitely play again. He's got a lot more talent than a lot of people going around. He's very dedicated and very hard-working, perhaps a little too hard-working, given the injury problems he's suffered."

THIRTEEN

The Odd Couple

GIVEN their awesome achievements it sometimes is hard to comprehend that the Waughs have their human faults. But they have, which is some comfort for all those who enjoy giving the little green-eyed monster that resides in everyone's breast a workout. To be fair, it is as human as the desire for warmth and company and to feel envy. It's more of a reason for that classic Aussie tendency — the tall poppy syndrome — than most care to admit. It may be nasty and petty but if and when you have trouble getting bat to hit ball or ball to hit wicket, then you must get your thrills in less savoury ways. Super sports they may be but Mark and Steve do, in fact, have their fair share of human faults and foibles.

Despite earning their keep as professional sportsmen and having an unquenchable enthusiasm for games, both of them hate jogging with a passion. They don't mind training hard, it's just that running is terribly dull. "It's boring," said Mark. "I'm used to doing things. You can still run as long as you're doing something at the same time, like playing soccer. But just plain running I find boring and hard work at the same time. I don't enjoy it. I don't know how you can enjoy running. Funnily enough I used to be good at cross country at school."

An incident on the 1991 West Indies tour confirmed Mark's prejudice for all time. It was during a match on the island of St Vincent when Mark, Mike Whitney, Craig McDermott and Geoff Marsh had the game off. The other three are certified fitness fanatics and one lunchtime Mark foolishly allowed himself to be talked into going along on one of their runs.

"Billy (McDermott), Swampy (Marsh) and I were very fit at the time and while Junior is anything but a runner I talked him into tagging along," said Whitney. "It was a hectic pace and there was a good incline for about a mile and a half. By the time we got to the turnaround Junior was gone. He was dropping further and further behind. Just then Swampy and Billy upped the ante and I thought the worst thing he could do was stop and walk. If he gave in he was never going to get out on the streets again. So I turned around and jogged back about 400m and we stopped for a while and did some stretches before slowly making our way back. For the rest of the tour he had blisters and sore calf muscles. "

Whitney said Waugh didn't let him forget about it for the rest of the trip.

"I couldn't believe how far they had run," said Mark. "Bloody idiots. I had blisters on my feet and a strained tendon in my knee. I couldn't walk for three or four days. I would have been struggling if there had been a Test straight after."

Neither is Mark keen on the gym, though Bankstown team-mate Andy Divall did share a few sessions with him pumping iron. "We used to go to the gym at Panania and Mark ran up there one day — I think it's the last time I saw him run," said Divall. "He'd wear his best sweat shirt and best tracksuit but he wouldn't exactly break into a sweat. I think he was there more to fill in the time than do the hard work."

While the twins' reputation as an odd couple because of their lack of chatter is

Above: Steve would rather fly than run. Left: Super-fit quicks Mike Whitney (left) and Craig McDermott talked Mark into joining them on a training run during the West Indies tour in 1991, with disastrous results.

(Photos by Greg Porteus)

undeserved, there is another area where it is more than appropriate. Tidiness is one area where the twins differ greatly. "Steve was always a nightmare," said Bev. "Mark always knew where everything was but he's changed since he went to England. He's deteriorated badly. Mark used to be organised. He knew where his school books were, you wouldn't need to touch anything of Mark's. His clothes would be neatly laid out. Stephen had the side of the room that you couldn't see into. He wasn't happy unless he was in a mess."

"Steve always looks the cricketer out on the field but behind the scenes he's a pig," declared former Aussie team-mate Tim May.

"He's a classic," said Mark Taylor. "He just throws everything in his bag and jumps on it. It's a wonder he looks any good when he goes out. And he's always losing the room key. I think once the cricket's over he switches off."

Just-retired NSW captain and fast bowling great Geoff Lawson provided documentary evidence in the account of the 1989 Ashes tour he did with Melbourne journalist Mark Ray. In the book he has included a photo of Steve, clad only in a jock strap, standing on his kit bag trying to get it closed.

"If you go into the dressing room I'm normally the worst," confessed Steve. "I don't clean up too well, I just tend to chuck my stuff around. I like it that way, I know where it is. If someone packs it away I don't know where it is. I've never been neat and I don't think I'll change too much. I'll room with Smally or Ian Healy (NSW opener Steve Small) or sit next to either of them and it's like the Odd Couple. Like Oscar and Felix. Smally's got it perfectly packed and I'm an absolute shambles. I suppose Mark is a bit neater. I think looking in his kit bag it always seems to be in pretty good nick. But I don't think I could handle it that way. I've tried it and it hasn't worked.

"But it's not really a problem. I think you learn to live with your room-mates. The only time it's really a hassle is if I room with someone like Brad McNamara. I end up going home with half of his gear and he's got half of mine. That's probably more of a problem than someone who's neat and someone who's untidy."

Steve's untidiness and disorganisation have, on more than one occasion, been more than an eyesore. In the mad scramble to pack various important items have tended to go astray.

"I'm one of the worst bag packers around," said Steve. "I hate it. That must be the worst part about playing cricket, packing your bags and unpacking them. I always seem to take too much stuff. I never get the right amount in my bag. And when I get there I've always forgotten something. I forgot my toiletries bag last year. And I've forgotten my cricket boots, my pads. I've turned up at games with half my gear and no clothes. I've got a bit of a checklist now so I've at least got all my cricket gear. But clothes I'm always a couple short there. And I get my climates mixed up sometimes. I went to the West Indies and took about five jumpers and never used one. I went to England and didn't take any."

One such memory lapse forced Steve to take a very inventive approach to tailoring. He had forgotten to ask Bev to take a pair of cricket pants up before he flew to Melbourne for his Test debut and didn't notice until he was taking the field. Ever ingenious, he used chewing gum to hem the pants but forgot about it. He did such a good job that it wasn't noticeable until Bev ironed the pants upon his return. Needless to say, the pants were ruined. And that's not all. "If the sleeves of his shirt are a bit too long he'll just cut them off," said Lynette.

Early on it was neither chewing gum, bad packing or forgetfulness according to Greg Matthews. "They were the worst-dressed cricketers you've ever seen," said Matthews. "Absolute shockers. Since he's come under my wing Steve's become a very good dresser,

(Philip Brown)

Left: Dean Jones did not look so cool after his luggage went missing in Adelaide. Above: Tim May (left) and Geoff Lawson have seen the worst of Steve Waugh's bag-packing techniques.

(Gregg Porteus)

he's probably the best-dressed guy in first class cricket in Australia, and Mark's improved tremendously since he started going out with Sue."

"I forgot my special orthotics for inside my boots before one Shield match," said Steve. "I need them because I've got nothing inside my boot except studs and metal on the bottom so I did get those sent down the night before. And I got out to the SCG for a World Series match last season and realised I hadn't put my boots out. So I had to ring Dean and get him to bring them out on the train. He got there about 20 minutes before the game was due to start. It would have been handy with no boots. I've done it a couple of times, the no boots trick. It seems to be my problem area."

Often he was not the only one to get caught short by his absent-mindedness. Steve tells of a time when he was rooming with Peter Taylor in Adelaide. The bags were delivered to the hotel and when they got to their room there was three in between the two beds. Steve thought that the middle bag was Taylor's and vice versa for three or four days when it was actually Dean Jones'. The pair didn't click despite the fact that a furious Jones went on the rampage in search of his gear.

"Jonesy's bloody screaming blue murder, abusing the porters and everyone on the hotel staff," said Steve. "He filled out insurance forms for about 10 grand's worth of stuff. On the morning we were leaving PT is out the door with his bag and I said 'PT I think you forgot one of your bags mate' and he said 'no, that's not mine'. I checked and it wasn't mine so we opened it up and it's Jonesy's gear. So we had to go and front Jonesy and tell him his bag had been in our room all that time while he wore the same set of clothes around. I don't think Jonesy's ever forgiven us for that.

"That's just one of the bag incidents. I always seem to be losing my bags in the airport. I don't know if it's just bad luck or someone doesn't like me but I must have lost them four or five times. I've had one go to Beirut."

Both have been in trouble because of their fondness for sleeping in. Both learned early that it wasn't acceptable conduct thanks to tough taskmaster Bob Simpson. Steve learned his lesson when he missed a plane to Adelaide for the Third Test against England in December 1986. Waugh caught a late afternoon flight and by the time he had arrived the Australians were back at their hotel after a lengthy hitout in the nets. To say that Simpson was less than understanding is an understatement.

"I've missed one flight," said Mark. "That was for a Tooheys Cup game. It was about a 6.15am plane and I got there about five past six and they had already sold my ticket to someone. I mean I was late but I was not actually that late. Six o'clock is pretty early anyway. But that was the only time I've missed a plane, fortunately. I'm usually pretty good. I've missed a few buses to the ground. Actually I did it my first game for NSW in Tasmania. Myself and Mark Taylor slept in for some reason. I don't know why; it was his birthday the night before. Bobby Simpson gave us a workout that time."

"I was rooming with Mark but I went out with Steve," said Taylor. "I was already out so I thought I could afford to have a few. I got in after him so I thought Mark had set the alarm but we got woken up by a call from Simmo at 9.10am telling us to get a cab to the ground. Simmo really nailed us."

Being late would have been bad enough but Taylor, who answered Bob Simpson's angry call at 9.10am, thought Simpson was joking, told him to get lost in no uncertain terms and hung up. He then noticed the time and realised the gravity of the situation. The pair moved very quickly. Steve recalled with relish that the two Mark's were almost at the ground before the team.

"And then there was me and Trevor Bayliss last season in Adelaide," said Mark. "He always gets up early. Always. So I didn't worry about a wake-up call. So he bloody sleeps in and we didn't get a wake-up call."

Another late arrival occurred in a grade game against Gordon. It was a one-day match but Mark got the time mixed up and arrived an hour late in company with Andy Crowfoot. When he finally went in to bat he was partnering captain Gary Crowfoot. The partnership didn't last long. "He was in there for about two overs and then ran me out," said Divall. "Not only did he turn up late but he ran the captain out for 49."

Putting aside the disputed claim over the misplaced box way back in their first ever cricket match Mark has had his fair share of embarrassing moments on the cricket field. When he was playing second grade for Bankstown at Rushcutters Bay it was his job to shift the sight screen when the batsmen required and he was so enthusiastic that he pushed it off the rails. And when he was playing Green Shield (under-16s) as a 13-year-old he jumped a fence at Waverley Oval to fetch a ball and couldn't get back over it.

Unfortunately he cannot dismiss such acts as the foibles of youth. This past season he managed to embarrass himself with a glaring act of absentmindedness. He was batting with England hopeful Nasser Hussain in a Sunday League limited-over match against Derby at Derby. When Hussain hit the ball into the gap and the pair took a single to take the score to 161, Mark started to head towards the pavilion, satisfied with another comfortable win.

Unfortunately the victory target was 162. He only woke up when his team-mates started yelling at him, and he barely made his ground.

Even some of the simplest physical activities are beyond Mark. Despite two trips to the snow and his prodigious athletic ability Mark has yet to master the mysteries of snow skiing and the Prichards are prepared to swear an oath that he cannot row a boat. The couples were out one day and Mark allegedly made a complete meal of it, unable to get both oars in the water at once. He actually ran the dinghy into the river bank where Jo-Anne Prichard had a nasty mishap with some of the local foliage. Her verdict: "totally unco-ordinated".

Mark claims to be not particularly superstitious but he has his little quirks. For a start when he is padding up he always puts his left pad on first, though he claims that may be more habit than anything else. Then there is his habit of marking a little stick man on his thigh pad after he scores a first class century. The origins of this interesting custom, according to Mark, are quite innocent and have nothing to do with superstition. Keith Fletcher, the Essex manager and former England batsman, drew 10 or so on Waugh's thighpad in a fit of boredom. Presented with a sort of fait accompli Mark then decided to give the artwork some meaning and turned them into hundreds.

But he does admit to a weakness for thinking too much about teams against which he has been successful. He says it invites bad luck. Steve has the opposite problem, mulling over his mistakes. "Sometimes I go over an innings in my mind. You realise you shouldn't have played that shot and you look to see why you played that shot or what brought about that shot. Pressure or frustration or whatever."

But a deeper and darker fault lies behind his aggression. "Sometimes I might have got myself out in the past just by being bored with myself. The way I have been playing, or if I'm not hitting the ball well and I expect to hit the ball well. I suppose that could be one of my weaknesses, not gutsing it out when I'm not playing well enough because I set my standards high. Whereas I suppose if I didn't have a lot of natural talent I could get through those tougher periods a bit easier. Just relax and say I'm going to get through it. But when I'm not playing well and scratching around like an old chook and not scoring quickly I think I bore myself out. I find it hard to go out there and bat for a couple of hours and not score many runs."

Cars in general, and petrol in particular, have never been a happy part of Steve or Mark's life. Bev tells of giving Mark a driving lesson which turned very scary very quickly. The car had been heading swiftly towards a pole when Bev told Mark to slow down. He didn't so she repeated her request and when he continued to ignore her she told him if he wasn't going to do what he was told he could just get out of the car. Which he did. Without stopping. Fortunately she was able to get things under control before any damage was done. That's her story anyway. "Mum exaggerates," said Mark. "She reckons she told me to get out of the car so I left it in drive and got out. I must admit it wasn't easy trying to teach me and Stephen how to drive. We didn't have any lessons. It was only Mum who taught us. Dad would have been too impatient."

Of the two Steve was the much more enthusiastic and adventurous driver. That became a bit of a problem as far as the constabulary were concerned. "Steve was a real lead foot," said Bev. "He was the first to be fined for speeding."

Technically, Steve had limitations. A former patron had promised to lend Steve his RX-7 when he made the Shield team, and Steve took him up because he wanted to impress Lynette. Bev got a call at 1.30am from Steve begging for help. He had accidentally turned the alarm on and couldn't switch it off. When she arrived she said it was quite a show. In trying to turn the alarm off Steve had turned on everything else in the car — wipers, radio, lights, etc.

Mark appears a pretty cool customer these days but the fact remains that he was, and still is, scared to drive a car with a manual transmission. "I was a bit scared of the old manual. I don't know why. I still haven't learnt properly. Although last year in Alice Springs I did a talk at a club and they hired me a manual car when I was up there. I had to learn on that pretty quick smart. I did all right, only one kangaroo hop."

The twins broke down countless times as teens and ran out of petrol on a regular basis. Mark was lucky that a memory lapse didn't land him in deep trouble. He was running late for NSW practice when he had to stop for petrol. He filled up and made practice okay but upon his return discovered that the police had been around asking after him. "I was in a rush," said Mark. "I filled the tank up and drove off. The police went to mum and dad's place and asked if Mark Waugh lived there. They said yes and the policemen told them 'when he gets back from practice tell him to go back there and pay for the petrol otherwise he'll be in jail tonight'." Fortunately for him, Waugh simply had to go and pay for the petrol he "stole". "There was no problem. I went there quite a bit. I'm not sure they knew who I was or not. I think they knew my face."

"I ran out of petrol twice in one day," said Steve. "On one occasion Lynette had to walk nearly all the way from Panania to Milperra."

The regular petrol droughts were caused not only by the cars, one of which Steve said used $5 to go around the block, but by the boys as well. "Both Mark and Steve were very careful with their money when they were young," said Tony Fort. "Most young men when they get their P's want to drive but these two were the exact opposite because whoever drove had to put the petrol in. Whoever lost the toss and had to drive would put $2 or $3 in the car even though the fuel gauge already read empty."

Mechanical troubles were also a bane of their lives and those of the people close to them. As has been previously mentioned, they had absolutely no idea about the mechanical workings of a car and became stranded by even the most minor problem. On one trip to Manly for a cricket match the car suffered a flat tyre but, as neither Mark or Steve knew how to change it, the NRMA had to be called.

"Once I picked Lynette up at school and the car would only go in reverse. We drove a couple of miles home in reverse," said Steve. "It was my last prac teaching assignment for college so I was very keen to make a good impression," said Lynette. "It was so embarrassing. He picked me up at the front of the school so all the kids could see."

Mark's fear of horses is not the only animal phobia from which he has suffered. He claims to be an animal person now but the list of animals he has shied away from is extensive.

Neither is he fond of fishing.

"I don't like seeing animals hurt and I just can't get the hook out of the fish's mouth. And it's a bit slow sitting there. It's not really interesting enough for me."

Mark and Steve's cricket may be sweet music to the fans but it's a different story when they try to make the real thing. The fact that someone asked them to record a song for the World Cup suggested that anyone really can do it or that the mastermind behind the project was tone deaf himself. "They certainly were never musical," said Bev. "They weren't very good singers. They used to always be told to mime in the school choir. Stephen and Mark are close to tone deaf."

FOURTEEN

Fit For Life

No STORY about the Waugh twins can be written without taking time to take a peek at their eating habits. If the first word that comes to mind when discussing the twins is competitiveness then the next would surely have to be food. And that's not to say the two were, or are, mutually exclusive. "They were even competitive to the point that when I served out dinner they would look at each others' plates to make sure that they didn't have any less than the other one," said Bev. "Now they have girlfriends around I feel embarrassed sometimes. They must think I haven't brought the boys up properly because they still eat fast and the girls eat their food really slowly and really precisely. I keep saying 'it's not a competition anymore. You can have what's here. You don't have to fight for your food'."

While their hectic lifestyle is a more than reasonable explanation, their appetite and love of food seems to be as natural a characteristic as their sporting ability. As small children they spent a lot of time with their mother playing in the kitchen. "When they were little I used to sit them up on the bench and let them stir the food with me," said Bev. "I had to make sure each got a go. I'm a bit far out. I'm a bit mad. I didn't care if they got in there and got in a mess and I got in a mess too. They would end up with stuff on their face and I would end up with it on mine too. Crazy. But a lot of fun. Sometimes we used to make toffees and had disasters with things like that where they boiled to the bottom of the saucepan and we had to throw the saucepan out.

"They used to love it when I cooked pavlova. They loved licking bowls, especially pavlova bowls. They loved making pikelets and pancakes because with those you could toss them to the top of the ceiling and try to catch them. They loved cooking those sorts of things because you could end up in a terrible mess and eat heaps out of the dish."

That's not to say that all this time in the kitchen and love of food inspired any culinary ambitions. Or even culinary competence in Mark's case. In fact his love of food stops most definitely at the end of his knife and fork. "They started to learn to cook things like fried rice but that was more Stephen. He was really adventurous. Mark would be more into things like a toasted sandwich." While Steve has become quite a handy cook, according to Lynette, Mark's cooking skills can be safely bracketed with his mechanical skills.

Both have always boasted prodigious appetites, and each has his little peculiarities and idiosyncrasies. Steve, for instance, cannot bear butter and has to have special sandwiches set aside for him at home and cricket matches. Such is Steve's dislike for butter that Lynette says if she makes a mistake and butters his bread and then scrapes it off he can still tell and won't eat it. Curiously, despite the fact of his enthusiastic long-term patronage of the establishment, he also boasted a long-term hatred of the pickles and sauce on McDonalds hamburgers. His friends swear getting trapped behind him in the queue at McDonalds was like doing penance. "He's fussy," said Brad McNamara. "It used to be a pain going to McDonalds with him. You'd have to wait half an hour while he had the pickles and the butter and the sauce taken off."

"That was hideous," agreed Richard Lane. "Punishing." Happily, it can be reported that Steve has almost overcome his difficulties at McDonalds now — it is only the pickles that he can't stomach.

McNamara recalls a colts game at the old SCG No 2 which was terminated after only an hour by a heavy downpour. "It might have even been our first pay cheque for a game," he said. "We got 80 bucks or something for the four days. So we went into town, to catch a midday movie, and ended up drinking and eating our first pay cheque. We had 400 Big Macs at McDonalds, then 5000 bourbons. The movie we watched was *The Natural*."

Steve's dietary atrocities were cultivated out of mum's sight at school and it has taken him a long time to reform his habits to the standards of decent society. "My diet was diabolical at school," said Steve. "Lunch was a couple of packets of Twisties, a chocolate bar and maybe a vegemite sandwich with no butter."

"When I first met him all he would eat was chicken and chips and meat," said Lynette. "We are eating a lot more vegetables, grains and lean meat."

The couple do most of their cooking together and Lynette said Steve has even become a dab hand at cooking.

Nelson's Mike Bradley recalled one incident where Steve's appetite and forgetfulness produced most unpleasant results. The team noticed a funny smell coming from Steve's corner of the dressing room. When he pulled his helmet out of the bag he plucked what Bradley claims were "the mouldiest egg sandwiches you've ever seen" out of his helmet. They had been there for ages. Lynette tells a similar story. Steve's cricket coffin had reached only as far as the door when he arrived back from a game. After a few days Lynette decided she had better fish out all the clothes and wash them. When she opened the bag the smell cleared the room. Again the culprits were some very old egg sandwiches.

Steve is also a very messy eater. His spaniel Chester always hovers nearby when his master is eating because he knows that a few crumbs, at the very least, will fall his way. Mike and Julie Bradley went so far as to put a huge bib on him for one meal of spaghetti. Eating with either of the Waugh twins can be a boots-and-all affair apparently. "They've both got shocking manners," said Mark Taylor. "They're both dreadful eaters. They get their fingers in the food and all sorts of things."

Spaghetti was the cause of one of Steve's more embarrassing moments at the dinner table. He and Lynette were travelling in Italy and because they could not speak the language had to put up with spaghetti every day. After about five days Steve tired of the situation and declared he was going to order something else. He did his best to decipher the menu before calling for the waitress. She, of course, did not speak English. He asked if a particular item was fish and when she managed to indicate that it was he ordered that. Much to his horror she emerged from the kitchen with a plate of fried whitebait. Steve took one mouthful before waving the dish back to the kitchen.

Steve also got more than he bargained for one day in primary school. Bev was going to the doctor's for a check-up one day and had to take a urine specimen. She put it in a brown paper bag on the bench. "When I handed over what I thought was my specimen bag the doctor opened it and it had biscuits in it. Steve had picked up the specimen thinking it was his play lunch."

Mark Waugh can be accused of many things but being fussy is definitely not one of them

*Both sides of the culinary coin ...
Above: Steve enjoys a joke with a
pretzel during his European jaunt
with Lynette. Left: He has his
epitaph written by team-mate
Simon Davis after an attack of
'Bombay Belly' in India in 1986. The
epitaph read:
"Stephen Waugh, RIP
Born June 2nd, 1965
Died October 17th, 1986
Victim of the dreaded Bombay
Belly"*

— unless you count his ritual request for tomato sauce. "Stephen is a bit fussy but I eat pretty much anything in large quantities," he said. "And we were all quick eaters, too. Because if we ate quicker and got our meal out of the way we would get a chance for seconds. With four boys if you scoffed it down quick you might get seconds."

Ian Davis was quick to cite two occasions when he came in contact with the Mark Waugh appetite. "Mark came around to my place for a barbeque just after he signed his first contract and he had two monster steaks, sausages, chips — he just never stopped eating. I couldn't believe it.

"Then we were doing a promotion at Myer and on the way back through the Queen Victoria Building he said: 'jeez I'm hungry, I'd love something to eat' so we went downstairs and I said: 'okay, I'll shout you lunch'. And he ended up eating the restaurant out. He started with avocado dip and we had toasted sandwiches and it cost about $60 for the two of us when it was only supposed to be a plate of chips.

"Every time I tell him I'll shout him a meal I know I'm up for a fortune."

Mark does have his dislikes though. "I can't eat anything that's not really well cooked. I hate undercooked meat, it's one of my pet hates. I don't like real spicy things. Although since I've played for Essex I've eaten a lot of curry. They're slowly trying to turn me around, trying to get me to eat hot curries, but I'm sticking to the mild ones at the moment."

England is not renowned for its culinary culture, but Mark had the blow softened in his time with Essex. "I was fortunate. The first couple of years in England I stayed with one of the committee members mother, so she cooked for me. Then the next year I struggled a bit.

I had a lot of takeaways. Can't remember cooking too much. I lived on takeaways virtually for four months in 1990."

This is still true. His partner Sue Porter arrived at his house well into the 1992 English summer to find a single chocolate bar in the fridge. She quickly put things right as she has done since the pair first started seeing each other. In fact Greg Matthews believes that Sue's steady influence has been a major factor in Mark's turnaround as a first class cricketer.

"I think Sue's been good for me," Mark said. "She spoils me a bit but I think I've matured since I met her. In dress sense and things like that. She's organised and I think I've grown up quicker than I would have normally.

"She's pretty good. I think she understands that cricket is very important to me and it's my livelihood so I've got to spend a lot of time on it. It's just a fact of life."

Mark had a couple of girlfriends before deciding to settle down with Sue. "There were two or three," he said. "Five or six months, that sort of thing. I don't know whether you call that serious or not. I was only 17 when I had my first girlfriend then when I came to England the first time in the Bolton League I met a girl and I was with her for about four or five months. Just one of those phases. Girlfriends come and go at that age don't they? I always put my sport before girls, really. I hate to say it but I think it is still the same. I always watched TV and I was always playing some sport so I probably didn't devote enough time to them. But that's bad luck, that's the way it goes."

Apart from the pure pleasure of eating, the central figure in Mark's dietary universe is tomato sauce. Apart from knives and forks that is the most important eating tool — and may in fact be No. 1. Ask anyone with even a casual relationship with Mark about his eating habits and they will remark upon his addiction. Ian Davis believes Mark keeps the industry in the red, if you'll pardon the pun. There is nothing he will not use it on. Paul Prichard's wife Jo-Anne tells of the time she cooked apricot chicken and Mark asked for the tomato sauce — and used it. Mark is quick to add that he didn't actually pour the sauce on the chicken — like Meg Ryan in *When Harry Met Sally* he had the sauce on the side. Then there was the time some friends of the Prichards held a barbecue in honour of the Fosters who were visiting Australia. The hostess is not a woman who does things by halves and turned the barbecue into a real event with all sorts of exotic foodstuffs and condiments. Mark allegedly sat down at this magnificent spread and his first question was: "Where's the tomato sauce?". Jo-Anne reports that he was also extremely reluctant to try the sausages that had been stuffed with oysters. His motto could well be ravenous but not adventurous.

FIFTEEN

The Other Side of Life

THE WAUGHS have their interests and their hobbies, though, strictly speaking, hobbies is not quite the right word. It takes a bit of imagination to picture either Steve or Mark sitting down and laboriously constructing a model of a 17th century Spanish galleon or lovingly placing the latest expensive acquisition in their stamp album. Mark's great love is punting and he blames his father for that particular weakness. Rodger does not deny the charge.

"I used to take them to the trots a bit. I was only a very small punter but that's where he'd probably get his interest from, going to Bankstown or the odd race meeting," said Rodger. "Stephen doesn't like it as much. He had a big win his very first bet but he lost about the next 10 bets and he gave it away pretty quick smart. But Mark's always liked a bet. He and I leased a trotter but it never did any good. It had a couple of runs at Richmond and Wyong." Mark said the horse was well bred but that it was such a loser he can't even remember its whole name — something Blue. It had three starts and failed to complete the course each time.

"It wasn't a very good investment," Mark said. Despite that experience and the knowledge that the vast majority of horses never make it to the track, let alone win a race, thoroughbred ownership remains an ambition. "When I'm finished my career I want to get a few horses and have a bit of a go at ownership," he said.

The twins were about 10 when they first went to the trots with Rodger. They also went to the greyhounds with him where he and three of his mates had a system of backing the one and the eight boxes in every race. Cricket coach Glenn Russell was also a punting mentor later on, taking them to the greyhounds at Wentworth Park every Saturday night. Armed with $10 from Bev, and not wishing to waste it on something like the entry fee, they usually jumped the fence. "We got caught jumping the fence once and we had to go around and pay but most of the time we didn't pay," said Mark.

"I've always been keen on the races, mainly horses and the trots," admitted Mark. "I'm not really keen on casinos or cards. I don't gamble much there. It's a way I can escape from cricket because I get on the race course, put my head in the form guide and do my own thing." Mark spurns the formality of the members enclosure for the paddock where he can relax in his tracksuit either by himself, which he does quite often, or with a couple of close friends like McNamara, Lee Sterrey or Bill York. He has his good days and his bad days but doesn't deny that the bookies and the government are well ahead at the moment.

"I think it's cost me a few dollars. I'm definitely behind, but the thought of winning big money quickly keeps me coming back. I'm a good loser. I don't really get upset although sometimes I think of what I could have done with the money I've lost. But there's the old saying 'if losing worries you, don't bet'. The next morning I think it's probably stupid but then I think I'll have to have another bet so I can get the money back."

You can see why those few unkind souls refer to Mark as a desperate. "Any amount, anywhere, any time" could be another appropriate motto for Mark's family crest. But he is not completely lost to society — he has limits and sticks to one golden rule. No vision, no way. And he never lets it affect his cricket. "If I can watch the race I'll have a bet but I usually don't bet when I'm playing. Very rarely. Maybe if I'm out and the TV's on. Stumper (NSW coach Steve Rixon) is a bad influence. If I haven't got much to do I'll have a bet most days or at least wander down to the TAB and have a look. But I don't like having a bet and not being able to see the race."

The TAB covers races midweek from some very exotic and out-of-the-way Australian towns as well as the bigger country centres. Often the form in the papers for these meetings contains the bare minimum of information but that is no deterrent. Waugh doesn't think there is anything strange about gambling on horses and courses he knows little about. "It doesn't matter where the race is. Something's got to win." In fact he claims to have had quite a bit of success on the Albury races.

Mark is very much an intuitive punter. Which is perhaps why he does okay at meetings in far-flung country outposts. He admits to perusing the form guide for information but doesn't take it too seriously. All he really needs are the numbers, weights, barriers, jockeys and previous couple of placings. "I enjoy having a look at the form guide, it's part of the scene, but I don't know if it helps too much." And his punting demeanour is in keeping with the way he conducts himself on the field. "Sometimes I cheer and get the whip out if I'm losing but if I back a couple of winners I don't get too excited. I have a bit of a yell if I've backed the horse with some of the other cricketers like Brad."

Sydney's now-defunct Sun newspaper once gave Mark a chance to show everyone his talent and expertise but he didn't do too well. He claims that he was hampered by the ridiculously early deadline for his tips. He had to make his selections on just horses and weights, the barriers and jockeys not having been released that early in the week.

Mark's affection for the punt can adequately be gauged by the fact that the Revesby TAB sent him a telegram congratulating him on his Test debut. He refused to divulge the size of his bets, though he did say he has never followed a system, his wagers have increased in proportion with his earnings and if he is having a good day he'll weigh in heavily on something he fancies. Likewise he would not discuss his worst day at the track and was very coy about his best, but he did tell about a couple of memorable collects.

One night he could only get to Bankstown trots for one race but made the effort because he was keen on a runner called Western Langus. To make the trip worthwhile he had $150 each-way on the pacer and it obliged by saluting at the lucrative odds of 12/1 — a payout of $2550 which gave Mark a tidy profit of $2250. Not a bad effort.

A win smaller in dollar value but which would have given him just as much satisfaction was the $1 each-way he had on a grey horse called Long John Silver. It was owned by Peter Sterling, and it greeted the judge at odds of 150/1. He said he was only young and probably losing, so the win was particularly sweet at the time. He also had a soft spot for an old trotter called The Cracker, NSW fast bowler Wayne Holdsworth's nickname, which has taken the money a number of times at good odds.

Mark said he has had plenty of good luck on the first Tuesday in November. He has backed a number of winners including Empire Rose and What a Nuisance and was also given a great sight by Noble Comment which was run down on the post by Kiwi, whose stunning finishing burst is one of the highlights of Melbourne Cup folklore. "I always go to Randwick

Steve mobbed after taking the wicket of Kim Barnett during the Third Test at Edgbaston in 1989.
The other Australian players are (left to right) Terry Alderman, Mark Taylor, Dean Jones, Allan Border
and Geoff Lawson.

(Philip Brown)

on Melbourne Cup day," said Mark. "But I never go to the members. I'd rather go in a tracksuit and wander around in the crowd. I prefer to go on my own. Once I get there I'm in my own world, head in the form guide. And I bet everywhere, unfortunately."

Brad McNamara is Mark's chief punting partner, and is well-qualified to provide a profile of Mark Waugh the punter. "He's a lunatic, an absolutely lunatic punter," said McNamara. "He's a touch punter. He doesn't bother looking at the form guide, doesn't care what people say. He just goes for the long shot. He's fearless."

Mark may claim that the races are his relaxation but the experience is apparently a much more hectic one than he lets on. "For a start, you're not allowed to miss a race in any state or any province anywhere in Australia," said McNamara. "If it's on Sky Channel or there's odds on it you've got to bet on it. His idea of relaxation is having a bet on every race. Not having one in Sydney and waiting 40 minutes and having a beer and having another one. It's helter skelter all day. You need a holiday after a day at the races with him. He turns over quite a bit of money in the course of a day at the races. Six meetings and eight races a meeting – – that's 40 or 50 bets. He doesn't lose all that often, he's pretty good."

As McNamara said, Mark is much more comfortable backing the value horse. But one Miracle Mile Lee Sterrey got Mark to go against the grain. Village Kid was the hot favourite and Sterrey, who said he loves a favourite, told Mark they would put their combined winnings, about $400, on Village Kid if they could get 11/8 on. They were having no luck and were leaving the ring with their cash still in their pockets when the last bookie they passed put up 11/8 on by mistake. Sterrey, who said he was sweating on the bet and had the money in his hand, quickly claimed the bookie for those odds. Unfortunately Village Kid got trapped in the "death seat" and was pipped on the post by Master Mood who had enjoyed a perfect rails run. "I looked at Mark and he was almost crying," said Sterrey.

Lee is amazed at Mark's luck on a race course. "He's one of the few blokes I know who can turn $30 into $2000. And he's not done it once, he's done it a dozen times."

An example of Mark's astuteness on the punt occurred on *Wide World of Sports* last season. The show had crossed live to a training session and Max Walker asked Mark for a World Cup tip. He told Walker people couldn't go wrong if they had something each-way the Pakistanis.

Steve may not be in Mark's class as a punter but he has his moments. Teddington's Michael Welch recalls receiving a 4am call from Madras back in 1987. "I'd had a big night and wasn't feeling particularly tasty," said Welch. "It was a telephone operator from Madras. Steve comes on and says, 'Welchy put 50 pounds on Australia to win the World Cup. "I said 'Don't be silly'. At the time Australia was the rank outsider at about 12/1, but I popped down in the morning and put the bet on. I'm glad I did because nine times out of 10 I would not have bothered."

That was a tidy little collect but his greatest success dates back to his time at Nelson. Steve had a bet with Nelson seamer Peter Cochrane about the 1989 Ashes tour. "He bet his plot of land in Sydney for my house that Australia would come back and beat England for the Ashes, which Steve duly did on his own. He hasn't been back to collect fortunately," said Cochrane. Steve had forgotten about the bet, but when reminded immediately started plans to collect.

True to the restlessness of their competitive natures, Steve and Mark can be found gambling on anything at any time. Their golf games often end up with significant sums changing hands and they will even add an extra bit of interest to their pinball parlour duels. Yes, the twins still love simple pleasures like pinball machines and video games.

(Above and below by Philip Brown)

Above right: Steve celebrates after the 1989 Test win at Lords. Top left: He relaxes with a round at St Andrews on that tour. Above left: Mark meets the former Australian Prime Minister Bob Hawke.

"We've spent a lot of time in amusement arcades over the years," said McNamara. "We've always managed to find the closest one to the hotel. I think people are often surprised to walk in off the street and find the two Waughs battling over a racing car machine or pinball machine in an amusement arcade, carrying on like three-year-olds. We all do.

"They're very competitive in everything they do. If you go into an amusement parlour you've got to come out on top. We were in Perth for three-and-a-half or four weeks in the 1991-92 season and found this one called Monaco Grand Prix or something. It's fantastic, it's one of those new ones that you sit in. It's almost like the real thing. We spent at least an hour there every night . It was almost like a grand prix the way we were treating it."

Probably the favourite game over the years has been Hyper Olympics where you control an athlete that competes in a variety of events such as the hurdles and sprints. As in most things they've been very even. But, with Brad and Mark involved, it's not surprising that the pure thrill of competition is never quite enough. "We'd bet little things like dinner or the

(Gregg Porteus)

first round of drinks — that sort of thing. Half the time you'd treat that more seriously than batting or bowling in the nets. It was a life-or-death situation to get that car across the line first."

That famous competitive streak extends to board games as well. Lynette made the mistake of introducing Steve to the board game Othello, and then was forced to play it almost non-stop until Steve had worked out the tactics and could beat her. He took the game with him on tour to Pakistan and cornered his mate Tim May. "Once I finally got it I'd cream Maysie every time for months," said Steve. May, of course, finally twigged and edged Steve 3-2 for the Othello championship in Karachi. "He still claims to be Othello champ," said Steve.

One incident caused Blues team-mate Trevor Bayliss to question the twins sporting talent. He wondered if it was not, to use that rough-and-ready Australianism, more 'arse than class'. Someone had produced a putter in the dressing room when NSW were in Perth for the FAI Cup in 1991, and a putting competition ensued. Steve then decided to up the ante, according to Bayliss. "Steve announced he was going to hit the ball 20 yards through the doorway, into the hall, miss the plastic garbage bin, bounce the ball back off the brick wall, back in through the door, across the dressing room and into the cup. With a minimum of fuss Steve hit the ball and it followed his instructions to the letter. It was as if it had a scanner and a map.

Sarcastic remarks and general scorn were drowning out his obvious pleasure when I said to Steve that there was only one other bloke who could do that. Of course at that very moment Mark walked in through the door, wondering what all the fuss was about. When it was explained he said 'give me a go'. It was like that mental telepathy twins are supposed to have. That little white golf ball retraced every instruction Steve had given it two minutes before. Only this time, to show a little individual brilliance, Mark bounced the ball off the plastic garbage bin out in the hallway and back into the cup. While Mark and Steve carried on the rest of us were left standing there wondering if we'd missed out on something."

Despite the excesses of his youth Steve is pretty much a stay-at-home-and-relax kind of guy these days. He said he is happiest going to a movie or to a friend's place for dinner. Movies are to Steve what punting is to Mark — a way to tune out and stop thinking about runs and wickets and victories. "It is a good way of relaxing," he said. "I like sitting in the theatre and forgetting about everyone else, just watching a movie and relaxing."

Steve believes the first movie he and Mark saw was *The Invisible Man* at Bankstown with their Aunt Coral. These days his tastes run very much to comedy although he admits to liking *The Godfather* as well. He has seen movies like *Animal House*, *Caddy Shack* and *Planes, Trains and Automobiles* a number of times. Steve Martin is his favourite actor. Movies were Steve's main recreation during the heady Ashes tour of England in 1989.

"We used to go out and buy videos and we would play them on coach journeys so we ended up with 30 or 40 tapes and at the end of the tour we each got to pick a couple. It was a way of passing time on the motorways. Either that or playing cards. Half the guys would be playing cards at the back of the bus and the other half would be watching a movie.

"I somehow missed out on cards on the way through. I never really learned how to play. And once you don't know how to play you don't get invited. There is always a group playing 500 or whatever. I can play poker or blackjack but pretty poorly. My record at casinos isn't good. I would like to learn how to play but once you're out of that circle no-one spends the time to show you how to play the game. They are always too keen on beating each other. So you miss out and do whatever else is happening."

Steve practises his putting during a break in play at the SCG. Helping him to read the line are team-mates Mark Taylor and Michael Whitney.
(Peter Brennan)

Music is another form of relaxation for Steve but he doesn't get too precious about it. He and Greg Matthews are major contributors to the portable CD player that takes pride of place in the NSW dressing room. Matthews is the Blue with the eclectic tastes, Steve provides the balance with some good old rock and roll. "I cater more for the average person. I like a lot of Australian music. Cold Chisel was always my favourite I suppose. Anything Jimmy Barnes has got to do with. Bands like Noiseworks, Baby Animals, Screaming Jets, Dragon, Australian Crawl, Icehouse."

A childhood fascination that has yet to fade is an affection for aircraft. "The airport was another place they liked to go as children," said Bev. "We would often go out to the airport or even just sit along Brighton and watch the planes. Little did they know that one day they would be forever in them. But they were always fascinated by aeroplanes."

It's a fascination that has never left Mark at least. During the 1992 English season Mark was playing in a benefit match for Derek Pringle outside a village called Rochford. There was a huge airshow on nearby featuring all sorts of aircraft. Vintage fighters and passenger airliners, the newest Tornados and the Royal Airforce's aerobatic troop the Red Arrows all flew overhead. Not only did Mark spend most of his time in the pavilion staring at them but he even paused during his innings, while he was on strike, to watch aircraft sail overhead.

Steve is a fearless traveller and game for anything, whether it be temples in Bangkok, scooters in the West Indies, or craft classes and beach cricket in India. The cricketers on the scooters are: (left to right) Ian Healy, Peter Taylor, Steve and Mark. The batsman on the beach in India is Greg Dyer. Steve is behind the stumps.

One of the benefits of playing international cricket, apart from the obvious fame and fortune, is the opportunity to travel to some of the more exotic places in the world. England aside, which is interesting for totally different reasons, Steve has been able to indulge his passion for travelling in such locales as the West Indies, Pakistan, India, the United Arab Emirates, Dubai, Zimbabwe, Europe and the United States. "I like seeing new places," said Steve. "The only thing I find frustrating is when you go away on a cricket tour you don't get to see much of the place you are travelling in. That can be annoying. I suppose you are there to do a job and you're not expected to go on a sightseeing holiday but I do enjoy seeing new places and touring around. I have an ambition to see the seven natural wonders of the world."

Not so his more timid brother. "I'm not real touristy," said Mark. "I'm just happy to hang around the hotel." He says he has no desire to explore overseas when his cricket career is finished. "I'd like to travel around Australia if anywhere. I'd rather just stay at home and go to the north or south coast."

"I can't stand staying in hotels while on tour," said Steve. "I'd rather go out and see the people and see what's happening."

"He's always having a go at me for being a five-star tourist," said Aussie keeper Ian Healy who, along with Mark, Allan Border and David Boon, is a member of the group that likes to hang around the hotel and give the in-house videos and mini-bar a workout.

The first time he went to Europe with Lynette, following an itinerary worked out for them by Bob Simpson, the pair got lost every day travelling through Germany, Austria, Italy and Switzerland. On one occasion Steve drove the wrong way down a street. Of course the car coming the other way was a police car. It wasn't easy to explain and the Waughs had to endure a search before the police let them go on their way.

On another occasion in Germany the pair had trouble finding accommodation because it was holiday time. Things were getting tense as night was falling when they came upon a building with a nice big pebbled driveway. Lynette ordered Steve to go in and find them a room. "I realised my mistake when I got to the kitchen," said Steve. "They were all eating around the table. It was someone's house."

Steve says he and cohorts like Mike Whitney, who is a world champion traveller and adventurer, are always keen to get to the out-of-the-way places that tourists — particularly white tourists — don't go. For instance a couple of the Australian players went to a market in Jamaica and were mistaken for Americans. Jamaica can be a fairly heavy place at the best of times so things could have turned ugly. "They thought we were Americans so they wanted to get stuck into us," said Steve. "'Bloody Yanks,' they were saying. 'You people think we are monkeys' and stuff like that. Of course we didn't think that. Once we told them we were Australians it was okay, there were no problems."

When Greg Matthews had a chain stolen during a walk through town in Guyana the local mafia heavyweight organised its return. Steve made his acquaintance following the incident and along with a few others was taken on a tour through the ghetto. "He wasn't a bad bloke," said Steve. "If we hadn't been with him we would have been killed. We played pool in a dingy bar. It was scary in a way but exciting in another way."

That trip is in the same league but not quite as courageous as one excursion Steve took with Darren Lehmann while the team was in New York on a two-match tour of the States that followed the Sharjah limited-over tournament in 1990.

"Darren and myself might have had a few too many drinks one night when we said to the cab driver 'take us to Harlem and the Bronx and show us around'. He said 'you're joking aren't you?' So we ended up paying him a hundred bucks and he took us around for about an hour and a half. It was unbelievable. Nearly every building was burned out and there were people coming out of corners everywhere. They had 44 gallon drums with fires and people just hanging around. This was about three in the morning and there were hundreds of people on the streets and you could see them doing their drug deals. Next day we found out in the paper that a taxi driver was killed that night driving around Harlem. They reckon three a week get knocked off. And we were in the cab being white people. It was a once in a lifetime thing. People, even the locals, told us we were mad. We could easily have been killed.

"It was a damn scary place. I would never go in there again. A few people saw us and gave us some dirty looks. I don't think the cab driver was too happy either. Of course he was black, he had to be. If you're white and you go in there you're in a bit of strife. This is the worst part of New York."

The US trip differed from the norm for more than just that walk on the wild side. Because the players were only required for two exhibition games, one in New York and the other in Los Angeles, there was plenty of time to relax and explore. "Two games in 14 days," said Steve. "It was a tough trip that one. Jonesy is pretty good mates with Elton John so he rang up and got us a few tickets to see Elton. They were great seats. And myself and Ian Healy and Jonesy went to see Madonna. That was a fair concert. We went to a couple of basketball games and to Venice Beach in Los Angeles. We had a tough time there. We went to the top of the Empire State Building, did all that sightseeing stuff. It was a great trip. That was the only cricket trip I've been on that we had time to look around. It was more of a sightseeing trip than a cricket trip."

Steve and some of his Australian team-mates met a representative of Foster Parents Plan in India in 1987 and chatted to her about her job. The result was that Steve dragged a number of them out to a village to have a look around and witness the introduction of westernised toilets. Afterwards Steve and Mark Taylor decided to sponsor a child, Steve helping a child in Colombia and Mark one in India.

"It was pretty interesting actually. It was a real eye-opener," said Steve.

Steve may be a soulmate of Whitney's in the travelling and exploring stakes but is no match for his team-mate in the photographic stakes. "I used to take a lot of photos," said Steve. "I haven't taken so many of the last couple of trips but I normally get a copy of Whit's photos. I also always buy something from every country we got to, something I can remember each country by. I got some drawings in Dubai that are extracts out of old books, a rug from India, a sketch from the West Indies, a stone sculpture from Zimbabwe."

"He buys some absolute rubbish," chuckled Healy. "In the West Indies we went to great lengths to meet this artist who took us back to his studio. We bought two prints and his is crap. Lynette hates it." When reminded of this story, Steve remarked that Healy's print wasn't much good either!

The earlier charge that the Waughs weren't much on sedate hobbies like stamp collecting is not strictly true. While he, like Mark, was quickly bored by stamp collecting as a child Steve has nonetheless become a bit of a collector. Apart from the curios brought home after his foreign travels Steve is also building quite a collection of cricket memorabilia. Apart from a tangible record of his career it is a habit he has developed in tandem with a tremendous respect for the traditions of the game. He became very close friends with former NSW and Australian player Hunter "Stork" Hendry before he died. "He had some great stories about how they used to tour — staying at the maharajah's palace and things like that. When Hendry's team got off the ship in India three of the players got cholera or malaria and they

(Gregg Porteus)

Mark is not in Steve's class as an adventurer, but here he gets to know a West Indian musician.

didn't take any part in the trip. They stayed in hospital for four months and were picked up on the way back."

Steve developed an interest in the history of the game only after he arrived at first class level. Up until then his love of and for the game had been firmly rooted in the here and now. When he arrived on the first class scene he realised there was a lot more to cricket. He began watching films, reading books and columns by distinguished player-journalists like Bill O'Reilly. "It was just interesting to see how they played and what the game was like in those days. Reading Stan McCabe's book, I think the thing that came out of that was the way they played the game, the sportsmanship they had in those days, the way they behaved and carried themselves on the field. They were always polite. Not so much polite, but they played the game in the right way on the field. I think sometimes today you get carried away because you are playing for such big money and there is so much pressure on you. Sometimes you look back and say 'jeez, I wish I didn't do that'. If you think you got a bad decision sometimes you don't walk off like you should. So reading books makes you think that's the way you should accept it and that you should always show good sportsmanship on the field even if you play hard. But with today's pressures sometimes you get carried away and do things that you probably shouldn't."

Steve believes that when it's all said and done he hasn't let himself down too many times with his behaviour on the cricket field. He will admit to the odd lapse but nothing too serious. Things like over-reacting when an lbw is turned down or lingering at the crease after being given out. Things which are, sadly, routine these days.

"I think most of the time I have been pretty good," he says. "You sit down and you think 'it's only a game, you really should just accept it, but I think it was easier for them in those days because they weren't playing for their livelihood. There wasn't as much media pressure, I don't think, either. So it was a little easier to accept if you got a bad decision whereas today it could cost you your whole future."

Waugh admits to more than a little nostalgia, if not jealousy, when he looks back to those more relaxed times. "I think it would have been the best time to play cricket. They had big crowds and there were no bumper wars until Bodyline and I think people probably enjoyed themselves more than they do now. I would say there was less pressure from a public point of view and moneywise it was not their sole way of surviving like it is today for most people."

Steve is an avid collector of cricket memorabilia. Anything and everything is fair game, from routine things like caps, shirts, ties, autographed bats, stumps and balls to more esoteric items like the fibreglass cast he wore when suffering from stress fractures in his shin in 1985, a back cast, Tim May's finger guard and Geoff Lawson's boots.

"The trouble is I'm pretty slack and I chuck them into a big box and don't know which is which," said Steve, who fortunately has Lynette to organise that part of his life. She has stored away things Steve doesn't even know he still has. "I've got a fair bit of stuff," he said. "It's always good to look back on. When you collect something you can look back 10 years on and remember the story that surrounds the item. Like the ball that I took my 100th one-day wicket with. I think it's good to keep some stuff and remember the good times — and the bad times too, I suppose."

"I don't purposely collect caps or jumpers,"said Mark. "On the spur of the moment I might try to swap something. I should start keeping a few more. It's fair to say that's more important to Steve."

Steve has built a room in his home that will store all his memorabilia. He has installed lights that will showcase his exhibits like a gallery. It will be the bar room with the items on show constantly changing. While their exhibition might be carefully planned there is no reason behind their acquisition. That's not to say, though, that there isn't a good story.

"It's just on impulse," explained Steve. "I think it would be a good idea to collect that. I've got a stump from nearly every Test we've won, I've only missed out a couple of times." One occasion he remembers fondly is the World Cup final of 1987. When the game ended wicket keeper Greg Dyer threw the ball up in celebration. While he was doing that his team-mates were diving for the souvenirs. Boon and one of the other Australians each got one stump but Dyer seemed certain to get the third. "He turned around to grab the stump and I nicked in and grabbed the stump from underneath him," said Steve. "Just nipped in right underneath his nose. I grabbed both of the bails and I gave him one as a consolation. He's still a bit cheesed off about that."

One of the stranger, and funnier, things that Steve has hidden away is a hand-written message from Tim May. It was written under the influence of alcohol after the controversial declaration Geoff Lawson made against South Australia at the SCG in February 1989. Lawson had spoken with Hookes on the phone during a break in play and Hookes understood that an arrangement had been reached. He thought the deal was that if he bowled his part-timers so NSW could score some quick runs then Lawson would declare behind the South Australian total and thus give both sides a shot at outright points. Hookes met his side of the "bargain" but Lawson did not declare until NSW had passed the Croweater total. An outraged Hookes said he had been double-crossed and Lawson claimed he had been misinterpreted. He had said he had undertaken to "evaluate" the situation, not promised to declare. Anyway May wrote a very funny screed which took the incident as its inspiration. It didn't name Lawson but the point was still firmly made.

"It's a classic," said Waugh. "Maysie didn't even know he'd written it until I'd told him." Steve has kindly allowed this valuable document to be reproduced. It said:

"It is so depressing to realise that some prominent and 'respected' cricketers amongst this present Australian touring team regard the pursuit of Sheffield Shield points to be above the best interests of the game. I am one of many deeply disturbed cricket lovers who are witnessing the game being crippled by the self-interest of satanically possessed Hitlers who pursue victory with little thought of morality. The struggle for power and authority is fraught with danger. Progression may be made in the eyes of the beholder but at what cost? The game can well do without 'parasital maniacs' similar to those emerging east of Alice Springs. If our game is to continue into the next generation, we must learn from ancient Rome. They failed to heed the advice of their countrymen.

'FAC FORTIA ET PATERE' (do good deeds and endure) 1 July, 1989.

Steve caused a bit of a stir after the game when he was drinking with some of the South Australians. He called the incident the greatest set-up since *The Sting*. This became fodder for more press controversy but Steve claimed he was quoted out of context. "Things were a bit tense and I tried to break the ice," he said.

Steve also has spent plenty of time and money collecting cigarette cards. He has the complete sets from the 1930 and 1934 Ashes tours of England. He also has tennis cigarette cards and golf cards. "They're all original so they're pretty expensive," he said. As was previously mentioned it was not something he did a lot as a child. "I collected stamps but I soon gave that one up. I had a mate around the corner who collected them and he used to give us a few. Plus I used to knock off a couple when he wasn't watching. But that soon stopped. I don't think we collected coins or anything. I think stamps were the only one we really started on. We were keen for a couple of months and then got bored with it. We threw them out or gave them away."

SIXTEEN

Playing To Win

VIRTUALLY everybody who knows the Waugh twins has a view to offer about two of Australia's brightest sporting heroes. That is not surprising, given the fact that although both are obviously strong personalities, their unique characters are difficult to pin down. Interestingly enough, while there was almost unanimous agreement across the board on the twins' essential character, and even their little quirks, the question that really drew some disparate answers is whether or not the public, was able to get a good idea of what the Waughs are like from newspaper reports, the opinions of television commentators and watching them from the stands or on television. There were those who said 'yes', it was pretty much a case of what you see is what you get, but a more common answer was that perceptions were distorted by the one-dimensional context and the often misguided opinions of the commentators and journalists.

"I don't think people have got a clue what they're like," said Ian Davis. "They have a certain charisma. I think the average spectator is in awe of them. I don't think people are sure, they just see them as a talent."

Some are quick to categorise them, and there are plenty of stories which serve to sum them up. One who's always been pretty handy with an anecdote is NSW team-mate Mike Whitney. "Their 464-run partnership was the highlight of playing with them," he said. "They walked into the dressing room after Henry (Geoff Lawson) had called them in and Steve sat down, and as he was taking off his pads nonchalantly glanced across at Henry and said under his breath 'Hell, we could have put on six hundred'. That typifies what they're like. It was a world record partnership and Steve wasn't happy. I haven't scored that many runs in my first class career!"

But, as Mark Taylor is quick to point out, too many have been eager to pounce on this one aspect of Steve's character and make it sum up the whole. "He doesn't give too much away in interviews. But when Steve gets away from cricket he is a very relaxed sort of guy." Likewise all is not as it seems with his brother. "Mark comes over as a very casual guy but I've seen Mark get very upset at times."

That image as an intense tough guy is one that doesn't sit well with Steve. "That's what cheeses me off," said Steve. "Blokes writing stories about me who don't know me. People are different to the way they play the game. They don't know me so they assume that's the way I am. But I'm always having a joke with Phil Emery or Mark Taylor." He said he and the others used to drive former NSW and Australian keeper Greg Dyer crazy by throwing their wads of chewing gum on the ground when he was about to walk past. On occasion they even hit him in the gloves. Experienced practical jokers, they made sure to use green chewing gum so that it would be hard to see.

Taylor said his relationship with Steve has always featured a friendly rivalry. The occasion of Taylor's initial first class hundred certainly says something about both their friendship and Steve himself. "I got out in the last session on the second day for 118 and at

Steve and close mate Mark Taylor have shared a friendly rivalry since their school days, neither missing a chance ot take a little dig at the other. (Gregg Porteus)

stumps Steve was 1 not out. The next morning I took the camera out to take a picture of the scoreboard and Steve said 'hang on, save that photo for the end of the innings when I'm 119. And when we declared he was 119. It's always been a bit of a tussle. I got 136 at the 1989 Test at Headingley and when he passed me he waved his bat at me and went on to score 177 not out. So when I got 200 at Old Trafford I waved my bat at him when I was 178."

The person best qualified to sum up the Waugh temperament is of course their mother Bev. She is the glue that has bound the family together and has provided an example on which Mark and Steve have drawn deeply.

"I see lots of my father in them, in their character," said Bev. "Things like remaining cool-headed all the time. I can never remember my father being anything other than that, except on one or two occasions. And I think they show a fair bit of patience. My father had an incredible amount of patience in everything he did. I don't think I would know anyone who would ever had said a bad word about him. Everyone liked him. He was kind. All those good things.

"He never got angry. I know they get angry but, gee, when you are at the top of Australian sport these days it tests you, doesn't it? I think it is going to bring out anger in just about everybody at some stage or other. He very rarely showed any physical anger. So even though

Mark appeals unsuccessfully for LBW against Carlisle Best on the 1991 West Indies Tour.

(Gregg Porteus)

he hasn't been alive for a lot of their lives I think he has had a fairly big influence on them.

"The same with Rodger's mother. She's done things she was told she would never, ever do. She was a really beautiful young girl and she contracted polio when she was 18. She was belle of the beach, belle of the ball and all those sorts of things, and suddenly she's told she will never walk again. Told she would never have children. Well, she walked again. She was determined enough to do that, that was against all odds. And then she had Rodger. She's got heaps and heaps and heaps of courage. She's still not in a wheelchair."

Another obviously well qualified to comment, particularly on Steve, is his wife Lynette. "He's not as shy as he used to be but that's just maturity," she said. "The priorities he's got are still the same. Cricket's always been important but he still puts his family and friends first. He's gotten tougher as a person. He was a bit of a marshmallow.

"He's a steady person, he's not up or down. It affects me more than it affects him. When you're on the outside you never feel like you're quite in control. He's pretty quiet anyway so to get anything out of him you've sometimes got to ask 10 million questions.

"He's the same whether he gets a duck or a hundred. If he does well I'll be doing cartwheels around the room but the only time I can tell he's really, really happy is when he talks very quickly."

The twins can be curiously silent. Steve believes their relative silence is a product of the way they grew up. "Those days we did absolutely everything together so there was nothing new to talk about. We played the same sports, did the same things and had the same friends."

Steve said that often he has a feeling that Mark is going to do well. When he scored a double century in England last summer for Essex, Steve said he had a premonition as he picked up the paper that there was good news about Mark. "It's been too many times to be a coincidence," said Lynette.

Whitney is in a good position to judge the relationship between Mark and Steve. Apart from the time he has spent with them while playing for NSW and Australia his wife Debbie has twin sisters. He's known them about nine years and can't believe the difference between them and the Waughs. His sisters-in-law lived close by each other in Sydney and would be on the phone to each other numerous times a day, every day. Then when one moved up the coast with her husband the other visited and ended up buying the house next door!

"When I first met the twins they were very quiet but once you get to know them they are totally different," said Whitney. "For twins I've never met two blokes so different. "

While people are puzzled by Steve and Mark's apparent lack of communication Whitney feels there is a lot more there than meets the eye. He believes that Mark's explanation that they don't have to talk because they spent nine months in the same womb and 15 years in the same room is perfectly reasonable. "He didn't say it in a cruel way, a bad way," clarified Whitney. Still the Blues can't help joking about it once in a while said Whit.

"When they're batting together we'll sit and watch and at the end of the over someone will say: 'Yes and will they talk to each other?' And they'll move out to pat down the wicket, get about a third of the way down, look at one another and go back to their respective ends."

Mark revealed that words are exchanged but added that there was nothing particularly scintillating about the dialogue. "We don't make a scene of it. We always say something at the end of each over if we are batting together. Not much. You know, keep going or he bowls an out-swinger or something like that. Nothing too in-depth but a bit of encourage-ment."

Whatever the reason for their minimal communication Whitney is emphatic that it is not because they don't like or care for one another. He cites as an example one occasion early

Mike Whitney shares a "joke" with West Indian Desmond Haynes. Mark watches the fun. (Gregg Porteus)

in the twins' careers. NSW was in trouble with Steve already out and Mark at the crease when Mark got out playing what Whitney considered to be an indiscreet hook shot. He reacted angrily with a few earthy remarks and Steve, who was sitting next to him, reacted just as angrily.

"Steve just jumped down my throat, quick as a flash," said Whitney. "He said: 'You know that's the way he plays. If it had gone for six you would have been cheering. Don't bag him while I'm sitting next to you'. And he got up and left the room. A little later I felt a tap on the shoulder and it was Steve who asked me if I wanted to go for a hit. I said okay and on the way out he apologised for jumping down my throat. I think they really do have a deep-seated love for each other. I certainly don't think it's as bad as people make out."

"I think there's an enormous amount of respect and love," said Matthews. "They're very ferocious as far as defending one another. They're intensely loyal. They're not very loud people so you've got to listen." That loyalty extends to their friends. "Steve backs all his friends. He won't have anyone speak badly of them, always supports them in conversations when they are being attacked."

Both brothers deny there is any ill feeling between them. "People say we're not close but if someone says something bad about the other one then you know we stick up for each other," said Mark. "It would appear that we aren't close but obviously we care about each other. It's only natural. We're brothers. We sort of know what each other is feeling or what each other is thinking about. It's hard to explain. I think we can read each other's minds pretty well."

Cricket is about more than scoring runs and taking wickets. Mark, with Bruce Reid, preparing for a World Cup match at the SCG in 1992. (Live Action)

Mark wearing the colours of Essex. (Philip Brown)
Inset: Badges worn by an ardent fan of the twins during the Australia v Essex match in 1989. (Philip Brown)

Still, he confesses to little surprise that people are fascinated by the apparent lack of communication. "You don't see us together chatting away too often so it is pretty easy for people to say that. Well, it's true. We don't talk that much. We wouldn't go out together, go out to the movies or a restaurant, while we are on tour but if there was someone else with us then we would go out. No problem. I think we quite enjoy each other's company with someone else with us."

There is no doubt that the relationship the twins have is unique but, given their gifts, it is not surprising that the pair have developed a unique solution to coping with the pressures they have had to live with for most of their lives. After all, there's no law that says twins have to be inseparable and walk, talk and think in unison. If anything it is more natural for people that have lived almost the same life for more than 20 years to create a little space for themselves rather than living in each others' pockets. It shows a refreshing sense of self and the resolve that has helped them make the most of their tremendous talents.

"We've always done everything together," said Mark. "I suppose when we get the chance there is no reason to go out together. I mean, if we get the chance to be separate then we don't ring each other up and say 'what are you doing now, come over for a drink'."

The same goes for rooming together on tour. Steve usually rooms with Mark Taylor. "We spent years together. Why would we want to room with each other now?" said Steve. He added, nevertheless, that all the sharing and time spent together was not a problem in those days. "We just accepted it, you know. We were twins and went everywhere together and we dressed the same and we lived in the same room and we didn't think anything more of it. I suppose looking back people might think it's a bit funny but it was never thought of that way. Always off to bed at the same time, wake up at the same time."

Both said the constant close contact wasn't a hassle.

"We shared the same drawers and the same clothes," said Steve. "It was a matter of first in best dressed, I think, half the time. It never really became a problem until we were 15 or 16 and then probably started to worry about what we were wearing. But before that it was the same tracksuits, the same clothes, so jump in and grab them. We were never too worried about clothes. I mean we used to wear T-shirts and track suits and that's about all we used to wear."

A popular theory has been that the two talented cricketers are insanely jealous of each other as a result of all the competing for places in various teams. It is definitely not true and probably more the result of wishful thinking on the part of the mean-spirited. "People always ask 'are you jealous of each other' but we never really have been except for a couple of years there. About 13-14-15," said Steve. "If we were totally honest. I don't know, Mark mightn't say that. But I think we probably were because everyone was comparing us. Everyone you would run into would say 'have you heard about the Waugh boys' and 'who's the best one?' and, in a way, we probably listened to it and you try to be the best one at that age. But it stopped after that. I mean, you know you are your own person and you've got to do your best without worrying about other people. It was just the fact that everyone was labelling us and I think the pressure probably got to us a bit there.

"It never really became a big factor. I think you concentrated more on your own effort, but at schoolboy level I think it was sometimes a relief to score more runs than Mark. You didn't want to let him get too far ahead."

Steve felt their choice of sport has unfortunately given ammunition to those who want to compare and contrast the two. The abundance of statistics in cricket gave the mischievous the perfect measuring sticks. They just looked at the scorebook. Soccer on the other hand

Pakistani quick Wasim Akran gets one past Steve during a 1989-90 World Series match. (Gregg Porteus)

was a much more difficult vehicle for such comparisons. For a start because Mark and Steve played quite different positions it was difficult to play one off against the other. And there wasn't the concrete statistics of cricket.

"I think we probably enjoyed them both equally as much though there probably wasn't quite as much pressure at soccer," said Steve. "But even when we were young we were always the best two players in the side so people were always looking for us to do the special things and star in the game. If you didn't people would say 'what's wrong with you?'. I was probably the better player of the two at soccer whereas at tennis Mark was probably the better player. Cricket was the sport where we were dead even all the way. Soccer I probably developed more later on and could have taken that up as a sport whereas Mark was always heading towards cricket. So there wasn't as much direct competition in the other sports as there was in cricket."

Whether or not they consciously competed against each other there is no doubt they never stopped competing against the game, themselves and everyone else involved. Life has been a game for Mark and Steve in both respects. It has been an opportunity to have fun but it is also a chance to test their skills and try to win.

Mark said the origins of these particular urges is clear. "We got our competitiveness from both Mum and Dad. If we had a game of social tennis we would always try to win. Whenever we play mum at squash, or whatever, she always tries her hardest to beat us. She never lets up. She never likes to give us a point, really. The same as dad. We play table tennis at home and he'll always try to win.

"I don't know whether it is always playing to win, more playing to give your best. Always try, never give up. That sort of attitude. I think it was very important. That's the main thing in sport, I think, to always give 100 per cent. Never give up, keep trying. If you've got ability and determination that's the main two things."

A photo that says a lot about the spirit, and success, of the Australian team in the late 80s and early '90s. Match-winners Mark Taylor (left), Terry Alderman (centre) and Geoff Marsh laugh off a Merv Hughes beer shower.
(Gregg Porteus)

Getting out has never been much fun.

The twins appear all business when they're at work, but team-mates know better.   (Gregg Porteus)

Bev tells a story that more than any of the backyard anecdotes or third-party accounts sums up the Waugh twins and the family as a whole. "Once I remember we were on holidays and we had nothing, no food to eat, which was a tragedy in itself. But we didn't have any sporting equipment that day either. We usually had tennis racquets or golf clubs or something you could play with. All we had left were about 10 Macadamia nuts. The boys decided to have a competition. We all sat down in a little circle on the sand. We had two rocks, which we had to find ourselves, one rock was on the sand and you hit it with the other. Each person got one hit at the nut and it went around the circle. Whoever cracked a nut got to eat it. I can remember there were a few bloody fingers that day. We were all in on it though. Dean was the winner. We ended up playing lots of fun games like that. Usually with that element of competition."

It is that sense of fun that people don't get to see from a distance when Steve and Mark are giving their all for Australia. Steve, in particular, has copped some unfair comment for his on-field demeanour. Despite the pressure and the big bucks he is still the same guy who threw water bombs at school. "He's a mischievous bugger," said McNamara. "On the surface he doesn't seem like the sort of bloke who would even like a laugh but deep down he's got a mischievous streak. If he's not carrying out the practical joke or whatever he's the instigator. They're both like that really. They're both very funny blokes. They have a very dry sense of humour. They don't come out with all that much but when they do they come out with a fantastic one-liner that breaks everyone up."

"Steve appears to be a bit shy and quiet but there is a wicked side to him," agreed schoolmate Richard Lane. "A wicked sense of humour. He doesn't mind stirring the pot a bit." It appears the reason most people don't pick it up is because Steve doesn't employ the stadium-sized gestures of a Merv Hughes. His humour is far more subtle and thus more difficult to pick up if you're on the SCG Hill with a half-dozen schooners under your belt or at home, flicking between channels during the ads.

"He did it quietly, he wasn't boisterous," said Lane of Steve, the schoolboy prankster. "He'd instigate some of the stuff and sit back and watch somebody else carry it on. Steve used to enjoy watching other people get in trouble. I think he and Mark were immune. They were participants but because they were a bit quieter it worked to their advantage. They were usually in it up to their ears."

"He's terrible," said Lynette. "He's the biggest teaser of all time. He torments everyone from the dog to the kid next door to me. If, there's a practical joke to be played you can bet Steve's behind it. He was working on a McHappy Day at McDonalds where personalities cook and serve the food for charity and he was out the back in the kitchen making burgers and throwing the pickles at everyone." Steve chipped in with a tip for all the youngsters: "You've got to lick them before you throw them."

"Honestly, sometimes it's like living with a four-year-old," said Lynette.

Waugh is also a dab hand at nicknames, perhaps his best is the one he concocted for Australian wicketkeeper Ian Healy — Swahili. Steve said it came about because Healy talks in his sleep and it's pure gibberish. Healy, for his part, said that while he had never become a victim there were plenty of atrocities committed by S. Waugh in the name of fun.

"He and Veletta, it's a nightmare when they room together. They're just shockers those two. But Steve only mucks around with people he's super-confident with. Generally it's the larrikins, the Mays and the Waggy Velettas. They're outwardly very stable, that's why people wouldn't see that side of Steve."

"Wag's a funny man," said Waugh. "Get a few beers into him and he's like a time bomb." The pair shared a room in the West Indies in 1991. Because it was a self-contained apartment they cooked for themselves and lost a lot of food to birds that flew in from outside and helped themselves. One morning Steve woke to find that Veletta, who had risen before him, had laid a trail of crumbs across the room to Steve's bed and up his leg. Steve's revenge for that one was sweet.

Veletta and former West Australian and Australian batsman Graeme Wood are brothers-in-law and after a run out mix-up a few years back Wood had refused to talk to Veletta for about four weeks. On April Fools Day on the Windies tour, which should have alerted Veletta straight away, Steve slipped a noted under Mike's door. "It said 'Graeme Wood called from Western Australia just to say hello and to talk about running between wickets to sort out a few things for next year'," said Steve. "Waggy returned the 'call' and Woody didn't know what he was calling for. It cost him about 50 bucks."

The practical joker tasted a large dose of his own medicine on one of the most important

Steve is safely out of harm's way when better-known prankster Merv Hughes lets Terry Alderman have it during post-match celebrations. The Australian players are (back) Merv Hughes, Steve, (centre) Bruce Reid, Geoff Marsh, Mark Taylor, (front) Allan Border and Terry Alderman. (Gregg Porteus)

days of his life. He had already got off to a bad start when they ran late for his wedding and Mark Taylor had to drive like a madman to get him to the church on time. He is reported to have said: "I'm more nervous now than before a Test innings." Things did not get any better on arrival — well they did, but not at first. Tony Fort takes up the story: "Mark Taylor and I had sabotaged Steve's shoes while he was in the shower. Using a bottle of liquid paper we painted HE on his left sole and LP on his right. When Steve kneeled to say his vows etc David Boon was the first to notice from the congregation. From the front row he saw HELP, turned to us and said under his breath "Lynette's going to kill you two". The bridesmaids then

Windies woes ... Mark tries to stop the bells ringing after stopping a Courtney Walsh bouncer with his head.

(Gregg Porteus)

caught on and there were giggles and shaking of heads throughout the church. Steve had seen it on his shoes just before the ceremony and was trying to get the message off by scrubbing twigs from the churchyard against his soles. He wasn't too successful."

One of Steve's best mates since he broke into the Test team has been South Australian off-spinner Tim May. The pair forged a firm friendship during the dark days of the 1988 Pakistan tour and have remained close friends ever since. May is puzzled by the squeaky clean image Steve has with the public given his personal experiences. "Everybody thinks he is the sensible member of the team but I look at him in a completely different light," said May.

And with good reason. May's first piece of evidence for the prosecution occurred during the 1988 international season. Australia had just won the World Series Cup and during the big celebrations afterwards May said he noticed Steve "lurking" around his kitbag or, as the cricketers call it, coffin. Given what was about to transpire the cricketing slang is particularly appropriate. The side travelled to Sydney and enjoyed a three-day break before a Test match. When May opened his coffin to practice on the eve of the game he said he was greeted by an odour which he describes as the worst he has ever smelt.

"Steve had filled my boots with prawn heads and the smell was such that I had to get rid of everything on the eve of the game — gear, tracksuits, the lot," said May. To this charge the accused pleads guilty although he claims mitigating circumstances. "I was just mucking around. Maysie is always good to have a joke with, this one just went a bit further than I meant it to. He was a bit stiff there. I didn't realise he wasn't going to open his bag for four days," said Steve.

The bond that secured the pair's friendship is the aptly-named "Curse of Room 242". The pair suffered a horror run starting on the 1988 tour of Pakistan and May dubbed it the 'Curse of Room 242' after the hotel room the pair shared in the city of Quetta. It was at that time that everything went sour for them. Steve jokes that May, who has had a shocking run of injuries and lost a lot of ground in his battle for Australia's Test spin spot, is still suffering from the Curse.

"Everything was going pretty well until Quetta," said May. "The very afternoon we got there we dumped out bags and headed out to practice. We were doing our hamstring stretches when Steve experienced a tightness in the belly (which quickly took a turn for the worse) and the following day I dislocated a finger. Steve then got a string of horrendous decisions. I'm still finding it hard to shake."

May is a great fan of the teen film *Ferris Bueller's Day Off* (Steve says he thinks he is Ferris Bueller) and it was on the Pakistan tour that he found out Steve shared his enthusiasm. The last night they were in Pakistan they left their Karachi hotel and had a fantastic meal that cost them next to nothing. Across the road from the restaurant was a video shop and the pair, not believing their eyes, decided to investigate. May said Steve asked the shopkeeper if they had *Ferris Bueller's Day Off* and the man, looking at Steve as if he is an idiot, pointed to the very large Ferris Bueller picture on the wall.

"We just had to get it out to cheer up after eight weeks of pure despondency," said May, who also managed to souvenir the poster. Steve reports that he held on to it until the beginning of 1992 when the Mays moved house and wife Catherine took the opportunity to "lose" the poster. "He was distraught for about six weeks," said Waugh. "It was one of the most devastating times of my life," said May.

Steve and Tim, having rented the video, tried frantically to rent a hotel room so they could watch it. Because most Pakistani hotels don't have in-house systems they had to settle for a hotel viewing room. They differ on the number and nationality of the tourists who were

It's prank time ... the sly smile on Mike "Waggy" Veletta's face suggests some mischief brewing as he, Steve, Geoff Marsh and Mike Whitney endure a rain delay in Barbados in 1991. (Gregg Porteus)

settling down to watch a film, anywhere between 30 and a 100, but the two managed to persuade them to experience the delights of Ferris Bueller. While the hotel guests agreed, or were bullied into it by a fast-talking May, they didn't give it much of a chance and by the end of the movie Steve and Tim were the only people left in the room.

Since then May and Steve have used their own personal code to lighten up tense Sheffield Shield clashes between NSW and South Australia. Various players took on the names of characters from the movie: Peter Taylor was the headmaster, Ed Rooney, and Geoff Lawson was the nerd Cam Fry. Given that Lawson and Taylor have now retired there will have to be auditions to fill the roles.

"In the heat of the battle everyone would be very serious and halfway through his run-up Steve's got to stop himself because he's laughing so much or I've got to stop him," said May who suggested the story proves that there is more to Waugh than meets the eye. "When he's on the field he's pretty relaxed. Basically he's looking for a laugh but he doesn't show it. My mum still thinks he's the most serious cricketer she's ever seen and I don't dare spoil her little picture." Bad luck Mrs May — blame Tim.

"I can always make Maysie laugh," said Steve.

Talk to their friends and it becomes clear that the Waughs' supposed aloofness is a fiction. They have their fair share of friends. Mark, despite his apparently easy-going and gregarious nature, has a smaller circle. Steve, in contrast, has a large number of friends and that magic ability to maintain and nourish the friendships despite the hurdles of distance and the passage of time. "Steve doesn't really let people drift away if he values them," said childhood friend and schoolmate Mark Grant.

"They've still got time for the people they used to play against," said former coach Ian Gill. "They've gained a lot of respect from guys because of that. They still treat them as mates."

"I've got quite a few friends who are outside sport and I like to keep those friends as well," said Steve. "Especially from school. I've got five guys who I see regularly although I don't see them as regularly now because one lives in Cairns and another lives in Canberra. I rang six of them one night just to keep in contact. It's good to keep those friends away from cricket because they don't understand much about it. It's good to get away from it for a while and talk about school and if they're around go out for a drink or something."

Resident tiler Chris Madden declared the Steve Waugh residence the ultimate party place. "He loves to see his mates have a good time," he said. "The minute everyone gets here he won't let anyone have a drink out of their hand. And when things start getting rowdy and there's a bit of fun going on he's the first bloke to have the video out to catch the good times. He doesn't like to miss anything like that. All in all he loves seeing people have a good time."

Ironically, given the venue where Steve's friendship with Richard Lane was forged and the world he inhabits, sport, and cricket in particular, is not the pivot of their relationship. "I've never once asked him about cricket and he's never once told me about it," said Lane.

"You've got to get him alone to really suck his brain on cricket," agreed Madden.

"Steve's very, very quiet about his own successes," said Mark Grant. "He doesn't bring them up unless you do. Steve always talks about 'we', like 'we' the Shield side. He's more than happy to talk about other people, that's one of the twins' strengths."

Once Steve and Lane were in McDonalds and the girl at the checkout did a double take when Steve stepped up to order. She continued to stare while he did so. The Australian cricket team was on the paper placemat, and she had noticed that he was one of them. "He'd just made the Australian team but he said, 'Yeah that's me' matter-of-factly. There was nothing big-headed about it," Lane said.

While there always had been other things to bring the Waughs down to earth in the schoolyard or at home, when they played sport they were unequivocally No.1 in the team. But their honesty, modesty, loyalty and sense of humour have gone a long way towards ensuring that they haven't alienated their team-mates

"They're the sort of blokes who don't get all that close to too many people," said McNamara. "But they've got as many friends as anyone. Both have been incredibly supportive to me, absolutely fantastic. Even though a lot's happened to them they really haven't changed at all. They've always related to their team-mates very well. Being such fantastic players it's a lot easier to get respect out of guys. You know what it's like when you're young — usually the best player in the side is the most popular bloke. So they never struggled there. But as they've grown older nothing's changed. They're very level-headed and get on in the side just as well as anyone. They've never had any troubles in that regard."

Ian Healy said the Waughs valued that team morale highly, and loved to get involved. "Steve is very, very persuasive without being obvious," he said. "Generally blokes will follow him. He's a leader. Mark is not as self-assured. He probably tends to follow more than Steve."

People, particularly shy people, tend to try to overcompensate when they enter a strange environment. Thus the birth of the ugly Australian or ugly American tourist. When you're away from home it is natural to be really Australian or American as a sort of self-defence mechanism. But, as shy and insecure as he might have been, it was an option that Steve passed on when he stepped into the difficult role of professional for Lancashire League club Nelson in 1987. "The thing that first struck me when we met was how mature he was for 22," said current captain Michael Bradley. "He was the youngest player in the side and there was a lot of pressure because in our league the professional has a reasonably big impact. If they fail there's a good chance the side will be beaten. Steve handled that well.

"He fitted in very well. Initially he was fairly quiet but as soon as he'd played a game or two he started mouthing off and taking the piss. He was very popular with the lads. He has a dry sense of humour, very dry. Real quick quips. He's basically a really grand lad. People over here think most Aussies are bigheads but he'd fit in anywhere. He's not a person who'll be falling out in lumps with people."

As the professional at Nelson, in the Lancashire League, Steve had junior coaching responsibilities which he fulfilled without fuss. But he also went a step further and spent a couple of hours a week helping Julie Bradley, the wife of the current skipper, coach her school cricket team. And they weren't some spoiled private school brats either. The clumsy title given to them was "social priority area disadvantaged" children.

"He absolutely adores kids and kids love him," said Mike Bradley. Wife Lynette refers to him as the king of the kids.

One kid in particular is Michael's son Lewis. Lewis was just a baby when Steve was at Nelson but over the years the bond between the two has developed to an amazing extent. The Bradleys came to Australia for a month in January 1991 and the pair were inseparable. "Lewis completely forgot I was there," said Michael. "He adopted Steve as his surrogate father."

As has been mentioned, Steve also sponsored a child in Columbia for a number of years. He recently discontinued the sponsorship and is considering doing something in the local sphere. "I'd rather do something closer to home," he said. "Homeless kids is a good cause. I don't like to see kids suffering. I think homeless kids are a tragedy. I don't want to sound like Mother Theresa but I think it's a good idea for sportsmen to get involved in charities because they can help."

Steve has done work for Camperdown Childrens Hospital. Lynette remarked upon the positive bedside manner he has developed on his hospital visits. "You've just got to be natural," said Steve. "You've got to have a good laugh with them. I learned that from watching Michael Whitney. But it's always sad. When you go you realise how lucky you are."

Mark and Steve's shyness, reserved public personas and preoccupation with sport might lead some people to suggest that they would be all at sea in the business world. Steve may still feel a little uncomfortable but he is a tough negotiator and no mug when it comes to organising contracts. And if anything having to deal with sponsors has been a positive influence on Mark, who has also proven to be a smart and diligent operator in the business world. He is currently under contract to Ian Davis' sporting goods company Slazenger. Because the two are in contact on a weekly basis Davis has had the opportunity to observe Mark in action . "Mark has been an absolute breath of fresh air," said Davis. "I think his performances and his attitude towards his contractual agreement have been absolutely impeccable. He's really been outstanding. He knows the value of a sponsorship. He's promoted our product to the fullest.

"I've seen a tremendous transition in Mark. When I first met him as a kid he was as shy as they come. And even when he was playing with the State he was still really shy. If you were talking to him or Steve face to face it would be very hard to get anything out of them. But just in the last year or so, since Mark's been successful at State level and since he's been to Essex, I think he's really matured and he's got plenty of confidence in himself, in his own ability. And I think that's portrayed by the way he presents himself now. And I've got to say that he really does go over very well, he handles the situation in meetings and store appearances. Generally, he has really come of age."

Mark doesn't just sign his name and bank the cheque. He is involved in the various processes — right down to the little things like photos and the swing tags that go on the bats. He has taken part in shoe design but has shown little interest in bat design. For others that is, he is very particular about the tools he uses himself.

"He knows what he likes," said Davis. "He basically designed what he wanted in a cricket

(Gregg Porteus)

Mark blew away his "easy-going" and "soft" tags with his brave displays on the 1991 Windies tour.

bat. It's very interesting because not many people would have thought of it. He likes the bat 3.75cm longer in the blade, with the normal standard-length handle, and he likes the handle to be forward about 2cm. He likes the weight of it about 2lb 10oz. The bats are handmade in England for him to those specifications. Not too many people would ask for that sort of thing but he's gone to a lot of trouble to find out what he wants."

Mark is very much a here-and-now kind of guy. Whereas Steve has grown to appreciate the more peripheral aspects of cricket Mark has lagged behind. He's also a little more concerned with statistics than it has appeared. "I'm reasonably interested in the history of the game," said Mark. "I don't know a great deal but I think as time goes on I'll get more and more interested. I know all the statistics, I'm big on statistics. I think it was there most of the time, ever since I've been playing grade cricket. Reading what people scored, knowing what is going on. Keeping an eye on other people who were playing for the same spot. It's only natural. It's still the same now really. You don't hope that they will fail but it's always nice to know what people are doing."

His statistical interest is purely confined to the fortunes of others. "I never used to worry about my average as a kid. It still doesn't worry me. You've got to be selfish in cricket but at the same time you've got to put the team first a lot of the time. People soon work it out if you are not playing for the team. We are not overly selfish really. We have always done our best and hopefully it's been good for the team as well. We've always played for the team rather than ourselves. It's just our nature I suppose. It's just something we've always done. I suppose because we're in a big family, we can't afford to be too selfish, we've got to share things."

Although he has said he is happy with the way the media has treated him Mark admits to be upset about some of the things he reads and hears. Particularly a few of the myths about him that are perpetuated. The biggest bit of baggage he has had to carry is the "lazy" tag. He doesn't deny that there was some basis for the criticism early in his career but he feels it's definitely old news these days.

"I suppose when I first played first class cricket I might have been a bit lazy but since then I don't think so," he said. "I never miss a training session or anything like that. It may sound like I'm blowing my own trumpet here, but if you do things easy, say you take a catch easily or you look like you're running slower than other people, people think you're not trying or you're lazy. It's just the way I play. Sometimes I make things look easy which means it doesn't look like I'm trying or putting in 100 per cent. But I am.

" I was a bit soft for a couple of seasons. I'd read it in the papers and hear it on the grapevine that other players were saying I should be doing better, that I had to toughen up, that I was too casual.

"I think people still do think I am a bit casual," he said. "Even Keith Fletcher, from Essex, was always at me at fielding practice. But when it comes to on the field that's where it counts in my book. How you perform on the field. My record speaks for itself at the moment."

Team-mates say any lingering doubt about Mark's desire is cured by playing with him. "Steve is more verbal and will say something if it needs to be said whereas Mark's a guy who'll try to lift his own performance to lift the team," said Taylor, though he did agree that Mark was not afraid to speak his mind. "I've seen them go past the line of what is acceptable on the field. Because they want to win so badly they say things I wouldn't say on the field, but that's their competitiveness."

"When they first started playing they wouldn't say boo but now they're a lot more narky

(Gregg Porteus)

Mark salutes the crowd after notching his cavalier century against the West Indies in the Fifth Test. The other batsman is Dean Jones.

on the field," agreed Matthews. "It's amazing how they always get away with it. Some of the stuff they get away with is awesome."

Mike Whitney believes Mark was unfairly saddled with the "too casual" tag. "It was just a perception. We always knew he was a great player."

"Because he's such a gifted player, so natural, rather like David Gower, if he gets out to a bad shot it'll look worse because it's him that's played it," said Neil Foster. "At times he probably finds it too easy but I've never had cause to question his commitment."

Ian Davis also believes the tag is unfair. He agrees that it is a bit of the "Gower Syndrome". "Every time he went out he tried," said Davis.

"I've always believed that Mark is a really good player," said Mark Taylor. "He's not going to be the bloke who's going to run 2000 miles — that's not his idea of putting in. He can work out what he needs to do. He doesn't need to run 10km and take a hundred catches at training just to look good. He puts in when he needs to."

Greg Matthews agreed.

"Anyone who knows the guy knows he's as hungry for the game as anyone," said Matthews. "When I think about it I've never seen him say no to a bat. He always does the job, he never shirks anything. When he's at fielding practice it may look like he's skylarking but they're all things he's practising for the game. He and Steve can be misconstrued as not putting in, but they're honing their skills in a particular way."

Another thing that still annoys Mark is the press' perception, which went hand-in-hand with his alleged softness and dates back a couple of years now, that he only got runs in the second innings. The largely unspoken inference was that the runs were cheap because he had performed when it didn't matter and the pressure was off. He did string together a succession of first innings low scores, often ducks, and second innings hundreds, but he feels it's not valid to draw the conclusion so many journalists did.

"They were on that bandwagon for about two months that I could only get runs in the second innings, which I reckon wasn't a fair statement," said Mark. "I still scored my fair share of runs in the first innings. And quite often it was harder to get runs in the second innings. The pitch had deteriorated. It certainly wasn't easy. I think if you went through a lot of players' records they might have scored more runs in one innings or the other. That's just part of cricket.

"Actually it would be interesting to see of all my first class hundreds how many were in the first innings and how many in the second. I got a bit annoyed about that at the time. It doesn't matter if it's the first or second innings, you've still got to bat well to score them. It's not a valid argument."

The resentment must have loomed large in Waugh's subconscious during his marvellous 1990 run, because of the 11 first class centuries he scored in his 3079 tally every one was in the first innings. He did, however, offer a possible explanation for times when he does fall swiftly.

"When I go into bat I'm half asleep with worry. I don't often get nervous but if I do I'll fall asleep, nod off on my bat, before I go in. Then it takes me a little while once I get out there to adjust and wake up. I need a good thump in the ribs or something to wake me up. And that's why I think I've had a lot of ducks over the seasons. It didn't happen to me when I was a kid, it started when I began playing first class cricket. It's a way of getting rid of the nerves, it's just a natural reaction. I can't explain it, it just happens."

Then there's the matter of nicknames. Everyone knows him as Junior and his Bankstown team-mates have called him Eddie (his middle name is Edward) but his pre-Test nickname

Steve is comprehensively bowled, but only after hammering a big score for NSW in an FAI Cup match at North Sydney Oval in October 1991. (Gregg Porteus)

of Afghanistan is purely a press invention. Mark says his team-mates have never called him Afghanistan—derived from being the "forgotten Waugh (war)". The only place he ever saw or heard it was in the media. But such annoyances are merely that, irritants. Waugh does not lay awake at night stewing over the nasty things that have been written about him. Instead he favours the philosophical approach.

"You've got to accept the good with the bad," he says. "When you do something good people say 'well done' and I suppose if you're not going so well then you've got to accept criticism. But a lot of it is not justified at the time and naturally you get upset. You can't do anything about it. The only thing you can do is just get out there and show them that they are wrong. But it is just part of the job. You've just got to accept it. Some people don't like the way you play or like your style and they're going to write about that."

To complain is not really in his nature anyway. "I suppose if I'm worried about something I probably keep it to myself. I won't come out and say I'm worried about something, I'll keep it under my hat."

That level-headedness, the ability to get on and produce despite the many distractions,

Steve is run out trying to keep the strike against England during the 1992 World Cup match at the SCG. The English keeper is Alec Stewart, the other batsman Michael Whitney. (Gregg Porteus)

is a great help to Mark said Neil Foster. "One of his strengths of character is that he is fairly even-tempered the whole time. No highs and lows. That's important. You notice with most young players that if they have a good day they're on a high and if they have a bad day they're down in the dumps. The more they play the more they get used to the highs and lows and they find the middle ground. Mark's always been a bit like that, he's always found the middle ground anyway.

"He's very even-tempered, has a nice quiet sense of humour and a calming quality. He's just a nice bloke, a genuine nice guy."

Paul Prichard is one who believes the general public, and even his friends, have still yet to understand the real Mark Waugh. "I think they're guessing it. I still don't think the real

Mark Waugh has emerged. I don't think even I know the real Mark Waugh yet. I don't think anybody does. Obviously it's still very early days in his cricket career. And basically he could be anything. He could still be the world's greatest player. He has the ability to do it."

Prichard said he has known Mark off and on for five or six years because of his off-season playing stints with Waverley in Sydney. He didn't really get to know him well, though, until Mark came to Essex in 1988 and says the pair struck up an instant friendship. They spend a lot of time together socially as well as rooming together on tour. When Prichard planned his wedding in Sydney in late 1991 he asked Mark to be his best man, feeling he was the natural choice. Unfortunately Mark had to drop out because NSW was playing a tour match against India in Lismore. "He is someone I would like to call a very, very good friend," said Prichard. "He's a very generous guy. He's always got time for you. He definitely realises the value of having a good friend.

"There's not an ounce of selfishness in him. It's not in Mark's nature to be selfish — in life or in a cricket situation. He's always keen for other guys to do well and play well and get the right result at the end of the day. As a friend he is never selfish, he's always willing to help out ... and he adds quite a lot to the dressing room humour."

And apparently a man who is not to be trifled with either, said Prichard. "We were playing at Southhampton and one of the young guys put a room menu on Mark and Sue's door ordering kippers for breakfast which duly arrived in the morning. The whole room stank, but Mark didn't say anything. When this young bloke went out to bat he found one kipper in his gloves and the other one in his helmet. He had to go out to bat smelling of kippers. I think Mark's comment was 'you mess with me and you pay the price'."

Steve and Mark have developed different defence mechanisms to survive the battering that comes with the territory. Whereas Mark is deceptively casual and easy-going, Steve has developed a much more obviously tough exterior. It was born in the grim early days of his Test career. These days, although he is still the same good bloke with his friends, he wears that shield off the field as well. "I think you get tough, tough with the people around you," said Steve. "Especially people who want to hang on to you and take you for a ride. I think I can pick those people a bit more easily. I think I can take the highs and lows a little bit better too. It helps to get through the tough times. We had four years there when we didn't win too many games. It really toughens you up and when you get into winning mode you don't want to get back into that losing frame of mind. You want to succeed. You've had all those failures. It's not a great way to live when you're not scoring runs and your team's not doing well. People get stuck into you left, right and centre so you don't want that to happen too often."

That's not to say he wishes the tough times had never happened. Steve has no doubt that the experiences, the tough times he has been through, have made him a better player and a better person.

"No cricketer can go through their career just having highs all the time. You've got to experience the lows just to make you appreciate the highs when they come. And as a person you are always going to have highs and lows outside of cricket so it is probably a good preparation. Plus being a team sport you've got to learn how to enjoy other people's successes. If you don't do that you're going to be a pretty sad character in the dressing room if you haven't scored any runs. You are going to sit there and mope all the time. It is a good test of a person's character when they haven't scored any runs or had a bad day, how they take it at the end of the day. Whether they go off in a huff and drive home or not talk to anyone or whether they are happy with other people's success. You can see through most people by the way they take failure. You've got to learn to accept it. It's part of the game."

Media personality and Balmain Rugby League coach Alan Jones has offered the twins plenty of support over the years. The subject of their treatment, particularly by the selectors, is one about which he feels strongly. Jones says the Waughs' difficulties are a symptom of one of the less-desirable Australian characteristics. "I think Australians are uncomfortable with extravagant talent and, oddly enough, put pressure on those who once or twice in a lifetime exhibit it," Jones said. "Therefore it has always been difficult for those two blokes. They are, without using the words loosely, immensely gifted. In many ways I think Stephen Waugh has been treated badly. My own view about this is you've got to treat such people differently. The opposite has happened. I don't think people understand. At the end of the day these are two simple young fellows. They are the kind of people who inspire something in others. I hope that the way in which Stephen has been treated we haven't put out the flame.

"You've got to be lucky if you've got that sort of person and you've got to encourage and cultivate them. Their talent deserves it. Now if Stephen Waugh feels that his position is not secure or there are question marks over his ability, well, he could become another statistic. There have been a lot of them. It's all related to how you treat them. And quite frankly the way Mark Waugh was treated in his last Test was shameful. Asking a bloke to go out on the paddock after he has been told he's dropped.

"For that sort of person I would walk from Sydney to Melbourne because they are worth cultivating, they are worth encouraging. I like the roll-up-the-sleeves, unpretentious way they go about things. They would bat all day if you asked them. And they've come back under pressure and made a mountain of runs. Talent of that kind is rare. It's got to be fostered and cultivated wherever it exists. You've got to water that garden all the time. You can't afford to have that plant not grow.

"They are loyal and I hope cricket is as loyal to them as they've been to it. These blokes are not devious people. They don't fit the world of sporting politics. They embody the fresh-faced approach to the game where you go out, hit the ball and get on with it. They are a typical family, a simple Australian suburban family and it's a tragedy when you find those values betrayed when you move up into the sophisticated world of international sport. They're undevious people. We live in a world of bastards and we've just got to out-bastard the bastards. That's true. It's the only way to survive."

There are plenty of people who qualify to deliver the last word on this fascinating pair but I'm going to let Mark provide it with the answer he gave when asked if he thought that he and Stephen had enjoyed the perfect upbringing for an aspiring sports star.

"I don't know what a perfect upbringing is but we had a good upbringing," he said. "We weren't given anything on a platter. We had to work for it, so that was good. We lived in an average suburb, we went to an average school. And everything we did we had to do ourselves. It wasn't given to us. I suppose it was fortunate Mum and Dad were good sportsmen and keen on sport and encouraged us and gave us a bit of natural ability. Mum and Dad were good parents to have for kids playing sport. You see a lot of parents yelling at their kids 'don't do this, do that'. Mum and Dad were interested, they used to come and watch, but they sat back and didn't say 'why aren't you doing this, why didn't you do that?' They just more or less encouraged us all the time. Whenever we went away on primary school trips we'd always get money. We never struggled. I think Mum and Dad were pretty good. We weren't spoiled but we didn't go without.

"I suppose being twins might have helped as well. We always had someone to play against. It gave us that competitive edge, I think, playing against each other all the time."

"Playing to win."

Steve and Mark Waugh in First-Class Cricket and One-Day Internationals

Compiled by Ian Russell

As at 30 September 1992

STEVE WAUGH

In First-Class Cricket

Batting

Season	M	In	NO	Runs	HI	100	50	Avge
1984-85 (A)	5	7	–	223	94	–	2	31.85
1985 (Z)	1	1	–	30	30	–	–	30.00
1985-86 (A)	7	12	2	378	119 *	2	–	37.80
1986 (NZ)	5	8	–	124	74	–	1	15.50
1986 (I)	6	7	3	227	82	–	2	56.75
1986-87 (A)	13	21	2	741	89	–	6	39.00
1987 (E)	4	6	3	340	137 *	2	1	113.33
1987-88 (A)	10	15	1	517	170	1	3	36.92
1988 (E)	15	24	6	1314	161	6	4	73.00
1988 (P)	6	9	–	160	59	-	1	17.77
1988-89 (A)	14	24	1	711	118	1	3	30.91
1989 (E)	16	24	8	1030	177 *	4	3	64.37
1989-90 (A)	12	19	3	704	196	2	3	44.00
1990 (NZ)	1	2	–	50	25	–	–	25.00
1990-91 (A)	8	11	1	598	216 *	1	4	59.80
1991 (WI)	6	7	2	229	96 *	–	2	45.80
1991 (Z)	2	2	–	130	119	1	–	65.00
1991-92 (A)	8	11	–	472	115	2	2	42.90
TOTALS	139	210	32	7978	216 *	22	37	44.82

Record in each country

	M	In	NO	Runs	HI	100	50	Avge
In Australia	77	120	10	4344	216 *	9	23	39.49
In England	35	54	17	2684	177 *	12	8	72.54
In India	6	7	3	227	82	–	2	56.75
In New Zealand	6	10	–	174	74	–	1	17.40
In Pakistan	6	9	–	160	59	–	1	17.77
In West Indies	6	7	2	229	96 *	–	2	45.80
In Zimbabwe	3	3	–	160	119	1	–	53.33

First Class Centuries

107	NSW v Tasmania	Hobart (TCA)	1985-86
119*	NSW v South Australia	Sydney	1985-86
111*	Somerset v Surrey	The Oval	1987
137*	Somerset v Gloucestershire	Bristol	1987
170	NSW v Victoria	Sydney	1987-88
115*	Somerset v Hampshire	Southampton	1988
103*	Somerset v Warwickshire	Bath	1988
137	Somerset v Sussex	Bath	1988
101*	Somerset v Glamorgan	Taunton	1988
161	Somerset v Kent	Canterbury	1988
112*	Somerset v Middlesex	Uxbridge	1988
118	NSW v Queensland	Brisbane	1988-89
177*	Australia v England	Leeds	1989
152*	Australia v England	Lord's	1989
112	Australians v Hampshire	Southampton	1989
100*	Australians v Essex	Chelmsford	1989
134*	Australia v Sri Lanka	Hobart	1989-90
196	NSW v Tasmania	Hobart	1989-90
216*	NSW v Western Australia	Perth	1990-91
119	Australians v Zimbabwe	Bulawayo	1991
115	NSW v Western Australia	Perth	1991-92
113	NSW v Western Australia	Perth	1991-92

*Indicates not out

Bowling and Fielding

Season	Ct	Ov	Runs	Wkts	Best	5/	Avge
1984-85 (A)	2	72	156	3	1-15	–	52.00
1985 (Z)	–	20.5	85	2	2-57	–	42.50
1985-86 (A)	4	68	190	4	2-36	–	47.50
1986 (NZ)	4	53	151	7	4-56	–	21.57
1986 (I)	4	97	367	10	4-71	–	36.70
1986-87 (A)	24	258.3	772	25	5-69	1	30.88
1987 (E)	4	112	348	11	3-48	–	31.63
1987-88 (A)	12	218.3	499	23	5-50	1	21.69
1988 (E)	20	23	60	3	2-33	–	20.00
1988 (P)	4	126	362	4	1-15	–	90.50
1988-89 (A)	12	365	1114	36	6-51	2	30-94
1989 (E)	6	176.1	571	23	3-10	–	24.82
1989-90 (A)	5	9	19	1	1-13	–	19.00
1990 (NZ)	–	–	–	–	–	–	–
1990-91 (A)	3	107	319	4	1-7	–	79.75
1991 (WI)	1	78	234	3	3-76	–	78.00
1991 (Z)	3	27	21	2	2-2	–	10.50
1991-92 (A)	9	125	342	12	3-23	–	28.50
TOTALS	117	1936	5610	173	6-51	4	32.42

Record in each country

	Ct	Ov	Runs	Wkts	Best	5/	Avge
In Australia	71	1223	3411	108	6-51	4	31.58
In England	30	311.1	979	37	3-10	–	26.45
In India	4	97	367	10	4-71	–	36.70
In New Zealand	4	53	151	7	4-56	–	21.57
In Pakistan	4	126	362	4	1-15	–	90.5
In West Indies	1	78	234	3	3-76	–	78.00
In Zimbabwe	3	47.5	106	4	2-2	–	26.50

Best Bowling

5-69	Australia v England	Perth	1986-87
5-50	NSW v Tasmania	Sydney	1987-88
5-92	Australia v West Indies	Melbourne	1988-89
6-51	NSW v Queensland	Sydney	1988-89

MARK WAUGH

In First-Class Cricket

Batting

Season	M	In	NO	Runs	HI	100	50	Avge
1985-86 (A)	7	11	–	167	41	–	–	15.18
1986 (Z)	2	4	2	176	83	–	2	88.00
1986-87(A)	1	2	–	26	26	–	–	13.00
1987 (Z)	2	3	1	123	61	–	1	61.50
1987-88 (A)	10	16	3	833	116	4	4	64.07
1988 (E)	3	4	–	178	86	–	1	44.50
1988-89 (A)	11	21	3	727	103*	2	4	40.38
1989 (E)	24	39	4	1537	165	4	8	43.91
1989-90 (A)	12	17	4	1009	198*	5	2	77.61
1990 (E)	22	33	6	2072	207*	8	8	76.74
1990-91 (A)	8	13	1	840	229*	3	3	70.00
1991 (WI)	9	12	2	522	139*	2	2	52.20
1991-92 (A)	12	226	–	924	163	3	4	51.33
1992 (E)	16	24	7	1314	219*	4	6	77.29
1992 (SL)	5	9	–	291	118	1	2	32.33
TOTALS	144	226	33	10739	229*	36	47	55.64

Record in each country

	M	In	NO	Runs	HI	100	50	Avge
In Australia	61	98	11	4526	229*	17	17	52.02
In England	65	100	17	5101	219*	16	23	61.45
In West Indies	9	12	2	522	139*	2	2	52.20
In Sri Lanka	5	9	–	291	118	1	2	32.33
In Zimbabwe	4	7	3	299	83	–	3	74.75

First Class Centuries

101*	NSW v Tasmania	Devonport	1987-88
114	NSW v Victoria	Sydney	1987-88
100*	NSW v Victoria	Melbourne	1987-88
116	NSW v Tasmania	Sydney	1987-88
103*	NSW v West Indians	Sydney	1988-89
100*	NSW v Tasmania	Devonport	1988-89
109	Essex v Hampshire	Ilford	1989
110	Essex v Middlesex	Uxbridge	1989
100*	Essex v Australia	Chelmsford	1989
165	Essex v Leicestershire	Leicester	1989
172	NSW v South Australia	Adelaide	1989-90
100*	NSW v Victoria	Albury	1989-90
100*	NSW v Victoria	Melbourne	1989-90
137	NSW v South Australia	Sydney	1989-90
198*	NSW v Tasmania	Sydney	1989-90
166*	Essex v Worcestershire	Worcester	1990
125	Essex v Hampshire	Southampton	1990
204	Essex v Gloucestershire	Ilford	1990
103	Essex v Warwickshire	Birmingham	1990
126	Essex v Derbyshire	Colchester	1990
103*	Essex v Sussex	Chelmsford	1990
207*	Essex v Yorkshire	Middlesbrough	1990
169	Essex v Kent	Chelmsford	1990
229*	NSW v Western Australia	Perth	1990-91
112	NSW v South Australia	Sydney	1990-91
138	Australia v England	Adelaide	1990-91 (Test debut)
108	Australians v Jamaica	Kingston	1991
139*	Australians v West Indies	Antigua	1991
136	NSW v Western Australia	Perth	1991-92
158	NSW v South Australia	Sydney	1991-92
163	NSW v Western Australia	Perth	1991-92
120	Essex v Kent	Chelmsford	1992
219*	Essex v Lancashire	Ilford	1992
125*	Essex v Gloucestershire	Southend	1992
138*	Essex v Worcestershire	Kidderminster	1992
118	Australians v Southern Province XI	Matara	1992

*Indicates not out

Bowling and Fielding

Season	Ct	Ov	Runs	Wkts	Best	5/	Avge
1985-86 (A)	6	124.4	352	11	4-130	-	32.00
1986 (Z)	4	43	110	2	1-25	-	55.00
1986-87 (A)	-	11	32	1	1-2	-	32.00
1987 (Z)	1	1	3	-	-	-	-
1987-88 (A)	18	46	158	6	3-49	-	26.33
1988 (E)	2	12	75	-	-	-	-
1988-89 (A)	9	43	163	1	1-46	-	163.00
1989 (E)	31	117.2	415	14	3-23	-	29.64
1989-90 (A)	18	131.3	465	15	2-7	-	31.00
1990 (E)	18	191	771	12	5-37	1	64.25
1990-91 (A)	9	31	138	2	2-15	-	69.00
1991 (WI)	13	93.2	271	12	4-80	-	22.58
1991-92 (A)	21	97.5	258	7	2-11	-	36.85
1992 (E)	27	184.4	671	22	3-38	-	30.50
1992 (SL)	5	40	129	2	2-77	-	64.50
Totals	182	1167.2	4011	107	5-37	1	37.49

Record in each country

	Ct	Ov	Runs	Wkts	Best	5/	Avge
in Australia	81	485	1566	43	4-133	-	36.41
in England	78	505	1932	48	5-37	1	40.25
in Sri Lanka	5	40	129	2	2-77	-	64.50
in West Indies	13	93.2	271	12	4-80	-	22.58
in Zimbabwe	5	44	113	2	1-25	-	56.50

Best Bowling

4-130	NSW v Queensland	Brisbane	1985-86
5-37	Essex v Northamptonshire	Chelmsford	1990
4-80	Australia v West Indies	Bridgetown	1991

STEVE WAUGH

In Test Cricket

Batting

	M	In	NO	Runs	HI	100	50	Avge
1985-86 v India	2	4	-	26	13	-	-	6.50
1986 v NZ #	3	5	-	87	74	-	1	17.40
1986 v India #	3	4	3	59	39*	-	-	59.00
1986-87 v Eng	5	8	1	310	79*	-	3	44.28
1987-88 v NZ	3	4	-	147	61	-	2	36.75
1987-88 v Eng	1	1	-	27	27	-	-	27.00
1987-88 v Sri L	1	1	-	20	20	-	-	20.00
1988 v Pak #	3	5	-	92	59	-	1	18.40
1988-89 v W Ind	5	9	1	331	91	-	3	41.37
1989 v Eng #	6	8	4	506	177*	2	1	126.50
1989-90 v NZ	1	1	-	17	17	-	-	17.00
1989-90 v Sri L	2	4	1	267	134*	1	2	89.00
1989-90 v Pak	3	4	-	44	20	-	-	11.00
1990 v NZ #	1	2	-	50	25	-	-	25.00
1990-91 v Eng	3	4	-	82	48	-	-	20.50
1991 v W Ind #	2	3	1	32	26	-	-	16.00
Totals	44	67	11	2097	177*	3	13	37.44

# indicates series played overseas

	M	In	NO	Runs	HI	100	50	Avge
in Australia	26	40	3	1271	134*	1	10	34.35
Overseas	18	27	8	826	177*	2	3	43.47

Record against each country

	M	In	NO	Runs	HI	100	50	Avge
v India	5	8	3	85	39*	-	-	17.00
v New Zealand	8	12	-	301	74	-	3	25.08
v England	15	21	5	925	177*	2	4	57.81
v Sri Lanka	3	5	1	287	134*	1	2	71.75
v Pakistan	6	9	-	136	59	-	1	15.11
v West Indies	7	12	2	363	91	-	3	36.30

* indicates not out

Bowling and Fielding

	Ct	Ov	Runs	Wkts	Best	5/	Avge
1985-86 v India	-	18	69	2	2-36	-	34.50
1986 v NZ #	2	36	83	5	4-56	-	16.60
1986 v India #	2	35	130	2	1-29	-	65.00
1986-87 v Eng	7	108.3	336	10	5-69	1	33.60
1987-88 v NZ	3	75	169	2	1-2	-	84.50
1987-88 v Eng	-	22.5	51	3	3-51	-	17.00
1987-88 v Sri L	3	28	47	4	4-33	-	11.75
1988 v Pak #	2	78	216	2	1-44	-	108.00
1988-89 v W Ind	3	139	472	10	5-92	1	47.20
1989 v Eng #	4	57	208	2	1-38	-	104.00
1989-90 v NZ	-	-	-	-	-	-	-
1989-90 v Sri L	2	6	6	-	-	-	-
1989-90 v Pak	1	3	13	1	1-13	-	13.00
1990 v NZ #	-	-	-	-	-	-	-
1990-91 v Eng	1	38	90	1	1-7	-	90.00
1991 v W Ind #	1	35	90	-	-	-	-
Totals	31	679.2	1980	44	5-69	2	45.00

# indicates series played overseas

	Ct	Ov	Runs	Wkts	Best	5/	Avge
in Australia	20	438.2	1253	33	5-69	2	37.96
Overseas	11	241	727	11	4-56	-	66.09

Record against each country

	Ct	Ov	Runs	Wkts	Best	5/	Avge
v India	2	53	199	4	2-36	-	49.75
v New Zealand	5	111	252	7	4-56	-	36.00
v England	12	226.2	685	16	5-69	1	42.81
v Sri Lanka	5	34	53	4	4-33	-	17.25
v Pakistan	3	81	229	3	1-13	-	76.33
v West Indies	4	174	562	10	5-92	1	56.20

MARK WAUGH

In Test Cricket

Batting

	M	In	NO	Runs	HI	100	50	Avge
1990-91 v Eng	2	3	-	187	138	1	-	62.33
1991 v W Ind #	5	8	2	367	139 *	1	2	61.17
1991-92 v Ind	4	6	-	83	34	-	-	13.83
1992 v Sri L #	3	6	-	61	56	-	1	10.16
Totals	14	23	2	698	139 *	2	3	33.23

# indicates series played overseas

in Australia	6	9	-	270	138	1	-	30.00
Overseas	8	14	2	428	139 *	1	3	35.66

* indicates not out

Bowling and Fielding

	Ct	Ov	Runs	Wkts	Best	5/	Avge
1990-91 v Eng	1	6	26	-	-	-	-
1991 v W Ind #	10	65	183	8	4-80	-	22.88
1991-92 v Ind	10	37	89	1	1-36	-	89.00
1992 v Sri L #	3	23	94	2	2-77	-	47.00
Totals	24	131	392	11	4-80	-	35.63

# indicates series played overseas

in Australia	11	43	115	1	1-36	-	115.00
Overseas	13	88	227	10	4-80	-	27.70

STEVE WAUGH

In International One-Day Cricket

Batting

M	In	NO	Runs	HI	50	Avge
129	112	30	2542	83*	12	31.00

Bowling and Fielding

Ct	Ov	Runs	Wkts	Best	Avge
43	843.2	3741	124	4-33	30.16

debut v New Zealand (Melbourne) 1985-86
highest score 83* v England (Adelaide) 1986-87
best bowling 4-33 v Sri Lanka (Sydney) 1987-88

MARK WAUGH

In International One-day Cricket

Batting

M	In	NO	Runs	HI	50	Avge
36	33	3	735	67	4	24.50

Bowling and Fielding

Ct	Ov	Runs	Wkts	Best	Avge
19	91.5	429	20	4-37	21.45

debut v Pakistan (Adelaide) 1988-89
highest score 67 v West Indies (Kingston) 1991
best bowling 4-37 v England (Melbourne) 1990-91